ELIZABETHAN ECCENTRICS

BLACK·FRYERS

LONDINI
Excusum impensis *I. Marriot* & *I. Grismand.*
1 6 2 5.

From Richard Hord, *Elegia de Admiranda Clade Centum
Papistorum*, 1625

ELIZABETHAN ECCENTRICS

Brief Lives of English Misfits, Exploiters, Rogues & Failures, 1580- 1660

BY
ARTHUR FREEMAN

WITH A FOREWORD BY
NICOLAS BARKER

DORSET PRESS
New York

For Steve and Helen, Sally and Ted
and

This edition published by Dorset Press
a division of Marboro Books Corporation,
by arrangement with Harvard Common Press Inc.
1989 Dorset Press

ISBN 0-88029-437-X

Printed in the United States of America
M 9 8 7 6 5 4 3 2 1

CONTENTS

FOREWORD

ONE OF THE TIRESOME THINGS ABOUT THE PASSAGE OF TIME IS ITS TENDENCY TO WHITEWASH. IF HISTORY WERE solely based on the lives of the good and respectable, how dull it would be! The evil that men do, it is true, lives after them, but only the spectacularly evil: petty wickedness, as well as good, is oft interred. And this is what happens to the morally distinguished. A worse fate attends the morally indistinct, the put upon, the eccentric, the failures: no one knows where their bones are.

It is not the least of Professor Freeman's achievements to have found the graves of the ten characters whose odd careers he celebrates. To have put live flesh upon them, as he also has, is an even greater success. But there you are, you may walk up and view them. Edward Squire, the Martyr/Spy who Could not Make Up his Mind; John Gee, the Only Protestant to Survive the Fatal Vesper (and what was he doing there?); Gamaliel Ratsey, Soldier Turned Highwayman, with an irresistible streak of chivalry; William Banks and his Marvellous Horse Morocco, who climbed to the top of St. Paul's; Nicholas Wood, the Great Eater; Richard Vennard, Impresario of the Show that Never Was; Richard Ferris, who sailed in a green cockle-boat from London to Bristol (forerunner of Sir Francis Chichester *et hoc genus omne*); Will Kempe, the Nine Days' Wonder, who morris-danced from London to Norwich in that time; John Taylor the Water Poet, who sailed from London to Queensborough in a brown paper boat: and Moll Cutpurse, who led a man's life in a world not cut out for an independent woman.

It is an amazing gallery, in which every form of human failure and oddity is mirrored. Despite the conspicuous non-achievement of his *dramatis personae*, Professor Freeman's play is full of vitality and wit, with never a dull scene in it. This is the real life stuff of which Shakespeare's clowns and bit parts were made. Here are the ephemeral exploits which brought the house down at the Globe (and have baffled posterity since). No more vivid picture of low life about the year 1600 exists, carefully resurrected from the forgotten records and unread books of the time.

Professor Freeman writes with a scholar's care for his sources, but with a poet's intuitive sympathy for his bizarre characters in their occasional success and more frequent failure. *Elizabeth's Misfits* is essential for the scholar of the period, but no one with the least interest in the odder sides of human nature will read it without pleasure and a sense of fellow feeling.

Nicolas Barker
London

PREFATORY NOTE

I CAN OFFER NO REAL EXCUSES FOR THIS BOOK BEYOND THE VERY EXISTENCE OF ITS SUBJECTS, WHOM I FOUND ODD AND provocative, and the promptings or seductions of amateur antiquarianism. In choosing fundamentally ignominious figures for biography, all of the late Tudor and Stuart reigns, I have been led in part by the belief that none has been accorded much historical equity in the past, and in part by the feeling that each is distinctly interesting, in his own period and in ours, both individually and as a "type"—a pattern of misfit whose own peculiarities illuminate the times and places around him, and cause us to consider certain problems of culture and justice which greater men seem almost to dwarf. I have added "type" and "pattern" perhaps retrospectively, as the individual has in fact been my earliest concern, and his implications my afterthought. In all cases I have gone to the primary available materials, manuscript and printed, but recorded the secondary accounts (often, and understandably, quite poor) in notes. These short biographies have been designed for continuous reading, with practically no bracketed citations, no footnote numbers, and with most spelling and punctuation modernized, and manuscript abbreviation expanded. For the purposes of scholarship, sources and evidence have been accumulated in appended notes, keyed by page and line-number to the text. I realize I am riding two horses, but my hope is to allow the reader to read without interruption, while not unnecessarily annoying the student or historian by excising all *scholia*. I intend that every historical statement should be thus linked to a dependable reference or verifiable in the obvious source, cited in my bibliography or notes to its chapter.

I am obliged and pleased to record my obligations, first to the officials and attendants of the Houghton and Widener Libraries at Harvard, the British Museum, the Bodleian Library, the Library of the Society of Antiquaries, Guildhall Library, and Somerset House; in particular to Messrs. Antony Allison, Nicolas Barker, the late John Crow, Roy Davids, Theodore Hofmann, Ian Willison, and Miss Katherine Pantzer; and in general to all friends who were kind enough to read portions of the manuscript, or its entirety, whose criticism I hope I have mitigated, if not met, in what follows.

A.F.
Cambridge, Massachusetts

"It argueth a very rusty wit,
so to doat on worm eaten Eld."

Thomas Nashe,
Pierce Penilesse
1592

CHAPTER I.

THE HAPLESS CONSPIRACY OF EDWARD SQUIRE

O N 13 NOVEMBER 1598 A MIDDLE-AGED JACK-OF-ALL-TRADES FROM GREENWICH, EDWARD SQUIRE, WAS hanged, disembowelled, and quartered by the public executioner on Tyburn Hill for multiple crimes of high treason. He had been charged and convicted of conspiring, while a prisoner-of-war in Spain, with an English Jesuit named Richard Walpole, to assassinate Queen Elizabeth by smearing poison on the pommel of her riding-saddle, and subsequently to kill the Earl of Essex by so treating the arms of his admiral's chair. This curiously inept and spectacular attempt, the latest in a long line of Spanish and Jesuit exiles' efforts, left its scar on the age. A sensational trial whipped up popular indignation against Spain and native Catholics near to the pitch of '88, and, with its inevitable outcome, Squire paid more than the price of the commotion. The temporarily shadowed "war party" of Essex could celebrate a small *coup*, while the secular priests imprisoned at Wisbech Castle edged anxiously closer to the clean break with the Society of Jesus they would effect within five years.

But Squire's case, in history, is not yet quite closed. Commentators, particularly Catholic, from 1599 to this century, have found the official account of the plot—in its details above all—impossible to swallow. From the earliest Jesuit apologists to Alfred Pollard in the *Dictionary of National Biography*, there has been a tendency to qualify the conspiracy "alleged" (Pollard, 1898) if not wholly "a stratagem of state" (Fitzherbert, 1602), and, at a skeptical extreme, to declare with Lingard (1825) that "if Titus Oates had never existed, the history of this ridiculous plot would suffice to show how easily the most absurd fictions obtain credit, when the public mind is under the influence of religious prejudice."

Yet the historicity of Squire's chroniclers has been weak at best, and at worst simply dishonest. Details arbitrarily fabricated centuries after the case have snowballed and multiplied in successive retellings, and practically no one has bothered to re-examine the abundant contemporary records. Garbled as it has generally been, the story indeed seems incoherent and suspect, and the original testimony often contradictory. But with the evidence impartially laid out there is no real question, attractive as it has seemed, of massive injustice and a hushed-up inquiry, as with Oates. The outlines of the strange plot emerge exceptionally clear, the conspiracy itself no less than the following process, baroque and merciless, of Elizabethan justice. Its particular drama lies in its cast and setting: in the background a simmering cold war of global scope; in the fore a varied parade of Renaissance intriguers, the clever, ruthless investigators, Machiavellian missionaries, mendacious informers, helpless and intimidated defendants; and in the midst, insignificant among world powers and historical issues, the peculiarly compelling personal tragedy of a slightly-above-average and sensitive victim of others' grand designs, caught in the quicksand of his own complicity. Struggling sinks him deeper: he is perpetually between prisons or in suspicion, and no venture redeems him. The Inquisition of Spain and the equally formidable domestic "question" by turns rack and eventually break a tender will, and he concludes a career of lies and evasions in despair and violent remorse. Squire's is only one of a hundred similar histories laid in Elizabeth's England, but it is uncommonly well-documented, and interesting enough to deserve an unvarnished reconstruction. I have gone back to the original and contemporary materials in all possible cases, and quoted wherever I could from Squire himself, his accusors, and the accomplices who disowned him.

The date and place of Squire's birth are unknown, but his home had been in Greenwich, then not part of Greater London but an independent township, for about sixteen years at the time of his trial, or since 1582. He was married, as he testifies, had children, and maintained himself before 1593 as a "scrivener"—i.e., a letter-writer and notary. Many scriveners of Squire's period inclined toward the law, toward usury, and public office, and on the whole it was an affluent if execrated profession, demanding of its practitioners by company statute enough education for a "perfect congruity of grammar." The fathers of Thomas Kyd and John Milton were scriveners, and relatively well-to-do. Squire, however, in an outlying suburb, may have made less success of the profession than Lombard Street Londoners, and in 1593 we find him employed instead at the Queen's stables—presumably those in Greenwich—as deputy purveyor of provisions to "one Kaies." This "for some two years' space," but Squire chafed at his job, "being of wit above his vocation, disliked with that condition of life," and so he threw it up, and shipped out 28 August 1595 with Sir Francis Drake and Sir John Hawkins on their final privateering voyage to the West Indies.

Squire's ill luck began almost at once. Where previous expeditions had experienced dazzling success, this last, at all times disorganized and frequently unmanageable, only skirted disaster, limping home to Plymouth with small booty after losing several barks and both commanders. Squire, inevitably, sailed on one of the missing craft, the *Francis*, which separated from the fleet near Guadeloupe—the grand plan of attack on Puerto Rico having been needlessly compromised by small pillaging parties—and was captured by five Spanish frigates on 30 October 1595. According to Hakluyt, the realization that the Spanish might now discover all the details of his and Drake's Puerto Rican scheme, and thus be able to defend against it, so depressed Sir John Hawkins that he immediately sickened, and died less than two weeks later, on 12 November. And the Spanish in fact did extract the plan from the captain of the *Francis*, so that when Drake at last mounted an attack, the island was sufficiently prepared to repulse it. The fleet turned back, and on the homeward voyage Drake himself succumbed to dysentery, and was buried at sea. Squire, his friend Richard Rolles, and the rest of the crew of the *Francis* sailed into San Lucar near Seville as prisoners-of-war.

Beginning with Squire's experiences in Seville we must deal with essentially conflicting testimony and make allowances in crediting it for the interests of each narrator. We possess, to begin with, several statements made by Squire himself—some possibly under torture—between 7 October and 13 November 1598, and containing some details of his treatment by Church and State in Spain; and we have an "official" account of the case presented as a pamphlet (*A Letter Written out of England . . . containing a True Report of a Strange Conspiracy*, London, 1599) which may confidently be ascribed to Francis Bacon, and which is based fundamentally upon Squire's own statements, eked out by the examiners' inferences. In some details, the testimony of independent informers, and of Squire's friend Rolles, bear out the general description of his experience, and there is little reason to disown Squire's own version of it as of primary value.

But on certain points, and of these some crucial ones, a completely contradictory account is given by the other chief actor, Father Richard Walpole, who presented his version in a lengthy letter—now in the archives of the English College at Valladolid—to Father Garnett, some time after Squire's death. Walpole's testimony is echoed by Martin Array in a pamphlet giving the Jesuits' side of the case (*The Discovery and Confutation of a Tragical Fiction*, Rome, 1599), but there is no indication that Array based his narrative on anything more than Walpole's own statement. A seminarian's publication, Thomas Fitzherbert's *A Defense of the Catholic Cause* (St.

Omer, 1602), reiterates Array's account—as do Robert Parsons' *An Answer to the Fifth Part of the Reports lately set forth by Sir Edward Coke* (Douai, 1606), and Henry More's *Historiae Provinciae Anglicanae* (Antwerp, 1660)—and so these and all subsequent Catholic versions of the Seville portion of Squire's story derive strictly from Walpole and no one else. By the time of Oliver, Lingard, and Foley, Walpole's testimony has undergone considerable embroidery and accretion, but no corroborating witness can yet be cited.

The first encounter of an English prisoner-of-war in Spain with his compatriot Jesuits, says Squire, is likely to be early enough—in prison, or even before disembarkation, the fathers having taken upon themselves the semi-consular office of mediating between English captives and their captors. But it is important to understand the political role of these far-flung Englishmen in 1595, and their relations with the government of Spain. Since 1570 and Pius V's notorious bull excommunicating and deposing Elizabeth of England, her Catholic subjects had been forced to choose between literal adherence to the law of the Church and obedience to the law of the land. The urgency of the choice was aggravated by retaliatory crown policies, including a flat banishment from the realm of all Jesuits and seminary priests ordained abroad, and a slow but steady suppression of recusant activity among the laity who remained in England. To oversimplify unpardonably an extremely complicated matter, one result among the community of English Catholics, clergy and others, at home and abroad, was a profound political separation. Most recusants found it possible to render Caesar his due, and submitted to the Oath of Supremacy now demanded by Elizabeth; some did not, and suffered for it. Among the clergy, the moderate loyalists, many of them connected in some way with William Allen's pioneer seminary in Douai, deliberately confined their activities in the English Mission to ministering a widely established faith and quietly proselytizing, and even when compelled by the edict of banishment to carry on their English operations undercover, they did not, in principle, mix politics with religion. The Jesuit faction and their following, on the other hand, especially after the execution in England of Edmund Campion and the rise to pre-eminence in the Society of Father Robert Parsons, represented an extreme position which refused to compromise with *status quo* in their native land. If Elizabeth were a tyrant and usurper, any means to dethrone her and re-establish the lawful Church in her dominions deserved consideration, and ultimately active encouragement. Hence it was that in 1595 an English Jesuit in Spain could in good conscience and with Spanish aid—for while the Spanish were not fully at war with England, their co-existence was scarcely peaceful—compass the assassination of the English Queen and the overthrow of her government in the name of the Roman Catholic Church. And it is easy to imagine the embarrassment this situation caused among the loyal recusant laity in England and the moderate Catholic clergy (now that Parsons' grip on the seminaries had tightened they had begun to call themselves "secular priests") and how open it laid them to recrimination. Without wishing to disown altogether their radical colleagues, they were generally unsympathetic to the more extreme Jesuit plots and policies, and generally unable to convince the English administration that this was so. They could see extremists among the Anglican clergy putting each Jesuit discovery to good use in polemic, and as long as they themselves kept silence, they must be taken for accomplices. Their dissatisfaction with the position imposed on them was leading toward a declaration of independence; and Squire's case may have been one of the straws that broke the back of Catholic unity in England.

Near the end of 1595, then, Squire and his shipmates were

brought ashore and imprisoned in Seville; and soon afterward began visits from the Jesuit fathers. Squire's own account of these interviews and the procedure they followed can be to some extent confirmed by the independent testimony of other prisoners, as nearly all Englishmen in Spain were contacted at one time by members of the Society or their associates or students, and underwent a course, long or short, of reconciliation and persuasion to convert. Thereafter, most agree, the talk would turn on active participation in the campaign against Elizabeth; every discontented soldier would be sounded as to the depth and roots of his dissatisfaction, and his willingness to change masters. But the first step in the program Squire describes is conversion, and the details of his own—feigned or conscientious—make an interesting study. By the time he came to write, however, he was understandably both bitter and desperate to disown any lingering involvement with the Church, and his qualifiers are accordingly severe; he must let it be known that he now appreciates the diabolic subtlety of his instructors, where at the time he may have been genuinely convinced.

The Jesuits begin, Squire says, by expressing pity, love of country, and

> natural affection . . . telling that they are sorry to see them in so poor estate, wishing it lay in their power to release them, according to the present necessity *and their willing minds* . . . but they must take the cross which God hath laid upon them patiently and give him thanks which doth it to his children for their good, whose bodies he often times punisheth to the end he may bring their souls home to his sheepfold under the shepherd Christ Jesus.

God is indifferent to nationality, say the expatriates, "he gathereth his flock together out of all nations, for there is no exception of person with God, but among them every one that feareth him, and worketh righteousness is accepted." He is tolerant, they allow, "he hath many means to save them he hath elected in Christ," but nevertheless at last "none comparable to true reconciliation into the holy Church." The Jesuits conclude their first visit, says Squire, with a general offer of instruction in the faith and non-sectarian amity, "protesting that they will never omit their utmost travail both to save their souls, and relieve their bodies, now in the time of necessity; and also to procure their liberty, when time shall serve, by any credit or friend they have."

But the true aim is conversion. With indefinite confinement comes the chance for the Jesuits to experiment freely with special techniques. They distribute a little money; they cultivate favorites; and they begin to intrigue among the prison society, "singling one of the most capability and one of the simplest," and "use all diligence to inform themselves of every man's estate and friends . . . and not long after come again, or send, taking some other to taste (as before), gathering their opinion one of another, and of their education and manner of life past . . ." This intriguing rapidly takes the form of stirring up dissent and distrust: "they will nourish factions closely underground, and yet bind them, not take any knowledge of it one with another, whereby not daring to be resolved for fear of their displeasure, it cometh to pass many times (by conceiving ill one of another) that a man uttereth that which discretion would conceal. This they do to breed a certain bitter conceit one of another, that they may the more easily bring them to the mislike of their present estate . . ." And the ultimate point of the Fathers' policy, Squire says, "is to make a man desperate of liberty, and every other good thing without them."

"After this foundation thus laid," Squire continues, "they proceed very gently to persuasions of prevention in religion." Singling out a prisoner for particular attention—Squire certainly means himself—they begin a doctrinal discussion on a plane suited to the prospective convert. Corruptions in

Anglican practice are contrasted with the historical purity of the Roman Mass; hoary precedential arguments are tricked out freshly, tales of Henry's and Elizabeth's persecutions of unoffending recusants dwelt on; and at some time the subject is allowed to realize that a willingness to convert can result in immediate parole. Faced with persuasions like these, Squire accepted an offer of instruction, but whether for material advantage or out of conviction we do not know.

New methods come into play. With the beginning of instruction begins observation as well, and "they diligently observe, by secret espial, how he entertaineth their doctrine; and it shall be by some one fool among the company which shall be a telltale, whom they will feed with such a hope of their favor that he shall not hide anything from them." Later, when backsliding threatens the acolyte, "if he halt never so little they will set spies about him, what speeches, actions, and gestures he useth in religion, holding themselves unsatisfied until they have brought him where he cannot start back." Squire's emphasis on spying might strike us as paranoid, if the use of such informers even in their own conclaves were not a known practice of Elizabethan Jesuits: at Rome in 1594 a violent protest was mounted by English Collegians against the *Angeli custodes* employed by their Jesuit rector, spies who "at recreation-time and in other places, speak liberally against their superiors, of their government and usage toward them, of their apparel, meat and drink . . . all this to sound their companions. Now if one or two hap to discourse, as he doth, against the superior, these spies carry the whole discourse straight to the rector . . ." Dr. Ely concludes his admonition by pointing out that there is "nothing so contrary to an Englishman's nature as to be betrayed by him whom he trusteth."

A convert's education proceeded in a leisurely way. Squire says, with the priests attempting to make each step sure before going on to the next. "When they think a man to be well persuaded of this doctrine ('that the Pope can forgive sins, and from him, they and all priests') they will let him rest a while, observing how his zeal increaseth . . ." He is encouraged to be frank about his doubts, thus "putting him in mind of making his confessions"; he is given a catechism, a list of particularly moot points of belief (e.g., the commandment against graven images), a rosary, and special prayers. He is forbidden to read the scriptures themselves, "for fear of falling into heresy, because they are intricate, ambiguous, and obscure, which is the cause that the church hath thought good to forbid the reading of them by the lay people; because it is not good to cast pearls afore swine, nor holy thing to dog." Particular emphasis is laid on confession, and he is confessed "two or three times before he shall be admitted to the Sacrament, for that having lived so long, and not made even with God nor once thinking of the means, he must now have a great account to make."

It would seem that Squire is still unsure whether he is really converting or simply playing along to get away on parole. Confession is particularly difficult, he says, in either case: the hypocrite "must have another bout with himself, and perhaps invent a lie to satisfy his ghostly father; but he which persuades himself they mean good faith and believeth their doctrine ransacks himself from the crown of the head to the sole of the foot, for he must not omit a thought, a look, nor a kiss in earnest, nor in jest, no, nor a dream that he can remember."

Now at some time during their *soi-disant* conversions, apparently, Squire and Rolles with him gained their cherished liberty—within the limits of Spain—by the intercession of Father Parsons himself. But the parole was short-lived. "Giving new occasion of offense in matters of religion," explains Fitzherbert, he and Rolles "were taken again at San

Lucar and brought back to Seville, and there again, after certain months imprisonment, delivered out of prison and put in different monasteries for to be instructed." Fitzherbert's "new occasion of offense" has been amplified by certain historians to have Squire fulminating against Catholicism in the streets of Seville, but more probably the opposition of "offense" and "instructed" should be taken to imply that Squire's conversion was not considered satisfactorily complete. I think we can assume that he was liberated on recognizances as a convert through the agency of the Jesuits, and incarcerated once more by the same powers. Squire's account suggests the reason: "if they find that a man do but temporise, and dissemble only for liberty, and that he make not great show of zeal and constancy . . . they will get matter against him to accuse him to the Inquisition." Examiner Bacon goes beyond Squire's immediate testimony, and infers subtler motives in the second imprisonment: "Yet nevertheless, the better to prepare him and work him to his purpose, and the better also to give color (when Squire should return into England) that he was a man that had suffered in Spain for his conscience, subtly he [Richard Walpole] compassed that, upon a quarrel picked, Squire was put into the Inquisition." "By this means," Bacon continues, Walpole "got his heart into his hands, mollified by distress, and became secure of him that he was a fixed and resolved Papist."

In re-interning Squire, the opportunity to confirm his sincerity as a convert and to find out what use he might serve was re-opened. Perhaps before the parole Squire's instructors had already begun the long casuistical argument, familiar to Elizabethan ‹statesmen and pamphleteers alike, which concludes in justifying any means to advance a lawful end, or any act—individually illicit or not—which might contribute to the general good of God and man. Touching expectably on the dignity of martyrdom, the courage of early Christians in the

13

face of tyranny and constraint, on points of doctrine such as that the command of the Church is at all times just and unsearchable, but that a voluntary deed in its behalf is "more meritorious," that "God accepteth the will for the deed," and so forth, it works up to suitable projects of penance and service for the acolyte, mingling promises of redemption with threats of damnation for infirm souls. A glib subject like Captain John Stanley might suggest the betrayal of Flushing, or burning the English fleet at Plymouth, but if Squire boggled at the particular end of his instructors' arguments, that might account for his abrupt recommittal, as unregenerate, to prison.

Let us consider Squire's character at this time, as Bacon describes it: he is

> a man of more than ordinary sense and capacity for his quality and education . . . a man that hath passed his middle age, well advised, and yet resolved enough, and not apprehensive at all of danger (for I do affirm this unto you, that never man answered upon his trial for life and death with less perturbation, nay, scarcely any alteration, as if he understood not his peril and calamity), and yet as sensible for speech as insensible for passion . . .

Squire himself might modify the estimate of his resolution: the declarations are full of hints of uncertainty, and unwillingness simply through fear to comply with Walpole's plot until he had been persuaded of its comparative safety. And the history of Squire's experience in Seville is one of a gradually disintegrating will. Nevertheless, fortitude he must have had, and we have no reason to think him cowardly or mean, nor even fundamentally dishonest; neither Walpole, nor Fitzherbert—who excoriates John Stanley and Edward Coke—will vent anything very damaging about Squire himself. The examinations reveal a man of some education, a scrivener's perhaps, a tag or two of Latin but no real knowledge of it, and a certain shy awareness of his own wit, of what Bacon calls his "very good reach." It was in fact his intelligence and exceptional qualities, says Bacon, which first recommended him to the attention of Walpole, which may have rendered him the more susceptible to the intricate reasoning leading toward the idea of the plot, and which finally made him a fit instrument for putting it into practice.

In the hands of the Inquisition, now, Squire's treatment was no longer gentle. A hard line follows where persuasions fail, and for a suspected apostate the severity of the punishment may conduce, says Squire, to an unintentional reaction:

> his keeper shall hold such a hand upon him, that he shall have good cause to wish himself out of the life; and every base rascal shall be suffered to wrong him, and yet complain, and be hard against him, but none to take his part or pity him; and if he have any kind of ease it shall be taken from him, and the best language he shall hear of himself spoken shall be: *Herro, Luterano, enimigo de dios, y Traydor a su Christo.* If he have any allowance of the King it shall be withheld from him, till he be ready to starve, and hunger will compel him to speak that he never meant.

And once he has begun to harden his heart, says Squire, the Jesuits will neither encourage nor restrain him, but let his own nature carry him to extremes:

> they will let him run on till he be a very Devil incarnate, never making any show of acceptance into favor, but let him glut himself, and even surfeit with discontent, until he be desperately resolved to undertake the greatest villainy that may be devised by the Devil himself. And yet they will not make any show of believing him till he hath vowed and sworn God out of his throne with hellish execrations to perform of that [the assassination], and a worse, if it can be imagined.

Now Squire knows he is "caught," as he puts it, and like Faustus, unable to repent; his keepers are convinced of him at last, and particulars of penance may be broached. Caresses replace cudgelling, and the Fathers "gently entreat him, encouraging him to continue his good purposes," urging him to propose a plan to promote the fortunes of the Church. Now they will "propound something unto him to search his capability," and suggest ways and means, "in giving whereof they show much exactness, as of things not only studied, but practiced."

The process Squire describes, with its alternation of tenderness and severity, its techniques of selection, isolation, and intensive persuasion, repetition, physical punishment and emotional reward, is what we now call "brainwashing," the criminal victims of which we are nearly prepared morally and legally to pardon, as we do offenders of constitutionally incapable or deranged mentalities. For its day, the process was sophisticated enough to cope with impressionable subjects, and given the nearly two years Squire passed in Spain, had the added advantage of long-term habituation and continual opportunity to test sincerity. Unfortunately for Squire, temporary insanity, irresponsibility, or action committed under post-hypnotic suggestion were no pleas for an Elizabethan court; but for us, if we wish to explain Squire's case by his own testimony, it is necessary to take "Devil incarnate" seriously, and consider him from that moment as a man "possessed," an essentially helpless agent of another's will. If indeed he did what he is charged with, there is simply no other explanation; he had nothing to gain from the crime, and he was not the stuff of which martyrs are made. Fitzherbert's argument that Squire must be innocent because to do the deed would require deep conviction, which Squire's death—reconciled to the Anglican Church—did not exhibit, is psychologically naive. The possibility that Squire is still merely acting, and that, as on different occasions he testified, he acquiesced to Walpole's bidding, accepted the charge and the payment, and then after setting foot on English soil wholly ignored the former, along with all relics of his promises, must not be completely discounted; but as we shall see, the tone of his last declaration, when hope of delivery had nearly evanesced, suggests strongly that at the time Squire made his covenant, at least, he expected to fulfill it.

Richard Walpole enters the story for the first time not long after Squire's installation among the Carmelites, where he and a priest named Jackson began to visit the despondent prisoner. Walpole himself says he came originally at Squire's request, which may be true; or perhaps as Bacon has it, he had already perceived in Squire a potential agent and engineered the new imprisonment to make sure of him. Walpole was the third of six sons of a Norfolk recusant, and a younger brother of the celebrated Jesuit martyr, Henry Walpole, executed at Tyburn in 1595 for little more than illegal entry into England. Richard was baptized a few months after Shakespeare and Marlowe, and would have been thirty-one or two at the time of his meeting with Squire. He was ordained at Rome in 1589, inducted into the Society of Jesus at Seville, probably by Parsons himself, in 1593, and at Valladolid occupied the position of Prefect of Studies in the English College during the Squire affair; Bacon calls him "a kind of vicar-general to Parsons in his absence." In 1605 Sir Charles Cornwallis described Walpole as "a hot-headed fellow, as full of practice as he is of learning, yet therein they say he hath attained much perfection."

Considerable ridicule has been cast on the nature of the plot which Squire says was broached to him by Walpole. Fitzherbert and others objected at once that no poison administered in the manner Squire claimed he was instructed could possibly have done any harm to the Queen, and at least one writer, taking Squire's word and assuming Walpole's guilt in the matter, has attempted to divine a subtler underlying reason why Walpole might send his protégé on such a "fool's errand." But was the plot in fact hopeless and fantastic to begin with? Consider what the Elizabethans themselves believed poison could and could not do.

When Walpole first questioned him, says Squire, he recalled, from Tartaglia's *Inventioni*, a ball "whereof the smoke would put men into a trance, or cause them to die." Stanley the informer speaks of a perfume "which should be cast in the way of Her Majesty to cut off her life." Such imaginings are scarcely peculiar to Squire and Stanley: witness the extravagant accusations levied by another informer in 1600 against Sir Walter Leveson, that "he could so poison a silver cup or bowl that whosoever drank thereof would be poisoned," that he could compound "a perfume that would poison those that smelt it," that he could poison salt, and the feed of live fowl, so that later "those who ate them would be poisoned," and so forth. Sir Walter's arsenal of ingredients, incidentally, compares advantageously with the three Weirds'. One may also recall Isabella in Webster's *The White Devil*, murdered by kissing the poisoned lips of a portrait, and Julia in *The Duchess of Malfi*, by kissing the Cardinal's prepared Bible, or the poisoned clothing mentioned by Mistress Kiteley in Jonson's *Every Man in his Humor*. John Dee was charged with elaborate machinations of this sort against the Queen, and in real life, Sir Thomas Overbury was unquestionably murdered in the Tower (1613) by means of a slow and mysterious poison. Squire's device may seem almost comical to us today, but contemporaries, including Walpole, might have allowed it a fair chance of success.

Moreover, Squire's explanation of the nature of the device was that he had justifiable fears of being caught. Walpole accordingly arranged a method to insure that Squire might apply the poison and then absent himself, and be miles away by the time the treason took effect. "Walpole said . . . to apply poison to a certain place was the most convenient way; I said I had no skill therein, to which Walpole replied 'You shall have directions'." Walpole then presented him with a prescription, Squire begins by saying, "under his own hand," for a poisonous confection which would remain operative for some time after being spread out. Its constituents were opium, white mercury, and three powders, "one yellowish, and the others brownish, and called by Latin or Greek names." Squire was "to cause some other to buy one of the ingredients at one place, and another at another, for fear of suspicion"; he was then to beat the powders and opium together, steep them in the mercury water, and let them set a month in the sun and congeal.

Now the exact constitution of this poison must have troubled the examiners, for they questioned Squire closely about it. Curiously enough, although he begins by giving an elaborate circumstantial account of destroying Walpole's scrip, purchasing each ingredient (the three powders cost eightpence, the mercury water came from an apothecary's shop in Paternoster Row) and experimenting with it on "a whelp of one Edwardes of Greenwich," the very next day after specifying so much, Squire breaks down and asserts that he received the poison *itself* from Walpole: "I do not know whether there is any opium or mercury in it, nor what was in it; I received it in a double bladder, wrapped about with many parchment wrappers." This odd turnabout, which seems also to have struck the examiners ("*Now* he confesseth," etc.), is difficult to account for, and is one of the most puzzling loose ends in Squire's case. Why did he change his explanation? If he were lying at first, why did he lie? Surely not to protect Walpole's reputation. And if the latter version is false, is he now attempting to shield accomplices—the agents Walpole suggested he make use of in procuring the materials? Or did the examiners prefer to have the poison an unknown Spanish confection furnished by a treacherous Jesuit, and so force Squire to confess as much? One tentative reconstruction, assuming for a moment that the poison itself was obtained from Walpole, would be to suppose a sequence of questions, and Squire desperately trying to evade admitting his actual use of the poison:

OCTOBER 19
1. Did Walpole give you poison? No, just instructions.
2. Where are they? I destroyed them.
3. What did they call for? Opium, mercury, and some other powders.
4. Did you create the mixture? Only out of curiosity.
5. Where did you buy the materials? Paternoster Row, etc.
6. Did you try it on anyone or anything? Only on a whelp.

OCTOBER 23
7. What were the "other powders"? I don't know, Latin and Greek names, cost eightpence.

Now at this juncture, for the first time—on October 23—Squire admits actually applying the poison to the saddle, and thus, as we might reconstruct the order of evasions, there would remain no reason to continue lying about obtaining the poison. Prodded further about it the next day, he confesses its actual provenance. Perhaps the whelp-story is true; at any rate, the confection is still "of a darkish color, and the whole about the bigness of a garden bean."

Now Walpole's persuasions to put the treason into effect were no longer hinted at, says Squire, but overtly urged. "He said it were a meritorious act to stab or kill the Earl of Essex, 'but this against the Queen is all in all, for there shall need but little else than to do that well, which I charge you to perform before all other things.' Seeing me very sad, he demanded if anything troubled me; I answered no, but my mind was in England. 'Be of good cheer', said he, 'you may come there, to the great joy and comfort of your wife and children . . . '"

Further instructions concerned the administration of the poison; little was left to Squire's discretion. He was to obtain "a double bladder . . . pricked full of holes in the upper part, and carried in the palm of my hand, upon a thick glove, for safeguard of my hand." He was to pay a visit to his old comrades at the Queen's stables—Walpole's plan revolved primarily around Squire's familiarity with the stables—and "converse with all, drinking a pot of beer or a quarter of wine . . . and so by little and little grow into familiarity, so I might come in time to help on the Queen's saddle, for expedition." Still holding the perforated bladder, Squire was now "to turn the holes downward, and to press it hard upon the pommel of Her Highness's saddle." The poison, Walpole promised, "would lie and tarry long where it was laid, and not be checked by the air." Soon the Queen would mount up and ride, the poison before her, grip the pommel from time to time, "and not unlike," says Bacon, "for her hand to come often about her face, mouth, and nostrils," whereupon the administration of the dose would have been accomplished.

The remainder of Walpole's supposed instructions to Squire are scattered among the declarations, perhaps as Squire summoned them from memory. He was also "to poison the Earl of Essex," he was to convey a letter into England and deliver it to Dr. Bagshaw at Wisbech Castle (of which more later), and after doing the deed he was to go to the home of Mr. Woodhouse of Beccles, speak to his wife (Squire insists that Woodhouse himself knew nothing about it) and by a token be directed to one Upton, a priest, who would carry the affair forward from there. "Walpole said the poison would speedily work, and that after the act was done, the Spanish fleet should come, being then in readiness for that purpose." Squire says he promised solemnly to execute his part of the plan, swearing on the sacrament he received at Walpole's hands, "and then, taking me by the arm, he lifted me up, and took me about the neck with his left arm, and made a cross upon my head, saying, 'God bless thee and give thee strength, my son, and be of good courage; I will pawn my soul for thine, and thou shall ever have my prayers, both dead and alive, and full pardon of all thy sins.'''

So much for Squire's account of his relations with Richard Walpole. We must now record that Walpole, for his part, flatly denies conspiring in any way with Squire, or encouraging him to perform any treason. Walpole's letter to Garnett, as epitomized by More and by Jessopp, declares that after Squire was sentenced to two years in a Carmelite monastery, he summoned Walpole, professing a desire to convert. Walpole says he complied "reluctantly," as Squire's sincerity seemed open to question. And he became more suspicious when Squire inquired after Catholics in England, wanting Walpole to supply him with the names of those who kept priests, or chapels—which Walpole refused to do. Squire himself seems partly to confirm this last allegation, as he mentions in passing having asked Walpole about Catholics in Norfolk through whom he might communicate with Walpole, and also Walpole's failure to provide any names; but Squire seems not to have taken the refusal as a rebuff, or anything further than saving both men the trouble of communicating at all. Finally, then, the only real conflict between the accounts of Walpole and Squire is on the main point of the conspiracy, and there is of course no way to corroborate beyond dispute either man's side of that story. For the Jesuit apologists and Catholic historians, Walpole's character and reputation have been his defense; for the Elizabethan examiners and court, no doubt, precisely what would insure his complicity and guilt.

In the early summer of 1597, at any rate, nearly two years after his arrival, Squire came out of Spain. But the actual manner of his departure is shrouded in confusion: according to Bacon, the plan was to exchange Squire for a Spanish prisoner held by the English, that "to give an apt colour; there was devised there should be a permutation, treated by the means of

22

a canon in Seville, of two Spanish prisoners here taken at Calais, friends of the said canon, for Squire and Rolles." On the other hand Walpole, and Fitzherbert after him, assert strenuously that Squire and Rolles fled the monastery, escaped to the seacoast near San Lucar, and thence to England without any authority at all. As Fitzherbert puts it, "they fled away to the sea side, and excused their flight afterwards to Father Walpole, that was most in daunger by that flight, which letters are yet extant." The contents of these supposed letters of Squire and Rolles are unknown, though Fitzherbert promises that either he or Martin Array will publish them in subsequent editions of their books. This has the familiar ring of a campaign promise (there were no further editions of either) and we are bound to be at least somewhat skeptical when Father Walpole as well, in his letter to Garnett, asserts that the letters (or as he has it, one letter, Squire's) were seized by the Inquisition, leaving him no more than a copy. Now Squire himself is silent on the means of his escape from Spain, mentioning of the prisoner-exchange only that the Jesuits had great influence in determining who should be chosen to go home. At one point he indeed does suggest that his departure may have been surreptitious, or at least ostensibly so, and winked at by the authorities: Walpole, says Squire, told him to go to England, "but not tell him when I went. The reason of this is, as I take it, because they may not be directly acquainted with any matter which concerns the King or the Inquisition, but they must reveal it to the superiors of the house or the Inquisition within a short time, and he is of council to the Inquisition." The stress laid by Fitzherbert on the manner of Squire's departure may thus be misplaced, if not wholly irrelevant.

A far more important point, in closing the account of Squire in Seville, is to establish if he accepted money from Walpole for the attempted assassination. This alone, whether or not he fulfilled his promises, would have sufficed by law to convict him of high treason, and Squire is understandably silent on the subject, as of course is Walpole. But Bacon says suggestively that Squire "was sent away conveniently moneyed, that he might be the better in heart, and yet not so abundantly as might make him love his life too well, and go away with his fare quietly; though indeed there were more money stirring, though not in that hand." The hand Bacon has in mind, I think, is curiously enough Dr. Bagshaw's. But John Stanley, the informer whose testimony began Squire's downfall, accuses him and Rolles of having accepted 1500 crowns from Walpole to do the deed. Stanley's word is generally worthless, however, and therefore a very important third testator is Richard Gifford of Chichester, one of Drake's captains, who was imprisoned in Seville after the same disastrous voyage involving Squire. He escaped and made his way to England by February 1600, and was thoroughly interrogated—as well might occur, after the Squire case. He alleges that Squire and Rolles "had 2000 crowns from the Lords of the Contraction House . . . this he heard from a woman in Seville who saw the money paid, her husband being then in prison where he and the other Englishmen were . . . ," and goes on to discuss the roles of Walpole and Stanley in the conspiracy. Now of course we are dealing with unsubstantiated hearsay, but even hearsay indicates that the story of Squire's mission was current in Seville at the time, where Stanley as well may have picked it up.

Squire arrived in England at the end of June, 1597, apparently still in the company of Richard Rolles, who had however, by April and the commencement of Walpole's urging to Squire, begun to distrust his friend, "to hold me in suspense." On precisely what happened during the next week depends Squire's innocence or guilt of actual poisoning, but it must be remembered that for the court the intent, the commitment, or the receipt of payment, singly or severally, would constitute high treason and be so judged. Thus Squire's naive willingness, at first, to confess the plot but not the putting it into practice had perhaps, unbeknownst to him, convicted him out of hand; for the examiners, his admission of a physical attempt would merely complete the picture and provide better propaganda against Spain and the Jesuits. But for any disinterested reader capable of excusing a promise made under stress and a deed contemplated only, not accomplished, the truth of what occurred between Squire's arrival and 9 July remains central to the case. And as Squire only gradually confessed his actions, or was gradually coerced into fabricating them—perhaps after being made aware that he had volunteered enough already to hang him, perhaps with a promise of clemency hypocritically held out—and both at his trial and at the gallows retracted parts of his account, we can never be entirely sure of what happened that day in July, whether poison ever lay on the pommel of the Queen's saddle, and whether the risk she unknowingly ran, and which reduced her attorney at Squire's trial to tears, was real or chimerical.

"Within an hour" of their arrival in London, Squire says, "I and Rolles made means to an honorable person in the council chamber to go with the Earl [of Essex] in his last voyage, and obtained leave"; he desired, he says, "to go to sea to be revenged" on Walpole and the Spanish. Essex was completing the preparations for his ill-fated expedition against the Spanish Azores and Canaries, and Squire recommended himself to the great Earl with a relation of news and secrets—Spanish defenses, preparations, strength, invasion plans, Jesuit conspiracies—he had gathered in Spain; he sent a copy to Secretary Cecil as well. The Walpole plot, however, he kept to himself. But far from heeding Walpole's admonition to conceal his knowledge of Catholic affairs, insists Squire, he went shortly to a "Mr. Wootten"—probably either

25

Essex' chaplain Anthony Wotten, or his secretary, the poet Henry—and offered him additional details about Jesuit methods of collecting intelligence from England; this in order to "warrant my course" with them in Spain. Wotton recommended him to Essex, and gave him a letter, but the Earl had already gone from Court (he left on 2 July) and Squire was unable to deliver it. Furthermore, says Squire, he never approached either the Royal Stables or Wisbech Castle, he threw the letter to Dr. Bagshaw in the sea along with Walpole's recipe for poison, and the day after his arrival, being a Sunday, he broke with the Catholic Church and took Anglican communion.

But repeated interrogation drew Squire out further. Now he asserts that two or three days after his arrival, and after assuring himself of a berth in Essex' expedition, he purchased the ingredients of Walpole's poison in various shops—"an apothecary's shop in Paternoster Row, towards the further end, near Dr. Smith's house, . . . at the Plough, Bucklersbury, and the other two in Newgate Market." He carried them about with him "six or seven days," and then "compounded them and put them into an earthen pot, and set it in a window of my house at Greenwich, where it might take the sun." He experimented upon Edwards' whelp, "and never saw it afterwards, and therefore I think it died thereof."

As we have seen, however, Squire subsequently revised his testimony and claimed that Walpole had given him the poison already mixed; and that all the foregoing account was untrue. And where orginally he had sworn that he never approached the Stables, and called on his companions there to bear him out, now, two weeks later (23 October 1598) he confesses that on a Monday nine days after his homecoming, and with his next voyage assured, "understanding that Her Majesty's horses were preparing for her to ride abroad, as the horse stood ready saddled in the stable yard, I went to the horse, and in the hearing of divers thereabouts, said 'God save the Queen', and therewith laid my hand on the pommel of the saddle, and out of a bladder, which I had made full of holes with a big pin, I poisoned the pommel, it being covered with velvet; and soon after, Her Majesty rode abroad.''

"Thus was Her Majesty's sacred and precious life by the 'All-hail' of a second Judas betrayed,'' sums up Bacon, who reckons it "God's doing and power'' which prevented the Queen "in July in the heat of the year, when the pores and veins were openest to receive any malign vapor or tincture,'' from once laying her unguarded hand upon the contaminated pommel. And without waiting to try again, Squire embarked for the Azores with Essex' Vice-Admiral Thomas Howard in the *Due Repulse*, a frigate of 700 tons, 50 guns, and 350 men.

The fleet "so weakly and wretchedly manned,'' as Essex complained, collected at Plymouth by 8 July, and Essex' flagship *Mere Honour* was already behaving badly. Four days out of port a crippling storm scattered the fleet and aggravated the leaks in *Mere Honour*, the fleet put back into Plymouth and did not sail again until 17 August. Essex, meanwhile, after a motherly message from the Queen, distressed about the condition of his flagship, had shifted his colors to the *Due Repulse*, leaving Howard to move on to the *Glory*. After this inauspicious beginning, the expedition, hobbled by an inexperienced commander, proceeded to Fayal, Punta Delgada, and eventually St. Michael; but the harassment of these islands brought in little booty and less military advantage. Squire wishes to make it clear that he was neither spying for the Spanish nor in direct contact with the Earl himself; he stayed constantly on board at Fayal, he says, and even at St. Michael, where he was permitted to go ashore, he "never stirred forth of the town . . . but stayed in Sir Anthony Sherley's lodging, keeping company with Captain Davis and

Captain Greenway." His hand was injured, and a surgeon dressed it.

"If I had meant to give intelligence," says Squire, "there was time," but "I moved not"; and "when the Portingalls came in, I never offered to speak with them." Squire asserts he "never offered to speak with my Lord till he was coming homeward, at which time . . . I besought him to be careful of her Majesty and himself." When they had regained Plymouth near the end of October, Squire went to stay at a friend's house four miles out of town, and there remained until after the Earl's departure; he then journeyed directly to Greenwich, and never saw Essex again until the autumn of 1598, at Essex House, having been haled in as a suspect. When, he demands, could he have attempted to administer poison?

Two weeks of questioning, however, and Squire was no longer denying anything. The attempt against the Earl of Essex fell shortly before the fleet reached St. Michael on 9 October 1597. "I carried the poison to sea in the Earl's ship, in a little earthen pot closely corked," he confesses, "and applied it to the Earl's chair, where he used to sit and lay his hand, which chair stood on the spar deck where the Earl used to dine and sup; I did this of an evening a little before suppertime, when the Earl was at sea between Fayal and St. Michael. The confection was so clammy that it would stick to the pommel of the chair, and I rubbed it on with parchment; and soon after, the Earl sat in the chair all supper time."

It is possible, if unlikely, that Squire's second attempt was more nearly successful than his first, as the Earl reached England in considerably deteriorated health, and too ill, he claimed, to obey repeated royal summonses in October and November. But no death ensued, and Squire, perhaps considering himself quits with Walpole—especially if "God accepteth the will for the deed"—settled down, unsuspected, to his old job at the Stables. Nearly a year would quietly elapse before retribution descended upon him, in the form of a new messenger from Spain.

Captain John Stanley and his companion William Monday appeared unheralded in London early in the autumn of 1598, with tales to tell. Stanley had come overland out of Spain in sixteen days, showing a false passport at Madrid before 29 August, and having served in 1595 with Sir Walter Ralegh on board the *Exchange*, on his arrival he took himself and some curious documents to Ralegh's house. It is possible that he attempted first to see Essex, and failed. His principal message to Ralegh concerned certain gold mines unknown to the Spaniards in "Orinoco," discovered to him by "one Francis Sperry, a man of Sir Walter's," while Stanley and he dwelt in the same Spanish prison; he had a map of Sperry's to prove it, but also, unrelatedly, two letters he claimed to have stolen from the Jesuits, and a wealth of information about conspiracy, plots of assassination, and invasion. Most peculiarly, Stanley wanted a private audience with the Queen, and no one else, to divest himself of his secrets.

Aside from the irregularity of such an interview, and the suspicion which naturally might attach to anyone demanding it, rumors of new plots, Spanish and Scottish, to kill the Queen had been circulating quietly since May. John Chamberlain on the fourth of that month mentions certain men "apprehended for a conspiracy against the Queen's person and my Lord of Essex, whereof one should be a Scottishman or somewhat that way; much buzzing hath been about it, but either the matter is not ripe or there is somewhat else in it, for it is kept very secret." The Scot in this instance, Valentine Thomas, eventually had the charges against him dropped, for political reasons, but as he had first swum into the ken of Elizabeth's council as an eager informant of a wicked plot, and seemed later to be its very implement, any councilor now might have reason to be even more than normally wary of a mission and a request like Stanley's. Accordingly Ralegh passed on Stanley's information and person to the ministrations of that wily spymaster and hereditary Chief Secretary of State, Sir Robert Cecil.

Now it is quite possible that some inkling of Captain Stanley's character and reputation had preceded him to Cecil, and to the Earl of Essex, who soon joined with Cecil in the investigation. Spain was a nest of informers and a sounding board of calumny and gossip among aliens, for which no statesman had a greater appetite or resources than the Secretary, inheritor of his father's and perhaps the remnants of Sir Francis Walsingham's formidable networks of intelligence agents. Returning prisoners-of-war were carefully quizzed on re-entry into England, and continual packets of correspondence kept Cecil and other councilors momentarily aware of the activities of their expatriated, imprisoned, or fugitive countrymen in the domains of the enemy. Thus Captain Stanley may have been far from an unknown quantity at his first meeting with Cecil; and what there was to know of him was not to his credit.

Writing after the trial and execution of Squire, Fitzherbert says that everyone in Spain, his compatriots in particular, knew Stanley for "a notable drunkard, a common liar, a pilfering, cosening, and cogging companion," a pickpurse, highwayman, horse-thief, and jailbird, who "betrayed his own fellow prisoners in Seville, revealing certain treaties and practices they had on hand for their liberty." Fitzherbert asserts that any Englishman who knows Stanley will swear as much, and so in fact did Captain Gifford, on 12 February 1600, calling Stanley "a most lewd and pernicious man . . . who has denied his prince and country, abusing them both in lewd and vile terms, and betraying Her Majesty's well-affected subjects in Spain . . ." Stanley had passed fourteen years in and out of Portugal and Spain, involving himself in various dubious enterprises and consorting with such thorns in the English side as Sir William Stanley, the betrayer of Deventer. In 1592 and 1594 he was a liberated prisoner in Spain, and in 1595 he sailed with Drake's fleet in Ralegh's *Exchange*, and returned to Seville like Gifford and Squire a prisoner once more. Fitzherbert says at that time he disclosed the whereabouts of an English ship in a Spanish harbor, "not for any zeal to the King's service, but in hope to get a third part of the goods."

Now when Stanley came talebearing to Cecil and Essex, he brought along the two letters which he claimed to have stolen from Walpole and Fitzherbert, and which disclosed the intended conspiracy against the Queen and named Squire and Rolles the agents. But forewarned or not, Cecil and Essex received Stanley's professions with considerable skepticism, particularly as the two letters appeared to be written out in the same hand, with "one and the same busy knot to both names." "Hereupon," recounts Bacon, "it was collected that this was but an engine against Squire, and that he was an honest man. Yet because it was a tender matter, Squire was sent for . . ."

Stanley in the meantime was allowed to reconsider his testimony in prison. By about 7 September Squire had been haled out of Greenwich and detained pending examination in the Counter, perhaps after a brief visit to Essex House for preliminary questioning. Rolles and Monday may have remained free, under observation, but the principals were now safely shut up and the Council could proceed in its investigation without haste.

On 22 September Stanley dispatched a plea to Cecil, complaining that "my body is almost spent with imprisonments," and asking, "that you would call in question all such members and I have made mention of, and make trial thereof, and then if you disprove me, let me pay for it with my life."

Probably at the same time he similarly petitioned Essex, begging him to "suffer me to be brought once again before your Honour, where I will please God, serve my sovereign, right your Honour, and save my soul, which is most grievously perplexed . . . Vouchsafe me this mercy, and that Sir Robert Cecil may be there . . ." He enclosed a long and imaginative relation of his adventures in Spain and Portugal, and more "secrets"; but he could never resist embroidering a story, and his assertion that he had served under Essex himself is contradicted by the latter in the margin of the manuscript.

On 23 September, therefore, an apparently penitent Stanley was examined in the Tower by a panel of three distinguished civil servants, Lieutenant of the Tower Sir John Peyton, Essex' ambitious, young, and literate secretary Francis Bacon, and the militant hispanophobe and "chief persecutor of Catholics in England" William Waad. Stanley confessed that he and Monday had been urged by Fathers Walpole, Cresswell, and Fitzherbert to undertake various services treasonable to England. He spun out his tale with somewhat preposterous descriptions of meetings with Spanish ministers—later he claimed to have spoken with the King himself—and in closing "called to mind that he had heard Cresswell say that they [Squire and Rolles] had played the villain and broken their vow, after having received 1500 crowns . . ."

Ironically, as the author of *Essays or Counsels Civil and Moral* was leaving the Tower after conducting this examination—"a service of no mean importance," he calls it—he himself was embarrassingly apprehended for debt, at the instance of "one Simpson," a Lombard Street goldsmith. Bacon complained bitterly about the moneylender's timing, and his superiors bailed him out; but for one night in the custody of Sheriff More he shared legal footing with his examinants.

32

Now Stanley was shortly (by 29 September) committed to the Tower, and the investigators had time to ask themselves about the motives of this curious witness. At first, as Bacon admits, it would seem to be all a hoax, an attempt to implicate an honest man, perhaps devised by the Jesuits, perhaps by Stanley. Later, however, when both Stanley and Monday had independently expanded their stories to include a circumstantial scene between Fathers Cresswell and Fitzherbert, furious with Squire's perfidy, and Squire himself appeared confused on a few points of memory, the councilors must have reconsidered their doubts. It is clear that they were aware of Stanley's irresponsibility, and suspected in him "hidden treasons" of his own; nevertheless, whether they believed his story about Cresswell and Fitzherbert or not, they decided to make preliminary use of it, or as Cecil says in a private letter, to reap "our benefit of his accusation first." And indeed, when they came to examine Squire, there seemed to be "some circumstances which, concurring with the other's tale, gave it to be understood that there was somewhat true, and that all was not an invention against him . . ."

But it is not obvious what the Council themselves believed was Stanley's part in the plot. The testimony of a proven liar and conspirator scarcely could carry much weight against Squire in court, of course, and thus a complicated explanation of Stanley's action came into currency and print. According to the preface to the Prayer of Thanksgiving republished in commemoration of the event after Squire's execution "Walpole, having received intelligence that Squire, being in the Earl's company, had fit opportunity to execute [the treason], yet the purpose not effected, in an affrighted mind fearing that Squire had of himself revealed it . . . addressed over one Stanley and others to detect the plot and designment of Squire; by which mask of discovery an easier entry being made for the said Stanley into the Earl's affection and company he might more safely and with less suspicion execute and effect the intended villainy . . ." Chamberlain echoes the popular notion that Walpole "thinking [Squire] had either changed his purpose or bewrayed it, gave Stanley instructions to accuse him, thereby to get more credit, and to be revenged of Squire for breaking promise."

Walpole and Fitzherbert are quick to point out the improbability of such a reconstruction. "What revenge could we except to have of Squire," asks Fitzherbert, "by revealing that which we thought he himself had revealed? Were we so simple to think we could hurt him thereby?" And would Walpole be "so prodigal of his reputation" to give Stanley instructions to defame him, even in England? Granting that Stanley was suborned by Fitzherbert and Walpole in the way claimed, why are his allegations credited in court? If Walpole so hated Squire to wish to accuse him, why may not his own account of the plot, as transmitted to Stanley, be itself a lie?

Fitzherbert's reasoning is convincing, and it is probable that the Council privately believed Stanley's mission and motives a little less neat than the popular—and perhaps in-dictive—version makes them. Bacon takes into account the possibility that Fitzherbert or Cresswell, being "passionate" revealed Squire's intention and then was merely "content that one . . . should give information of this matter . . ."—in other words, that what began as an indiscretion concluded as a plan. And Robert Cecil explains to his correspondent Edmondes that Stanley "was purposely sent to do another such act (as now he confesseth) and set on by the Spanish Secretary [Idiaquez] and Christophero Mora, but because he should get credit, he had liberty to accuse this Squire" —leaving open the possibility that Stanley was sent by the ministers independent of Walpole, Fitzherbert, and Cresswell, and that the manner of accusing Squire was left to Stanley's discretion. Indeed Stanley's revelations were inept enough to suggest that he had no specific instructions in the matter, and suspending the question of his own intentions against the Queen, it is perfectly conceivable that he picked up the Squire story on his own—like Richard Gifford—and himself had the inspiration to use it for personal advantage. The examiners surely were aware of such alternative reasons for Stanley's peculiar conduct, but in their efforts first to get the truth out of Squire, and latterly to present a convincing indictment to the court, a little oversimplifying seems to have occurred, which Fitzherbert very justly reveals, and represents as tainting by implication the legality of the whole process.

Now for Squire, who had never even met Stanley and Monday, and "not knowing how far his confessor [i.e., Walpole] had broken trust with him," the problem was bewildering: how to parry the examiners' questions and admit what could be independently proven but yet conceal what could not? How not to contradict, save in undemonstrable points, a testimony he had no access to? "For a time," says Bacon, "he denieth."

Squire's denial took form by 7 October, in a holograph declaration forwarded by Waad to Essex and Cecil, "A Large Discourse of the Jesuitical Persuasions," which Waad allows is "in my poor opinion very well set down for so bad a matter." After giving some account of his imprisonment in Seville and detailing the plot, Squire turns to his own conduct in London, and flatly denies putting any of Walpole's commands into effect, denies visiting the Stables, or approaching Essex save once on their homeward voyage. "In this it is evident that I neither believed the Jesuits' doctrine, nor intended to perform anything that I promised, but the contrary in everything," he concludes, apologizing for not coming forward voluntarily with the tale: "Only fear of that which is now fallen upon me was the cause of my concealment."

"We can proceed no further until we have warrant to authorize us," wrote Waad, forwarding the declaration, "then we will not fail of our best endeavours." Now it is possible that the warrant Waad sought was permission to employ torture. But here again we possess conflicting testimony: seemingly the idea that Squire was stretched on the rack "for five hours at a time" to induce him to confess his treasons, or the examiners' fabrications, stems originally from a letter of an alleged witness at the trial, mentioned by Henry More in 1660 and now lost, and is independently put forward by Martin Array (in Rome), by an otherwise inaccurate Catholic correspondent (in Brussels, 19 November), and by Thomas Fitzherbert (in Madrid). Citing "divers relations that I have seen thereof in writing," and calling upon all present at Squire's trial to bear him out, Fitzherbert affirms that at the arraignment Squire claimed his confessions were extorted by torture, and disowned them. But quite contrarily Bacon makes a point of the *absence* of torture in Squire's case, that the confessions were made freely and "without any rigor in the world," and more important (as Bacon has an obvious commitment to popularizing the State's version of the story) we have the specific statement of Robert Cecil in a personal letter before Squire's trial, and little to gain by lying to a friend and fellow statesman, that "after one or two days denial, *without torture or any punishment save only restraint*, he revealed all above said . . ." Given the choice of Cecil's extant testimony and Fitzherbert's and More's unspecified and lost letters, one must lean toward the "official" version. After all, torture was an entirely commonplace tool of the English prosecuting examiners, and, despite Fitzherbert's extended arguments to the contrary, was both customary and legal in cases of suspected high treason. And Secretary Cecil is scarcely so squeamish a witness to persuade himself that a standard technique of interrogation was foregone when it was

36

not. And again, even if Squire cried torture to the court, when his signed declarations had condemned him out-of-hand, in such an extremity we cannot rule out his lying or temporizing; no warrant for the use of torture in Squire's case exists among the state papers and Council records which are extensive for this period. Of course there are tortures other than the rack, psychological and subtly physical—even "restraint"—and as Squire was susceptible to them in Seville, so might he have been in London.

On the seventeenth of October in the Tower Stanley finally admitted that the letters he had shown as Walpole's and Fitzherbert's were forged, both written out by the same Spanish amanuensis—at Walpole's behest, however, he insisted. And on the next day at noon he was interrogated again, by an awe-inspiring trio: Essex, Cecil, and that most devastating of legalists and implacable enemy of Spain and Catholicism, Edward Coke, at the time Attorney General and Crown Prosecutor. The dignity of the tribunal did not prevent Stanley from reiterating his fantastic story of an interview with King Philip himself on August fifth, involving instructions for sabotage and details of a plot to poison the Queen with perfume—whereas on 5 August the prudent monarch in fact lay sick to death at the Escorial, surrounded by doctors and priests and preoccupied with matters higher than intrigue, murder, and low-level bribery. Stanley implicated his companion Monday as well, who "was dealt with secretly," and now said that Walpole "gave me the aforesaid letters to deliver to the Council, saying Rolles and Squire had discovered their employments," and that Walpole as well told him of the original payment of 1500 crowns to both.

This was evidently enough for the Minister and the Earl, and Squire was the next day removed from the comparative informality of the Counter, committed to the maximum-security Tower, and at once re-examined. Now his questioners

37

were five, Peyton, Waad, Coke, Bacon, and Solicitor General Thomas Fleming. In the examination, which centered strictly on the attempted assassination, Squire repeated to a considerable extent what he had already written out for Waad, adding particulars of Walpole's instructions, and some details of the purchase of poisonous ingredients which he subsequently retracted. Later the same day, with Waad absent, the remaining four examiners witnessed a written-out declaration, in which Squire elaborated on his indoctrination at Seville, clearly repeated that he was expected to deliver a letter to Dr. Bagshaw at Wisbech, and enumerated the points of information he had prepared for Essex on his first return to England. He says nothing yet of the assassination itself, or of his voyage with Essex.

Four days later, however, when the same quintet examined Squire again, they found in the prisoner no further resistance. Whether by torture, remorse, weariness, or the questioners' skill, Squire was suddenly a broken man; he confessed poisoning the saddle, the Earl's chair, that he "came out of Spain a resolved Papist," and released the last names in his portmanteau, Upton the priest and Mistress Woodhouse. The next day before Coke alone, already preparing the case for court, Squire straightened out his story of the poison, and reaffirmed his declaration of the 23rd. Only a gathering of loose ends and the composing of a suitable indictment remained to occupy the examiners.

On November third, therefore, Peyton, Coke, Fleming and Bacon interrogated—perhaps for the first time—Richard Rolles and Stanley's companion William Monday. Rolles had probably come to the Tower along with Stanley, in any case before 6 October; on 3 November he entirely denies having anything to do with the Squire plot, confesses only to having accepted the sacrament of Walpole and to having been urged to serve King Philip, which he insists he refused to do.

Monday declares that like Stanley he heard Fitzherbert "in a great rage" complain that "Rolles and Squire were villainous rascals to deceive the Catholic King, and undo us all . . . and that Squire undertook to poison the Queen's saddle and Rolles to kill the Queen." "Two or three days after," he adds, Stanley told him that Cresswell and Fitzherbert had learned of Squire's treachery in a letter from Walpole. For himself, Monday says he had never spoken either to Rolles or to Squire and had no previous or further knowledge of the plot.

From the Temple on the same day Edward Coke submitted to Cecil the indictment he had drawn up against Squire. Uncertainties had arisen. Despite Squire's full confession to the examiners there were niceties of the case which inevitably would worry so astute and conscientious a lawyer as Coke, who, although he might act as he would one day at Ralegh's trial, and "make up for the weakness of the evidence by the ferocity of his presentation," clearly desired a clean conviction; despite his open persecution of English Catholics he had scruples against the use of torture which later broadened into principles, and he could probably anticipate that Squire—"a man of very good reach"—would disown the confession of 23 October as obtained by torture or the threat of torture, or otherwise unintentional. And there were justices—rare, to be sure—who demanded of a confession that it have been freely given. Moreover, Squire's was oral, preserved as an "examination," not a holograph "declaration," and the worth of Stanley's and Monday's evidence, hearsay to begin with, seemed equivocal at best. It is also possible that Coke was worried lest he might compromise Cecil's intelligencers in Spain by making public their testimony, or was in some way unsure of what evidence could aptly be exhibited: "what is convenient to be inserted and what omitted, it is my part to be directed by those that are able to give direction in so great causes."

Given the rough edges of the case and the undoubted concern of the court with its reputation for fairness at home and abroad, we can appreciate Coke's anxiety that all be "according to law," and understand the slight twist of simplification given Stanley's story in the circulated version. Perhaps a hint of war-party propaganda against Spain specially can be discerned in Coke's suggestion that "the whole composition of [the indictment] do . . . *tacite* set forth the whole manner and contriving of it to be not by P. Walpole alone . . ."

Much to Coke's advantage, nevertheless, was the quite open and traditional cooperation of bench with prosecution which could be counted on in cases of high treason, the fact that Cecil himself was a justice of King's Bench (although he stood down at the trial) and the fact of Coke's own indisputable eloquence, and of the steadily rising tide of popular anti-popery. At worst, anyway, there was enough to convict Squire in his original confession of *intent* to commit treason, or acquiescence—feigned or not—to Walpole's promptings, or acceptance of Spanish pay for a treasonable promise.

On 6 November Cecil wrote to Thomas Edmondes, the ambassador in France, describing the discovery, and mentioning that Squire "shall be arraigned for it on Thursday next." Stanley, he says, confessed that he himself had vowed to kill the Queen with a pistol—a detail absent from the extant examinations—"for which he shall also be arraigned and die . . ." Meanwhile the warrants to convene a grand jury of the Court of King's Bench in the Great Hall of Pleas at Westminster went duly forth; and on 7 November six eminent justices headed by the venerable Lord North met for a preliminary consideration of Coke's indictment. It was indeed a busy day for Coke, who on the same evening startled the courtly public and gave his rival-in-affections Francis Bacon

40

yet more to grumble about by abruptly marrying Cecil's wealthy and eligible niece Elizabeth Hatton. Coke's haste, and the improbability of so excellent a catch—she proved an affliction, in fact—accepting "a man of his quality" after rejecting many better, led John Chamberlain to hint caustically at "some mystery," and a shotgun wedding; but the Cokes' honor was vindicated when their child took some eleven months to materialize. Coke apologized to the Queen for his precipitous action, and Squire's trial continued without postponement.

But the strain of the moment may have affected Coke's work on the indictment, which is a wretched production. No one seems to have gotten Walpole's first name right, and he figures as "P. Walpole" in the letter of 3 November, and as "William Walpole, Clerk, the Queen's Traitor" in the indictment. Walpole himself pointed out this inaccuracy as typical of the Squire trial; other blunders in the indictment include setting the date of Squire's supposed visit to the Stables as 11 July, two days *after* Essex' fleet had sailed out of Plymouth with Squire on board. Nevertheless an Elizabethan court could overlook such *minutiae*, and as the defendant was not guaranteed aid of counsel, there was little he could do about it. Furthermore, in a treason trial hearsay evidence was considered creditable, the disused but fundamental principle of "two witnesses" was generally suspended, the hapless prisoner usually denied the privilege of confronting or cross-examining his accusors, and sometimes even prevented from submitting evidence or producing witnesses of his own. With a head start like this, and the good will of the bench assured, even the shakiest case for the prosecution would seem water-tight; and there was room for court-room histrionics as well: Coke worked himself into such a state picturing to the bar the enormity of Squire's crime, and the narrowness of Her Majesty's escape—the hypocritical bitterness of Coke's rhetoric can be gauged, and marvelled at, from the transcripts of Ralegh's trial—that he burst into tears and was compelled to interrupt his harangue.

No real witnesses appeared at Squire's arraignment on 9 November. Evidence filed for the prosecution consisted of (1) Squire's signed "examinations," (2) the declarations of his examiners, (3) Stanley's depositions, and (4) the statement of an unnamed privy councilor, present at the arraignment, that he had seen a letter sent from Fitzherbert to a kinsman in Rome which made mention of Squire's intent. This last may have been one of Stanley's forgeries, of course, and the letter itself was not shown—a remarkably flimsy and gratuitous fragment of evidence, even by treason-trial standards.

Now Squire determined to make a stand at the arraignment, and all contemporary accounts agree that he there disowned those parts of his confessions which dealt with the poisoning itself. "Finding that it had been his wisest way to have confessed the whole plot, which was known to Walpole, and there to have stopped, and not to have told of the putting it in execution, which was only known to himself, and which indeed was won from him by good following, he endeavoured at his arraignment to have distinguished, and avouching the first part to have retracted the second; pretending [i.e. claiming] that although he undertook it, yet he had not any purpose to perform it" (Bacon).

But this attempt to compromise the triumph of the prosecutors met with stern opposition. In Bacon's version, "one of the Commissioners, being well acquainted with all the particular circumstances, did set before him the absurdity of his denial, against his former confession, which was voluntary, particular, and needless (otherwise than in conscience of truth): upon which speech he being stricken by remorse and convicted in himself, acknowledged and justified the truth of his former confession in the hearing of all the standers by."

Fitzherbert explains this last turnabout as in "expectation perhaps of a pardon," and points out that Squire at his execution once again went back to disavowing the actual attempt. Fitzherbert also claims that Squire in his disowner exonerated Walpole as well, but this detail is almost certainly untrue. At any rate, following the outburst, Squire was induced to write out and sign one final "voluntary and particular" declaration, to contain all parts of his former confessions that he would now reaffirm, and any further matter he might want to get off his conscience. This ultimate confession covers six foolscap pages in Squire's small, neat autograph, and is titled "The manner how the English Jesuits do deal with our Englishmen which are brought prisoners into Spain." It is duly signed by Squire and docketed in Robert Cecil's hand, "1598, Nov:/ A declaration of Edw. Squire after his arraignment." As Squire's last words on the whole affair it is worth looking at closely; no previous historian has had access to this document.

Nearly half the declaration is given over to reiterating what he had said, often word for word, about the Jesuits in Spain; either Squire had copies of his former statements to hand or his memory was exceptional. The Walpole story is similarly close in language to the examinations of 19 and 23 October, but now Squire has settled on the poison being handed him by Walpole, in a bladder wrapped in parchment, which he was later to prick full of holes with a pin. Fatally, he also admits being paid.

But nothing whatever is said of the July attempt. As in his earlier confessions, Squire simply drops the story after Walpole's instructions, and goes on to discuss in very general terms the relations between secular priests and Jesuits (which he is convinced are close) and retail a few more anecdotes of aliens in Spain. But the extremely moving conclusion of this last declaration leaves little doubt that Squire considered himself a guilty man, and the depth of his remorse may finally explain for us why he would voluntarily confess enough to ensure his own conviction. Even as he angles dispiritedly for a pardon with his *envoi*, he seems aware that he is beyond help; forgiveness is what he is finally craving, not amnesty.

. . . wondering of myself what should be a reason why I did no better consider of mine own estate, the matter being no less horrible than dangerous, both for soul and body, I can give no better reason but that it is the deep policy of Satan, who when he tempteth a man which he suspecteth in some measure to be able to examine the cause (God withdrawing his grace) he stoppeth up all the passages to consideration, and so carrieth him blindfold from consent to action, and continue warm in drowsy security and oblivion, adding sin to sin, as in DAVID, JONAS, and PETER; and then having plunged a man in, he layeth the horror of the fact before him, exasperating what he can the conceipt of God's justice for the same, as in CAIN and JUDAS; and myself have tasted of his tyranny since I came into question [i.e., under examination], which I conceive to be the only cause that hath carried me into such palpable and gross absurdities, which I would have thought could never have happened unto me. Therefore let no man presume that of himself he is able to withstand the assaults of Satan, for if God withdraw his grace never so little, straightway the Devil is at hand to sow the tares of his envy, whereof he is never unprovided. And the end of all his temptations is destruction, and that which is worse; he is never contented, but procureth . to heap sin upon sin; I have had lamentable experience of his dealings, but the mercies of God are over all his works, which is my only comfort, for He is faithful and just that hath promised. And now with DAVID I confess my sin and acknowledge mine own wickedness, laying it ever in my consideration, with full purpose never to fall into the like, come life or death, most humbly beseech my God of pardon and forgiveness of that and all other my sins; and for her most gracious Majesty, mine honorable Lordship, and all others to take compassion of my weakness and forgive me mine offences; protesting by the assistance of almighty God to live and die her

Highness' faithful and loyal subject; and this I speak from the bottom of my heart (meaning to perform it) as God knoweth, whom I beseech to work me favor in her most merciful eyes, even as I speak unfeignedly between God and my soul.

Edw. Squire

Squire pleaded Not Guilty, as is customary in treason cases. He was found guilty, and condemned to be hanged at Tyburn; the sentence was carried out four days later on 13 November, and John Chamberlain recounts that "he died very penitent." But the dependable chronicler William Camden adds that at the gallows Squire once more denied administering the poison, and perished protesting that he had never truly intended to carry out Walpole's instructions, a last disowner which one later historian characteristically perverts to "he died asserting both his own *and Walpole's* innocence with his last breath" (Lingard, evidently following Oliver, but citing Camden and Speed. The irresponsible Foley slyly quotes Lingard and gives Lingard's references *ut dicat*, without noting that they in no way support him).

And so we conclude in a mist: was Squire guilty of the act? We may never be able to say surely. But the fact of the conspiracy, far from being a "stratagem of state" set forth by Elizabeth's Council, seems established, and the complicity of Squire, Walpole, and probably Stanley essentially indisputable.

The fate of the other suspects is curiously hard to trace. Dr. Christopher Bagshaw, the leader of the faction of anti-Jesuit secular priests at Wisbech Castle, a fairly comfortable Catholic detention center, was hard put to explain the letter from Walpole Squire claimed to have been entrusted with, and was seriously suspected as the paymaster of the assassins. It is indeed possible that Walpole himself believed he could count on Bagshaw's aid, but Bagshaw and his fellow seculars almost certainly were ignorant of the plot, and not a little annoyed at being implicated. After a spell in the Tower, Bagshaw eventually managed to convince the authorities of his innocence, and explain the widening political rift between Parsons' exiles and his own loyalists. And henceforth the seculars made no bones about accepting the official version of the Squire-Walpole conspiracy and washing their own hands of it, much to the disgust of Parsons and his associates, and the delight of all the anti-Catholic pamphleteers in England. In France as well the plot redounded ill on Spain and the Society of Jesus: Ambassador Edmondes informed Cecil that "it hath moved all men to wonder at so foul and detestable practices . . . and many are desirous it should be published to the world." Bacon's quasi-official account resulted, and to it, Array's quasi-official reply. For years afterward polemicists slung the case, from either standpoint, at each other, and Coke raised its ghost against Father Garnett at his trial for treason in 1606.

Of William Monday there are no further records in the State Papers. Rolles seems to have been still in the Tower early in 1599, and Stanley as well; when the Venetian ambassador wrote on 22 December that "two Englishmen have just been executed in London; they had attempted to poison the Queen," and added, in cipher, that they "were sent on this errand separately, one after another, *by two of the principal ministers of the late King of Spain,*" he can scarcely have meant Stanley, whose lodgings in the Tower were paid for through Christmas day, and who was "now in the Tower" when Fitzherbert composed his self-defense. But Cecil had told Edmondes "he will be arraigned and die," and despite the absence of court records one imagines he was and did.

Father Richard Walpole was still visiting prisoners at Valladolid in 1601, uring the captive English to serve Philip III, and working conversions at Seville in 1605. He himself died prematurely in 1607. Neither of the intended victims of

46

the conspiracy survived him, Essex having followed Squire to Tyburn within twenty-eight months, and the septuagenarian Queen finally expiring at Richmond within two years more of her impeached favorite.

CHAPTER II.

JOHN GEE AND THE EXPLOITATION OF DISASTER

O N THE FORENOON OF SUNDAY, THE TWENTY-SIXTH OF OCTOBER 1623, A YOUNG LANCASTRIAN MINISTER NAMED John Gee stood in the rain outside St. Paul's Cathedral listening to the public sermon.

Rain had fallen off and on all week. "A sad season, by reason of the continual wet," as John Chamberlain described it a day earlier, the dismal late autumn of London with its fogs rolling off the Thames and the wind whipping up drizzle in open courtyards like Paul's, where the uncovered pulpit stood by a monumental cross in the midst of the congregation, surrounded in turn by shut-up bookstalls. Six thousand listeners had been known to attend these public readings in Queen Elizabeth's reign, and occasional criminal executions or exhibitions of contrite penitents might draw even more; but today perhaps less. The fashion was waning, and winter close at hand; in ten years the cross would be down and the sermons transferred to a chapel inside the church proper.

On this occasion the preacher may plausibly have been John Donne, who had occupied the office of Dean of St. Paul's since November of 1621—or possibly a substitute or visiting celebrity designated by him, or by the Bishop of London, who shared that influential prerogative. But only three days earlier, on Thursday, Donne had been kept waiting unconscionably late to speak to the fifteen newly-elected sergeants-at-law and their party, who were celebrating their installation by "dabbling on foot and bareheaded save their beguins [i.e., coifs] to Westminster in all the rain" for a noontime feast, "and after dinner to Paul's, where the Dean preacht, though it were six o'clock before they came . . ." And ten days from now on November fifth, the legal fast commemorating Guy Fawkes' and the Jesuits' nefarious Gunpowder Plot of 1605, he might be expected to deliver an anniversary sermon—as he had the preceding year, when it was "intended for Paul's Cross, but by reason of the weather"—wretched

51

again—"preached in the Church." Overwork and the climate might partially account for Donne's coming down with a near-fatal "spotted or purple fever" by December sixth, which was to keep him in bed—and writing *A Hymn to God the Father* and *A Hymn to God my God in my Sickness*—until April.

So the sermon that John Gee braved the rain for may as plausibly not have been Donne's. And Gee's appetite for pulpit eloquence may thus have been scotched, not satisfied, for he found himself acquiescing to an unorthodox proposal within no more than an hour or two. It was all the fault, Gee might say, of "company, villainous company," of chance acquaintances both Catholic and persuasive. "Lighting upon some Popish company at dinner" after Paul's, he reports, the talk turned insistently on a different sermon and a different preacher—the young, celebrated, and proscribed Jesuit scholar Robert Drury, who was scheduled to preach to a select congregation of sympathizers the very same day in the afternoon. "The ample report which they afforded him," says Gee, "preferring him far beyond any of the preachers of our Church, and depressing and vilifying the sermons at Paul's Cross, in regard of him, whetted my desire to hear his said sermon: to which I was conducted by one Medcalfe, a priest."

Poor Medcalfe must have seemed to Gee in retrospect the devil's advocate chiefly responsible for his own subsequent discomfiture. The priest is condescendingly characterized as "a good companion, but not guilty of much learning; he is often deep loaden with liquor." He lodges, unfashionably, "at a tobacco shop in Shoe Lane," a few blocks north-west of Paul's in a thriving but inelegant commercial quarter. Together Medcalfe and Gee proceeded from dinner to the precinct of Blackfriars—five minutes by foot from St. Paul's—where Father Drury's performance and a celebration of evensong were to be housed.

The Blackfriars in 1623 was a kind of walled city within the city, like the Temple, originally a great friary, subsequently crown property, and now largely a high-rent but declining residential district with its own precinct administration more closely knit than that of most parishes. Shaped like the cutting half of a mattock-head, running from Ludgate downhill to the river, within the walls the leased and subleased structures of the old friary buildings had proliferated wings and interconnected outbuildings, until one complex of tenements might be owned or inhabited by a dozen different landlords. This crowded but expensive sector of London traditionally had accommodated more than its share of recusant Catholics, although the parish church of St. Anne's was now presided over by a vigorous and learned Puritan, Dr. Gouge—a man noted particularly at Eton and King's for his "strictness of life and constant attendance at prayers." This dour minister was to play his part in the ensuing events.

Other traditional residents of the Blackfriars included Italians, fencers and painters, and above all feather-merchants; Lovewit's houseful of society coneycatchers in *The Alchemist* dwelt there; but the true thorn in the side of the respectable citizens was and had been for decades the great indoor playhouse, Blackfriars Theatre, where the royally-sponsored King's Men of Burbage and Shakespeare had performed steadily since 1609. Four years earlier, a pair of citizens' petitions had protested the extreme disorder visited upon the precinct by the playgoers, the "quarrels and effusion of blood . . . the broils, plots or practices of such an unruly multitude," and especially their parked coaches, which blocked up the narrow streets from one to six every afternoon while the playgoers attended, and caused monumental traffic jams all through the area when arriving and departing. But a new royal patent frustrated city action to suppress the playhouse in 1619, and not until 1633 was anything firmly statutory done to remedy the congestion. Meanwhile the respectable residents grumbled and protested and moved away, leasing their holdings to newcomers, as Lord Hunsdon leased his to the French Ambassador Leveneur de Tillières. Two generations of Careys had stuck it out next door to the seething theatre; indeed they had sponsored—with mixed feelings—the very company which later played there; but a third gave it up and sublet.

Now as Gee and Medcalfe arrived at their destination about three o'clock, on the west side of the precinct along Water Lane, it might well have seemed to the beleaguered residents that the weekday affliction had broken out again Sunday. For a very considerable crowd had converged—"the first so solemn assembly of theirs [i.e., the Catholics'],'' says Chamberlain, "that I have known or heard of in England these threescore years and more"—and there would have been more and "greater" in attendance, he observes, "if the day had not been so very foul." One contemporary estimate asserts that seven hundred persons had been at mass in the forenoon, "but now at this time but about 400, of several qualities, English & Irish, of which 20 were priests." More modest estimates give between two hundred and three hundred, but by any account the gathering was both large and historically suggestive. For the very idea that so popular a demonstration of Catholic loyalty, in a time legally prohibiting all such manifestations, public or private, might openly be attempted and attract neither suppression nor interference, seemed most emphatically alarming to Puritans and more moderate Anglicans alike. There was something almost brassy about the project which set the cap on a series of Catholic outbreaks, perhaps designed at testing the current applicability of the anti-recusant legislation of James' early reign and Elizabeth's late; with the aged King, Catholic by heritage and persistently hispanophile, two years from his death, ecclesiastics as dissimilar as John Donne and

54

William Laud feared equally for the immediate future and its liberties. The "Spanish Marriage" now being broached between Prince Charles and the Infanta Maria represented a gaping danger, as they conceived it, of Catholic alliance and enfranchisement, and what might come of it: the subversion of religious self-determination by wily papists, and the deterioration through amity of the truculent and vigorous national character. The very independence of England seemed at stake. Young Symonds D'Ewes, staunchly Puritan, records in his diary that "during Prince Charles his being in Spain, the English Papists began to boast of a toleration they should have shortly; yea, after his return they proposed to set up a Popish lecture publicly in the French Ambassador's house in Blackfriars in London." Whether insolence or optimism better characterized the attitudes of these recusants late in 1623, there is no doubt that they as well as their observers sensed a change in the climate of ecclesiastical control; and the significance and audacity of such a gathering as this of October 26, "whereby you may see how bold and forward they are upon a little connivance" (Chamberlain), escaped nobody. Yet their enterprise, opportunistic and calculated, may have been after all fatally premature, and their open demonstration of faith in James' indulgence have served only to consolidate the factions of their most formidable opponents at court and in the city. Given its outcome, the conclave of 26 October could not have been more unfortunately timed. Pride, as innumerable homilists observed *ex post facto*, would have an appropriate fall.

* * * *

Now the site chosen for Father Drury's performance to some extent depended on the implicit protection and diplomatic immunity of Ambassador de Tillières, who, as a

Catholic envoy, was of course permitted to maintain a chapel and a chaplain in his residence. He had leased that wing of the old main friary building formerly occupied by the Careys and now known as Hunsdon House, adjoining which stood a narrow three-story structure of timber, loam, and brick, raised over the vaulted stone arch of a gateway into the precinct. Unreconstructed examples of such gatehouses, pinched between more substantial buildings, may still be seen here and there in today's London, a particularly fine specimen surviving at the Smithfields end of Cloth Fair. Wherever complexes of buildings surrounded courtyards, or walls divided precincts, were gates, and where property was costly, gatehouses. In 1613 William Shakespeare, on the verge of retirement from playwriting, purchased for 140 pounds—possibly as a *pied-à-terre* near his company's playhouse—a similar gatehouse not far from this one, likewise in Blackfriars, and likewise by tradition a seat of Catholic intrigue.

De Tillières personally took over the lowest story of the gatehouse, abutting his own bedchamber, for a "gard-robe"—a wardrobe or armory. But the apartment above the gard-robe, constituting the second story of the gatehouse and corresponding to the third story of the adjoining houses, was let independently to a Catholic priest, one William Whittingham, known widely by his *alias* of Father Redyate. And the ultimate story, slightly narrower than Whittingham's because it was "gathered in" under the roof, but twice as long because it straddled the building, extending about ten feet over to the north and south, was the garret designated for Drury's fatal appearance. Its dimensions, William Gouge records, were forty by sixteen feet (where the floor below measured 20ft x 20ft), with an interior dividing wall of deal—removed for the sermon—cutting off twelve feet from one end; its front and back outer walls were made of brick and stone, and the shorter end walls, contiguous with those of Hunsdon House, of loam. But the most important feature of its construction was the underpinning: a main beam or "summer" ten inches square ran under the floor from end to end, and despite mutterings after the fact, was neither rotten nor half-sawn-through by saboteurs. At its center, however, it was knotty, and to make matters more hazardous it was mortised to central cross-beams from both east and west walls at the same untrustworthy juncture. Whittingham's story below was more dependably supported, the main beam being thirteen inches square, unknotted, and of course only half as long.

Into this garret chamber by three o'clock had crowded, with Gee and Medcalfe, two and perhaps three hundred worshippers. Leaving a space for the preacher at the middle of the back wall of the room and providing chairs only for the most eminent guests, the majority found themselves forced to stand ranked to the walls like the auditory at Paul's Cross. Late arrivals, unable to penetrate the upper rooms, overflowed instead into Whittingham's chamber below.

Inevitably the architecture betrayed the effects of such strain. According to the earliest chronicler of the event, even before Drury had made his appearance, a frightened gentlewoman sensed the floor seeming to sag beneath her, and when the priest had come she "told him that she thought it would prove an action full of danger if he should offer to preach in that place." But in the brilliance of the occasion her premonition went unheeded: "being led on by a divine and fatal necessity, which blinds the judgement of the wise men of this world, he [Drury] told her that he did mean as then to preach, and to go forward with the greatest expedition he could, with his intended sermon."

At thirty-six, Robert Drury stood at the zenith of an illustrious recusant career. Born in Essex the youngest son of an eminent law-professor and judge, a death-bed convert, and a kinswoman of the poet-martyr Robert Southwell, he had received an extended Catholic education at Douai and St. Omer in France, and the English College at Rome. As early as 1608 he had entered the Society of Jesus, and by 1620, as the rector of St. Omer's, had gained a fair reputation as preacher and controversialist. With his older brother William, a Latin playwright and schoolteacher, he had served in the mission to England, been imprisoned, deported, and proscribed. Even his ideological opposites allowed him eloquence and zeal: church historian Thomas Fuller called him "a Jesuit of excellent morals and ingratiating converse, wanting nothing saving the embracing of the truth to make him valuable in himself and acceptable to others," and a pamphleteer tells us that "the generality of our nation, both protestants and papists" held him "by the outward circumstance and appearance of his actions, to be a man of good moral life, and of a plausible and laudable conversation." But like Caesar before the Ides of March, and Cassius before Pharsalia, says one account, he had passed "all the day before . . . wondrous sad and pensive, contrary unto his wonted humor and disposition . . . as though that some spirit of prediction had foretold him of that fatal disaster which was at hand."

Yet having crossed the Channel at the usual risk to address this significant conclave, he made an impressive entrance from an inner room, "clad in a surplice, which was girt about his waist with a linen girdle, and a tippet of scarlet hanging down from both his shoulders," wearing "a red cap with a white one underneath." He was attended by a man bearing an hourglass, both to measure the duration of the sermon, and "to suggest to him, his auditory, and us all, that their and our lives pass away continually with the defluxion of that descending sand." Much significance was divined in this emblem by later commentators.

Drury took his place at the elevated chair near the east wall, and kneeling before it, offered a private prayer "about the length of an *Ave Maria.*" Then with no "vocal audible prayer at all . . . wherein the people might join with him"—an omission repugnant to one Protestant chronicler—he abruptly entered upon his sermon. Taking the Rheims New Testament from his acolyte, he read aloud the text as appointed for the day—26 October by English computation, but November fifth according to the Gregorian calendar, a coincidence later to be dwelt upon—namely Matthew xviii, 23, the parable of a King who generously forgave his servant the debt of ten thousand talents, but whose servant would not follow in turn his master's example with a matter of one hundred pence. Drury's exposition upon the text covered "three principal points of doctrine," viz.:

1. The debt we owe to God
2. The mercy of God in forgiving it
3. Man's unmercifulness to his brother

Now most accounts agree that Drury passed rapidly over the first two points and had begun to concentrate on the third, dwelling upon the cruelty of Protestant England toward the Catholic minority, and perhaps, as some say, insisting upon the efficacy of penance and the sacrament in redeeming the universal debt of original sin. But whether or not he allowed himself to inveigh bitterly against the English church, "not hesitating to rail," as one reporter has it, "where God himself had held his peace," remains in question now, as contemporaneously it figured in debate. "Whatsoever the matter or manner of his last speech was, I do not curiously enquire," says Thomas Goad, "as making interpretation of God's judgement in stopping the current of his speech at that instant." Whatever direction Drury's sermon took, midway through its passage disaster struck.

"Most certain it is, and ever manifest by lamentable evidence, that when the said Jesuit had proceeded about half

59

an hour in this his sermon, there befell that preacher and auditory the most unexpected and sudden calamity that hath been heard of to come from the hand not of man but God, in the midst of a sacred exercise of what kind of religion soever: the floor, whereon that assembly stood or sat, not sinking by degrees, but at one instant failing and falling, by the breaking asunder of a main sommier or dormer of that floor—which beam, together with the joists and plancher thereto adjoined, with the people thereon, rushed down with such violence that the weight and fall thereof brake in sunder another far stronger and thicker sommier of the chamber situated directly underneath; and so both the ruined floors, with the people overlapped and crushed under or between them, fell, without any time of stay, upon a lower third floor, being the floor of the said Lord Ambassador's withdrawing chamber, which was supported underneath with arch-work of stone (yet visible in the gatehouse there) and so became the boundary or term of that confused and doleful heap of ruins . . .'' (Goad). What had happened was that the main beam of the garret-floor had snapped where mortised, and a section of floor 20ft x 20ft over Whittingham's chamber had fallen through, bearing its freight of humanity, which, combining impetus with the weight of those gathered below, crashed through the solider flooring to the stone-arched gateway—a total distance of twenty-two feet—while the floor of Whittingham's chamber, in turn, fell over the garret floor, ''just as the two halves of a larking net, and so overwhelmed those which till then were upon the floor and not under it'' (Mead). The walls and roof of the gatehouse remained standing, but the shattered interior timbers served in the collapse to bury, transfix, and maim the victims, leaving ''a spectacle of men overwhelmed with breaches of mighty timber, buried in rubbish, and smothered in dust.'' ''Here you might have seen a man shaking of his legs and striving for life,'' records a pamphleteer, ''there you might have seen another putting forth his bloody hands and crying for help; here you might have seen one like some poor spectre thrusting out his head out of the grave; there you might have seen his fellow half dead and half living, entombed in that grave which he was not long to keep. Here you might have seen the living thus pressed as they were mourning for the dead, and there the dead senseless as they were embracing of the living . . ."

"Such was the noise of this dreadful and unexpected downfall," asserts Goad, "that the whole city of London presently rang of it." Dr. Gouge was preaching in St. Anne's a short distance away, adds Joseph Mead, "when the noise of the fall and the shriek of the people so amazed his hearers that they ran out of the church and left him alone." And from all corners of London curiosity-seekers gathered outside the gates of the precinct, with the result that police protection was soon deemed necessary.

Meanwhile, some twenty or thirty who had been positioned at the south side of the garret, beyond the partition which limited Whittingham's chamber below, had not fallen with the majority, but seemed trapped on the fringes of the abyss, as the only stairway to the room was at the north-west corner. Shock and terror seized them, and "some through amazement would have leaped out of a window almost forty feet from the ground; but the people without told them of the danger if they leapt down, and so kept them from that desperate attempt." At length they broke through the common loam wall of the south-west corner into the Ambassador's house and made their escape. Likewise, those standing at the stairhead and in the doorway of the garret were saved; and some half of the fallen apparently survived with varying degrees of injury—like Lucy Penruddock who fell with a chair which protected her from the rubble, or Lady Blackstone, who survived although at first thought fatally hurt. But the toll was heavy, by final count nearly a hundred perishing directly, among them Drury, Whittingham, some lesser nobility, and a host of respectable middle-class London merchants, professionals, and servants.

John Gee, however, was fortunate. Apparently he fell between two pieces of timber, which shielded his head and chest from the falling bodies and wood. Although completely buried by rubble, he was able to break through the laths of a ceiling (at the cost of his cloak) and squeeze beneath a pair of joists or corner supports to where a light appeared. He turned out to be in the Ambassador's house, and was set free by one of the Ambassador's men, he being "so astonished that he scarce was apprehensive of the courtesy done to him." When he had taken a little wine and recovered from the initial shock he returned to the gatehouse area and began assisting the rest.

In this enterprise he had both help and hindrance. Helpers with pickaxes and shovels tried to raise the debris and uncover the main concentration of bodies—"at the opening whereof, what a Chaos! What fearful objects, what lamentable representations! Here some bruised, some dismembered, some only parts of men . . . some putting forth their fainting hands and crying out for help . . . some gasping and panting for breath, others stifled for want of breath . . ." A girl about ten years old came to Gee crying, "O my mother, O my sister, which are down under the timber and rubbish." He advised her to be patient and trust in God's grace, but was surprised and somewhat chastened when the child replied that nevertheless "this would prove a great scandal to their Religion." A sympathetic pamphleteer found such a response "worthy admiration in all men," and even Dr. Goad conceded that "to have a deeper apprehension of public scandal than of private loss" was "a lesson fit for far elder to learn: *Out of the mouths of babes and sucklings thou hast ordained strength. . . .*"

But other Londoners were not so charitable as those who urged the few trapped above not to jump. A turbulent, savage crowd had assembled, Chamberlain reveals, and not only "refused to assist them with drink, *aqua vitae*, or any cordials in their necessity, but rather insulted upon them with taunts and gibes . . . and even in Cheapside, where they should be more civil, they were ready to tear them out of the coaches as they passed to their lodgings or their surgeons." The Venetian Ambassador Valeresso, whose home de Tillières was visiting at the time of the accident, reports that "a girl taken half dead from the ruins nearly fell a victim to some fanatic Protestants when she was being carried through the city, and almost lost the little amount of life in her . . ." Both to forestall riot and to protect the French Ambassador's property, the city officers raised a guard from among the Blackfriars inhabitants, shut up Ludgate, locked the entries to the precinct, and doubled the watch at every passageway. Secretary Calvert at his lodgings in St. Martin's Lane heard of the tumult and summoned the Recorder of London, ordering him to aid the sufferers and disperse the crowd, "intending myself to go with him and offer [de Tillières] my service as soon as the press of people shall be removed, and the passage to his house be free." Despite these precautions, the Venetian Ambassador records that "this accident provided the unhappy occasion for a general and bloody riot."

At the scene of the disaster, rescue operations continued all that night and into the following day, and it was reported (but questionably) that living persons were still being extricated from the rubble on Monday morning. At one o'clock in the afternoon the Recorder and sheriffs met as a coroner's jury at Hunsdon House to evaluate the evidence of the accident and assemble a list of the dead. They assured themselves that no foul play had occurred, no sapping of the supports, measured the timbers and area, and examined the causes of the collapse. Never subsequently was an allegation of sabotage made seriously by anyone, Catholic or Protestant, though at first, apparently, some of the victimized suspected the agency of Puritan terrorists.

The Court had by now been informed of the fall. George Calvert, perhaps the first high official to be reached, had sent a message—doubly woeful in that he himself was a Catholic—to the new Secretary at Court, Conway, dated seven o'clock Sunday evening. Conway replied that "His Majesty was very sorry for the mis-accident," and was sending "one Mr. Maynard" to condole with the Ambassador. John Maynard (a curious choice of the King's, for he especially despised the Jesuits, and bore the reputation of a brawler) reported back to Conway on Wednesday, making "no question but your Honor hath a list of the dead men's names."

Various states of the Coroner's List have survived, in varying conditions of accuracy and fullness. At first the figure seemed to approach eighty, but more corpses were discovered in time, and a few who were "inquired after and not found" turned up living after all. Robert Drury's brother William was at first suspected dead, but in fact lived well into the 'thirties and may not even have been present at the meeting. Gee's much vexed friend Medcalfe figures in all the earlier Coroner's Lists, but probably had merely gone into hiding, for Gee records him as extant about London the following February. Gee also insists scurrilously that one unnamed "Catholic maid," presumed dead, was actually being concealed at a physician's house while she recuperated from an infection contracted from priests. Even the French Ambassador was believed a casualty by one diarist on the outskirts of London, while he in fact had been with Valeresso during the fall, and now, "suspecting that part of the house to be weak built," transferred his quarters to the Earl of March's in Drury Lane.

The final toll reached ninety-five, a rough estimate at best, and some suspected that a number of the more eminent victims had been conveyed away secretly by relatives for private burial. Among those recorded, however, were Drury, Whittingham, Lady Blackstone's daughter, and Lady Webbe, the sister of Sir Lewis Tresham—a Gunpowder Plot suspect—who was interred solemnly in the back courtyard of Ely House, the Spanish Embassy. Twenty-six parishioners of St. Andrew's Holborn were accounted, and three buried there; Mistress Sommers, the wife of a Captain, and known to Chamberlain, was placed in the vault beneath Gouge's St. Anne's; and two more male victims in the churchyard of St. Bride's. But the Bishop of London presently delivered himself of an edict summarily forbidding any of the dead, Catholic or Protestant, grave-space in any of the City's consecrated ground—a shocking expedient—and so two pits were dug on the site of the accident, one before it and one in the courtyard. About sixty-three were buried there communally and their mourners set up two large black wooden crosses over either pit. These were subsequently ordered removed, as a precaution against riot. The next Monday a memorial mass was held at Ely House, with Donne's friend and Chamberlain's *bête noire* Sir Toby Matthew present as chief mourner, "clad in black cotton or bays down to the heels."

* * * *

Through unofficial channels the news spread rapidly, often incorporating curious inaccuracies and distortions which in time were to prove almost as significant as the event itself. Factors like Henry Bannister and young Dudley Carleton passed along routine reports to their land-holding sponsors, Carleton pausing to reflect that the assembly had been "the greatest the papists have had in England these fifty years, and therefore the accident the more remarkable"; members of the Privy Council exchanged letters among themselves, and

Ambassador Valeresso bitterly informed his Doge and Senate that "the wisest restrained their tears, as it is a dangerous crime to weep for those innocents who are considered guilty even in death by the rabid opinion of the heretical multitude." John Chamberlain, still indefatigably inquisitive and garrulous at seventy, took a special interest in the accident, forwarding to his correspondent Sir Dudley Carleton extended reports of his own, pamphlets, ballads, and printed ephemera occasioned by it, and late in November yet more notes about after-effects and reactions. Meanwhile in Cambridge, the more antiquarian-minded Joseph Mead lent his characteristic discrimination and skepticism to the narratives sent him from London, and added his own careful analysis of the news before passing it along to his cousin in the country, Sir Joseph Stutevile.

But it is with the diarists that we find the most striking elaborations and distortions, and as indications of what the common citizen believed actually had happened, these deserve a look. The idea that the hand of God was active must have occurred almost at once to any resolute anti-Catholic, but just what particular retribution He had intended to signal may have required a little time to specify. William Laud records the downfall thus in his journal:

> Oct. 26. The fall of an house, while Drury the Jesuit was preaching, in the Blackfriars. About 100 slain. (It was in their account, November 5.)

This most provocative coincidence simply could not pass unnoticed: by the Gregorian calendar, ten days out of step with the English, Drury's Sunday lecture fell not on 26 October but November fifth, a date inextricably identified in the English memory with Guy Fawkes and the Gunpowder Treason of 1605. The force of suggestion was enormous: not only did it seem to prove that divine intercession had caused the accident, but by circular logic it seemed also to fix the blame of the Gunpowder Plot squarely on the Catholics now so obviously "punished." What began, then, as a pitiful "mis-accident," rapidly devolved in contemporary opinion to an awesome judgment. Every writer on the disaster weighed the evidence of the date; even Catholic apologist John Floyd felt compelled to consider it, and to object—weakly—that if God had intended to make such a point, he would have revealed it more clearly by choosing either *stilo veteri* or *stilo novo* for both dates, not mixing the systems.

More "causes" were sought. Walter Yonge's diary confidently records that Drury's lecture was "an invective sermon," and that he had "inveighed bitterly against Luther, Calvin, and Doctor Sutton, a reverent preacher sometime of St. Mary Overy's, in London, who, travelling beyond the seas was drowned. The preacher said the sea swallowed him because he was not worthy the earth should receive him. At which words the house sank." This last detail, unconfirmed by any witness or serious writer on the fall, is fairly typical of the direction the story took in successive re-tellings. Another popular and probably apocryphal anecdote makes Drury a temporary apostate to Protestantism, who was just now rejoining the Roman Church, and his sermon "a sermon of recantation from the reformed religion, into which the author was fallen of late years, but brought up in papistry, and now returning *in gremium matris ecclesiae*" (Carleton).

Other diarists like Father John Southcote, William Whiteway, Symonds d'Ewes, and the splenetic Mr. Foord, vicar of Eltham, give succinct, slanted, and generally inaccurate versions of the story. Least accurate of all, however, was the usually dependable annalist William Camden, who epitomizes the breakdown of hearsay transmission: "By the fall of the playhouse in Blackfriars in London, 81 persons of quality were killed." But most probably the aged chronicler was

67

unable to confirm his information, for this scrambled report forms the very last entry in his manuscript 'Annals of King James I', written in the extremity of his final illness; only three weeks later, at seventy-two, he was dead.

And within the precinct of Blackfriars itself, the accident and its significance reverberated as elsewhere. On Guy Fawkes' Day Dr. Gouge preached a stirring and interminable sermon, pounding home the point of the date, and holding up the disaster as a terrible emblem of mortality to Catholic and Protestant alike. But next door to St. Anne's, the personnel of the Blackfriars Theatre were understandably eager to play down the fall—they too, after all, occupied an upper story of an old building adjoining, and filled it daily with audiences far greater than Drury's. Thus in Philip Massinger's play *The Bondman*, registered the following December third, a character reflects scornfully upon the ballad-mongers who hawk "damned ditties" concerning events as petty and un-newsworthy as the fall of a chapel, a lover's suicide, "or any such-like accident."

Meanwhile, though unharmed, John Gee was in trouble. At the time of the accident, when the gates of the precinct had been locked to prevent looting, one man—"through the favor of the constables and watch, who were all my neigh-bors"—had gained free access to the scene. Armed as well with a warrant of the Bishop of London, Dr. Gouge had proceeded "to view the dead bodies, and to inform myself in all the material circumstances . . . whereupon I did not only view matters myself, but caused carpenters to search the timbers, to take scantlings thereof, and to measure the rooms." Naturally he took note of Gee's presence, and when a few days later the Archbishop of Canterbury evinced an interest in the matter and desired information, Gouge rounded up four survivors of the fall, including Gee—all "men of good understanding, able to conceive what they saw and heard, and to relate what they conceived"—and conveyed them to Lambeth.

At the palace Archbishop Abbott and his two domestic chaplains, Featley and Goad, confronted the witnesses. The testimony taken, and three of the four discharged, there remained a somewhat ticklish problem concerning the last. For John Gee provided a complex emblem: as a miraculous escapee, he represented the work of God's mercy, and as a Protestant among so many Papists, a particularly fitting object for salvation, and one well worth propagandistic exploitation. But as a minister of the church his presence at a meeting of Catholics could not but raise questions of orthodoxy, the more serious for the limelight he would soon find himself in. Abbott and his chaplains weighed these conflicting considerations grimly while the young cleric was left to re-examine his conscience.

Finally it was determined to give Gee a second chance. After interrogation, finding him "inclining to [the Catholic] side"—a defection Gee freely admitted—the Archbishop and his chaplains vigorously set themselves to reviving the apostate, Abbott with "his holy counsel and monition," Goad and Featley with "some other speeches" as well. In conclusion the Archbishop "rung in his ears" Christ's *caveat* to the Magdalene, *Vade et ne pecce amplius, ne deterius contingat tibi,* and the rest was up to Gee.

This, then, was the crisis of John Gee's young life, a point of choice from which he might never again retreat. Halfway measures would not serve him, he could be certain; he was a responsible twenty-seven years old, of comfortable and conspicuous family—traditionally churchmen—and "a man of very strong able body." From 1612 to 1621 he had passed his time at Brasenose College, Oxford, taking degrees of B.A. and M.A.; now beneficed in Newton, near Winwick, Lancashire, he would eventually accede to a more elegant living at Tenterden, in Kent. So fashioned a career was now on the line: Gee could persist in his religious uncertainty and endure the disfavor of his superiors, or he could thrust the devil entirely behind him, owning up to his sins, and doing his utmost to repair them. His decision was predictable. "Albeit my foot was stept into the Babylonian pit, yet I often meditated of [the Archbishop's] fatherly admonitions," until his course was obvious. He put himself abjectly in the hands of his confessors, promising to behave in the future, and offering, as a sop to the authorities, whatever he had by now learned of recusant activity in London. Evidently his recognizances sufficed.

Now one of Archbishop Abbott's chaplains, Dr. Thomas Goad, found Gee's narrative especially intriguing. At forty-seven, in his twelfth year as chaplain to the Archbishop, Goad was well-established in the high echelons of the Anglican Church. A King's College B.A., B.D., D.D., fellow and lecturer (his father had been Provost) he had participated with his colleague Daniel Featley in several celebrated debates against Jesuit controversialists like Muskett and Fisher, bringing to them "a commanding presence, an uncontrollable spirit, impatient to be opposed, and loving to steer the discourse . . . of all the company he came in" (Fuller); but with the written word his experience had been brief and disappointing. Seventeen years earlier he had turned his hand, on the eve of ordination, to Latin poetry, choosing, as he would again, a Catholic disaster for his subject. But the Gunpowder Treason was year-old news in 1606, and without a translation to go along with Goad's elegiacs, the booksellers he canvassed refused flatly to publish him unsubsidized. Faced with humiliating alternatives, Goad chose to pay, but vented his annoyance in a scathing preface. Thus *Proditoris Proditor, sive Decachordon* came to the press in 1606, late, unwelcomed, and hastily printed for an obscure publisher at the partial cost of the author—but other of Goad's verses fared even worse. A Latin eclogue of 1606 celebrating the struggle between Shadowy Equivocation and the Light of Reason had to remain in manuscript until 1624, when the new notoriety of its composer had lent it currency enough for Henry Mason to include it in his anti-Jesuit diatribe *The New Art of Lying*.

But Gee's stories had rekindled the *littérateur* in Goad. The respectable chaplain arranged a second, private interview with his charge, and drew him out in detail; he visited the scene of the disaster, copied portions of the coroner's report, and as rapidly as possible set about committing the matter to prose. This time, however, he chose English, and good vivid English at that—a thorough and evocative account of the accident was to form the heart of his book, and the preacherly "application" or moral summing-up only the last quarter.

But Goad evidently could not resist beginning with the "application," and letting the news slide for the moment; the sixteen-page conclusion reached his publishers, Barrett and Whittaker, and the print-shop of John Haviland, first, where it was set up at once to save time while they all awaited the remainder of Goad's manuscript. By the first week of November he had made a good start on the factual portion, but either his hand was rusty or his heart was not in it, for the earliest draft of this part was not nearly long enough. Barrett, Whittaker, and Haviland expected forty-eight pages more from Goad; here were scarcely a dozen.

Faced with the burdensome necessity of fleshing out his narrative, and the consideration of time uppermost in his mind, what must Thomas Goad have thought, when, with no warning, and a scant week after the accident, there appeared at the stationers' of London a pamphlet on precisely the same subject, with some of Gee's own information in it, and under its provocative title the imprint of none other than Haviland and Whittaker? With the spectre of 1606 in his memory, how bitter must this new anticipation have seemed to him? One can only imagine Goad's "uncontrollable spirit, impatient to be opposed" confronting so infuriating an obstacle, and draw our own conclusions from what followed.

Like many other eminent ecclesiastics and noblemen, Goad possessed the privilege, loosely defined, of "licensing" or refusing to license for publication any book, of demanding changes in the unpublished manuscript, or causing offending printed copies to be "called in." In the case of *The Fatal Vesper*, by "W. C.," Goad through disinterest or ignorance had not exercised his prerogative of censorship at the earliest opportunity, when the title was registered on 31 October at Stationers' Hall; at that time it obtained an *imprimatur* from one George Cottington. Now, however, upon reading the printed pamphlet, Goad—or anyone else—could perceive a quality of moderation or tolerance in the report which coasted close to Catholic sympathy. It was not overt, to be sure, but it was enough for Goad. "We look for some relation of this mishap in print," wrote Chamberlain on November eighth, "and there was one two days since, but presently called in again for what reason I know not." Indeed the reason was obscure—Mead thought it "want of license," which, although untrue, may have been the explanation circulated; Mead also noted that "*The Fatal Vespers* . . . is affirmed to have been penned by a Catholic," although the author himself speaks of "us of the Reformed Church," and is at pains to protest anyone's identifying him as an "adiaphorist" or equivocator. At any rate, whether by Goad or Goad's agency, the distribution of W.C.'s report was stopped, the copies impounded, and for the harried chaplain a respite and a new chance of precedence or at least equal footing at the booksellers provided.

And what was more, Goad discovered, the temporarily banned pamphlet could be made to yield solid matter. Here was

Gee's story of the little girl who lamented the scandal to her cause more than the loss of her mother and sister; perhaps Goad had also heard it from Gee, but his earliest draft of the narrative omits it. In the finished version, however, the story is present, lifted almost word for word from the interdicted report—save that where W.C. finds the child's response "a speech which is worthy admiration in all men, as this Relator did truly admire it," Goad prudently tones the characterization down to "a *strange* speech proceeding from a child of so tender years." Other details found their way from *The Fatal Vesper* to *The Doleful Evensong,* and with the stalled rival report undergoing no doubt painstaking and slow scrutiny for traces of heresy, Goad rapidly concluded his own manuscript, although the final version still fell twelve pages short of the publishers' expectations. They, however, had in turn discovered a way of levying contributions from their own earlier report, now that litigation threatened to defer its appearance endlessly: the "Catalogue of the Dead," an early version of the coroner's list which was appended to the first pamphlet, had been left standing in type. John Haviland's assistants merely reshuffled the blocks of lead, made a few perfunctory corrections, laid them into another forme, and printed them up as "an exact catalogue" to be annexed now to Goad's work.

On Saturday, 14 November, *The Doleful Evensong* was at last ready for entry at Stationers' Hall. Who could be approached on a Saturday to provide the license? Thomas Goad himself was amenable, and no doubt none knew better than he the strict orthodoxy of his own book; appropriately, then, he allowed his own *imprimatur.* The book was available in bookstalls by Monday the sixteenth.

But Whittaker and Barrett were not yet through exploiting their new literary property. Presumably now *The Fatal Vesper* had been restored to grace, but, stripped of its particulars and deprived of its priority by *The Doleful Evensong,* no further printing seemed called for. Goad's pamphlet, on the other hand, might benefit from an old publisher's stratagem: no more than ten days after the initial publication, Whittaker and Barrett reissued it with certain changes. These in fact were almost wholly typographical, a few obvious errors being corrected, a few minor changes in the list of the dead—with a paragraph added drawing attention to them—and the signature to the preface altered from "T. G." to "T. Goade." Yet with these insubstantial differences the publishers and stationers felt themselves licensed to purvey the pamphlet as an altogether new work. Writing to Sir Thomas Wotton on 26 November, a London bookseller Francis Barnham craves that the "new" version be acceptable to him "as a work of a new edition and material addition to the former: for, in the first book the author under the epistle dedicatory subscribed himself, 'Thine in the Lord, T. G.,' but in this new edition and addition, of two days time, he hath plainly written himself, 'T. Goade '; by favor of which addition the book-binders sell them apace, even to those that bought of the first . . ."

Perhaps the exemplary action against W. C.'s pioneering effort discouraged other London publishers from above-board competition with Goad, Barrett, and Whittaker. For the only other surviving and strictly contemporary printed report, an ill-tempered, uninformed, polemical account called *Something Written by Occasion of that Fatal and Memorable Accident* [*STC* 3101], appeared without any attempt to obtain entry or license, and on the title-page prudently named neither author, printer, nor place of publication. A pro-Catholic apology, Father John Floyd's *A Word of Comfort*, was printed pseudonymously abroad and only smuggled into England. As for broadside ballads, which served the Elizabethans in disaster-reportage much as newspapers have come to serve us, several may have emerged at once: Chamberlain on 15 November forwarded to Carleton "such books and ballads as I can come by, touching that fearful accident''; but only one now survives, in only one copy, publisher Matthew Rhodes's spirited *A Dismal Day at Blackfriars*—printed in double columns in the form of a tombstone, surrounding a partial list of the victims. The conclusion is predictably pious:

> O Lord, defend thy Church and Commonweal,
> Maintain thy Gospel free in this our land,
> And since to us thy Truth thou dost reveal,
> In zeal to it let us ever stand;
> Protect our King still from his enemies' hand;
> And when we must resign our vital breath,
> Save us (O Lord) from strange and sudden death.

While not demonstrable, it seems likely that John Gee had entered into an agreement with Thomas Goad to hold off publishing his own account of the Blackfriars disaster until Goad's had run its course. At least Gee would certainly not expect to improve his case by immediate competition with an influential superior; while at the same time all the relations containing his tales would serve, as well, to pave the way for the first-hand narrative only he could provide. But by late March, 1624, when Gee's maiden effort of journalism finally issued from the press, the bare story had lost its sensational appeal. More matter would have to be incorporated.

Despite the hiatus, however, *The Foot out of the Snare* was evidently composed and printed in considerable haste. The publisher, Robert Milbourne, entered the title on March 20, despite the fact that Gee had not even finished writing it: one line in the printed copy refers to "yesterday" as "Good Friday, this present year 1624," i.e. March 26, the date subscribed to one of the appendixes as well. Possibly Milbourne's failure to provide a sample for licensing provoked the cancellation of his entry, for in the Stationers' Register this March 20 passage is deliberately scored through.

But the pamphlet was soon ready, and soon in print,

dedicated to practically everybody: "the most reverend father in God the Lord Archbishop of Canterbury his Grace, and to the rest of the reverent Lords Spiritual, and the right honourable the Lords Temporal, and also to the most worthy and religious knights and burgesses of the House of Commons," *et al.* From the start it stirred up profound controversy. For Gee had chosen to lard his unseasonable narrative with the most extraordinarily personal attack on any sect or group in the history of English journalism. *The Foot out of the Snare* is a startling compilation of scurrilous anecdotes, "providential" interpretations of recent history, and above all, *names*—names of Catholic priests, physicians, factors, nuns, lists of books, booksellers, writers, and even binders. Like the more articulate ex-communists of the 1950's, Gee apparently had left no stone unturned in his efforts to clear himself of suspicion. He explains his spiritual conversion and the fruits of his gratitude in inspirational detail:

> Being in the midst of the room that fell, and though that *omnes circumstantes*, all (in a manner) that stood about me perished in that calamity, and I involved in the downfall and falling, being covered with the heaps of rubbish and dead carcasses, yet it pleased God to hasten my escape, beyond my own expectations and human understanding . . . What was there, or is there, in *me*, miserable man, that the hand of God should strike so many on my right hand and left, and yet overpass *me*? Surely I was no Lot, to escape out of burning Sodom, no Noah to be preserved in a general Deluge. If the load of sin pressed them down that fell (alas! far be it from me to have uncharitable conceit of their persons) . . . &c.

The last expostulation may seem particularly disingenuous. Gee saw clearly, at any rate, the way to repay God for his deliverance: "*It becometh well the just to be thankful,*" he says, and glosses this sentiment in the margin: "I penned and published this writing as a monument of my thankfulness."

The body of Gee's monument consists of unrelieved invective—enlivened by illustrations. One new post-Blackfriars anecdote concerns a "friend" of Gee's, one Parker, a "trader and factor for the Papacy beyond the seas," who narrowly escaped the disaster along with Gee "and accompanied me that night to my lodging."

> He told me by the way that nothing grieved him more than that he had not been one of those that died by the aforesaid mischance. What should make him so prodigal of his life I know not; but sure, not long after, the Powers Divine cut the thread of his days; for the week following, he being the man that must carry the news over the seas to Douai, and going there to take priestly orders—there being a need of a supply, F. Drury, F. Redyate, and one F. Moore being so unexpectedly, as they term it, "martyred"—at London Bridge, at his very first setting forward, M. Parker was drowned, with a kinswoman of his bound for Brussels, there to take on her the habit of a nun. I will not comment upon these disasters, knowing that God reserves to himself three things: the revenge of injuries, the glory of deeds, the judgement of secrets . . .

Despite the almost nauseating sanctimony of such disclaimers as the last above, Gee's style remains curiously engaging to the reader; one follows avidly in spite of oneself. As a journalist Gee emerges a "natural"—but his reportorial honesty may raise doubts: where Gee is vague, Chamberlain (November 21) dates the death of Parker 17 November, far later than the "the week following," and specifies that "himself with one of the youths, one of the watermen, and the novice nun, drowned; the other two escaped." Now Gee calls the novice nun Parker's "kinswoman," but William Gouge adds further that she was Parker's niece. Why is Gee ignorant of these details, if indeed he is Parker's intimate? Similar suspicion may be attached to the catalogues of Catholic professionals Gee appends to his main narrative. In a list of 127 "Romish Priests and Jesuits now resident about the city of

London" we rarely encounter a Christian name; most of the surnames, as well, are quite common—Smith, Jones, Wood, White, Young, etc.

Perhaps the popularity of the catalogues of the dead offered with Goad's and W. C.'s pamphlets, and Rhodes's broadside ballad (we may note that the anonymous *Something Written &c.* apologizes for the lack of one) inspired Gee's voluminous tallies of men and books. If the public would eagerly devour a list of the dead, how much more so a list of living? Some of Gee's characterizations, indeed, are exceptionally vivid: among the "Priests and Jesuits" we find:

> F. Townshend, alias Ruckwood, brother to that Ruckwood who was executed at the gunpowder treason, a Jesuit, a little black fellow, very compt and gallant, lodging about the midst of Drury Lane, acquainted with collapsed ladies.
> F. Palmer & F. Palmer. Both Jesuits, lodging about Fleet Street, very rich in apparel; the one, a flaunting fellow, useth to wear a scarlet cloak over a crimson satin suit.

Gee pays the "Jesuits"—a term he uses with customary looseness—their due as soldiers of a learned, formidable order: Fisher is "a notorious Jesuit," Harvey "a very dangerous Jesuit," Fr. Armstrong "one that insinuateth dangerously, and hath seduced many." He can reflect of one Fr. Harris that he is "very shallowpated; and yet some say he is a Jesuit, which I much wonder at."

Often Gee's qualifications are captious, but nothing if not piquant: Fr. Latham "was sometime a bird in the stone cage at Lancaster," Fr. Medcalfe, "now lodging in Shoe Lane, a good companion, but not guilty of much learning; he is often deep-loaden with liquor," Fr. Heigham the "author of many loud-lying pamphlets," Fr. Stubbly "a boon companion," and Fr. Charles "a limping hobbling priest." Popish books as well as proselytes now particularly provoke the scorn of the new author, with their exorbitant cost—possibly a bitter retrospect—high on his scale of complaint. The two-volume Douai Old Testament, revised by Worthington, is "sold for forty shillings, which at an ordinary price might be afforded for ten." St. Augustine's confessions, translated by Toby Matthew, cost sixteen shillings, "being but a little book in Octavo, and might be afforded for two shillings sixpence"; others are "sold very dear," or "at an unreasonable rate," and the crowning insult is "the loud lying pamphlet termed *The Bishop of London's Legacy*, written by Muskett, a Jesuit, and reprinted with a preface of a new disguise; the book containing about sixteen sheets, they squeezed from some Romish buyers six or seven shillings apiece. A dear price for a dirty lie. Yet I wish they that have any belief in it might pay dearer for it."

Thus, with preface and errata, five-and-a-half pages of Popish books, and eight of priests, Gee fleshed out his diffuse attack until it covered a hundred and sixteen small quarto pages. With its catalogue of offenders as confident and vague ("two priests, lodging in Mistriss Fowler's house in Fetter Lane, whose names I cannot learn") as McCarthy's of "communists in the State Department," it issued from the press of Humphrey Lownes soon after March 26, 1624.

The reaction among the Catholic community was instantaneous. Anthony à Wood explains that the pamphlet was "printed four times in the said year 1624 because all copies, or most of them, were bought up by the Roman Catholics before they were dispersed, for fear their lodgings, and so consequently themselves, should be found out and discovered by the catalogues . . ." Furthermore, it was noised about that Gee was not really the author at all, "that the book," as he indignantly reports, "was none of my writing, but that I am hired to put my hand to it. Within these few days Palmer the Jesuit, with a bold wainscot face, bruited [this rumor] in a stationer's shop in Paul's Churchyard." But truth triumphed,

Gee records, when meeting Palmer in the street he convinced him to retract so insulting an assertion. Faced with the onslaught of following editions, few of Gee's former companions would deny him the propriety of authorship.

But at least one of the victims cited chapter and verse about Gee's accuracy. Fr. Muskett, the presumed author of *The Bishop of London's Legacy*, objected hotly to a number of errors of fact, including being himself called a Jesuit, which he was not. He sent word to Gee, bluntly, that he "must expect a knock" for his slanders; and in Muskett's wake Gee reveals that "others have vowed to do me a mischief." Undeterred by the threat of physical violence, and perhaps instigated by the disappearance of his book at the bookstalls, Gee replied to all such harassment in a second edition, entered for publication as early as May first. Here now were a satirical "Gentle Excuse to Mr. Muskett, for Styling him a Jesuit," dated April 22, an answer to the charges of ghostwriting, and a new list of "Popish Physicians in and about the City of London." The catalogue of Catholic books has more than doubled in length; the number of priests has risen sharply from 127 to 255, in the city alone, although there are "above seven times so many . . . that overspread our thickets through England"—an assertion which carried a scarcely veiled counterthreat. If his nominees wished to provoke him further, Gee proclaims himself ready and armed.

No doubt the hurried issue of his expanded edition accounts for its frenzied collation: working partly from standing type, and partly from new, the printers supplied an extremely confusing set of sheets. Presently, however, a third edition was called for, perhaps again made possible by Catholic purchase, and the text was re-set and regularized. This too was soon exhausted, and a new, fourth, and last edition appeared shortly.

By now Gee had incorporated extensive additions of his

own, some dictated by the original response, some ostensibly by the claims of conscience. At first he had concluded sententiously with an evocation of "my aged father, a minister of the diocese of Exon.," whose "divers letters of argument and exhortation" had contributed to Gee's evangelization. Now he adds fervent apologies—evidently an afterthought—to Parson Josiah Horne of Winwick, for an unspecified but apparently egregious slander Gee had circulated in his Lancashire days. Presumably the new notoriety of authorship had called down upon him old, and valid, recriminations. Now chapter divisions and "content" running-heads have been added, as befits a more elegant production; the length has risen from 112 pages to 146; the priests are up to 261 in number, the Popish books and physicians added to, and a one-leaf list of "the names of such as dispenses, prints, bind, or sell Popish books about London" has been annexed. One new post-Blackfriars anecdote now figures: "Somewhat remarkable," Gee recounts, "was the death of Master Richard Linton, clerk, late parson of Middleton in Norfolk, who was Popish in opinion and affection . . . This minister having heard of the fall of the house in London, the Sunday next before Christmas, preaching at a place called Cornard, a mile from his own parish, took his text out of Ecclesiastes, ii. 2: *Thou knowest not what evil shall be upon the earth.* In which sermon he took occasion to signify unto them the accident that had lately befallen some at the Blackfriars, and thereof made this construction: that he thought the most of them were martyrs and saints in heaven, and desired that he might die no other, or no worse death than they did.

"Shortly after, on Thursday, being Christmas day in the morning, there blew a very violent wind, which had continued most part of Wednesday night, and still did endanger a ruinous barn in his yard; whereupon he came forth to support it. And then, whilst he was upholding a tottering part thereof, a strong gust of wind throwing down the barn, a piece of timber struck him between the shoulders and pressed him down to the ground, that he instantly died . . . In this secondary mischance methinks I not only see a type of the greater disaster in those that died, but also a kind of parallel of myself in this man, that escaped, being at the brink of the same danger and downfall, and beholding that which the other tasted.''

Since the second edition, naturally, Catholic antipathy had increased. Where by May first, as Gee records, the threats had amounted only to "a knock" and "a mischief," by the fourth edition, "two of them [Catholics] have threatened to cut my throat." Still Gee persisted in his exposure. A sequel to *The Foot out of the Snare* was registered with extraordinary rapidity, on 24 May, *New Shreds of the Old Snare.* "After the sprain and dislocation which I have suffered by entanglement in Popish snares," Gee explains, "nothing hath been more available to me for my perfect cure than the view and search of those rotten ragged shreds of those cords of vanity and illusion, which a while did hold me captive in the time of my weakness. The best means, therefore, for the confirming of myself and arming others is and will be the further inquiring into the particular course of the great seducing masters, especially the Jesuits . . ." Particulars include new but not dissimilar attacks on superstition—apparitions and witchcraft—"copies of divers letters of late intercourse concerning Romish affairs," and lists of indulgences supposed to be available in Rome during the upcoming Jubilee of 1625. Supplementing the catalogues available in *The Foot out of the Snare* is now one of "the names of such young women as to this author's knowledge have been within two or three years last past transported to nunneries beyond the seas." Forty-six culprits are identified, among others a predictable "Mary Smith" and "Mrs. Jones," as well as one "Mrs. Townely," followed immediately by an undifferentiated and identical name. After this comes a separate catalogue of "Factors employed for the conveying over of the said women to the nunneries," numbering among them the intriguing character of "Spanish John, commonly called The Devil's Factor, or Forty-Pound John, which name was given him for cozening two gentlewomen of forty pounds, whom he undertook to transport."

Thus with four editions of *The Foot out of the Snare* and at least one of *New Shreds*, 1624 proved for John Gee journalistically a banner year. Official recognition of his achievement seemed almost inevitable, and indeed within the year was accorded. By 31 October 1624 the penitential career of John Gee had come full circle.

A year and five days earlier the young cleric had stood in the rain listening to a sermon at Paul's Cross. Now he occupied the pulpit. As near as practicable to the anniversary of the Fatal Vespers—perhaps appropriately, this corresponding Sunday fell on Halloween—Gee found himself delivering the most prestigious public lecture in England. For the occasion he had carefully prepared a sermon, *Hold Fast*, predicated upon Revelations, iii. 11: *Behold, I come quickly: hold that fast which thou hast, that no man take thy crown.* Beginning, perhaps nervously, with a dull, semantic interpretation of his text, Gee soon warmed to a familiar theme. Having likened himself to the Prodigal Son returned to the fold of his church, he proceeds to depict, enthusiastically, the pitfalls and defects of the discipline he has abandoned. New anecdotes and cautionary illustrations rapidly follow, and inevitably the conclusion evokes Gee's particular claim to fame, and the *raison d'être* of his present and honorific office: "This day wherein I speak standeth in center and equal balance between two days which I must never forget. The one of public danger, intended by men, but prevented by God; the other of danger and damage not intended by men, *but permitted and disposed by God.* The one by common gratulation ye are to celebrate in this place five days hence, being the fifth of November; the other is fit for me to record in my personal thanksgiving, being past five days since, namely the six and twentieth of October—I will not say the fifth of Roman November . . ."

"[The Catholics] gasped their last in the act of their devotions. In what manner or measure the chastisement or punishment of God came to them, when he cut off their days *tam cito*, by such a sudden downfall, I cannot, I may not judge . . ."

And so, perpetually protesting, Gee backs into history. Innuendos he so hypocritically disowns, but so deliberately supplies, came in time to dominate the bare history of the Fatal Vespers; Gee's own role as witness and publicist figures as crucially as anyone's in the spreading of the news and the formation of a popular attitude toward the disaster and its participants. By the fate of a hundred he himself evaded, and the bitter aftermath he contrived partially to implement, Gee's place in religious and political history, shameful or merely partisan, has been inescapably assured.

EPILOGUE

As always, the aftermath seems indistinct by comparison with events themselves: following their months in the limelight, the participants we have isolated seem properly to withdraw, once more, into the comparative obscurity they had earlier earned. Little or nothing, for example, is known of Thomas Goad's later life, beyond his death at 62 in 1638, and twenty-three more years would elapse—characteristically—before the publication of a last literary attempt, one solemn and substantial tract on predestination named *Stimulus Orthodoxus.* Likewise the mishandled "W. C." disappears from subsequent journalistic history; no more of Matthew Rhodes's ballads survive;

dependable John Chamberlain was dead by March, 1627, and King James himself two years earlier. And soon after his spectacular ascent in the public eye, the now indubitably orthodox leading actor accepted his meed of a living in the lush country of Kent—far from the asperities and animosities of his former northerly parsonage—and settled down to the small tasks of provincial ecclesiastic administration. A little garland of prayers, *Steps of Ascension to God*, 1625, constituted his last recourse to the printed word. It proved reassuringly and even permanently popular, as such things go, experiencing a sixth edition by 1636, and by 1677 a twenty-seventh. No one would deny so salable a homilist's impact on the book-market of his time; but in his personal relations following the accident, his reformation, and his retaliation, Gee appears to have been less fortunate. "For publishing of which books," says Anthony à Wood, "and for his mutability of mind, he was much blamed by both parties, especially by those of the Roman persuasion, as I have been several times informed by a grave Bachelor of Divinity, Mr. Richard Washbourne, Chantor of Christ Church in Oxon., who had been his contemporary in Exeter College. Which person having known Gee well, and what he was, as to his life and conversation, blamed the writer of this book much, for honoring the memory of such a *sorry fellow* as he was . . ." Gee died young in 1636 at Tenterden, willing the bulk of a modest estate to his widow, one otherwise unidentified Jane. No more is known of her, of him, or of any descent.

But the reverberations of the accident itself rang far into the century. Latin poets like Cantabrigians John Robotham and Richard Hord, the philanthropist Edward Benlowes, and schoolmaster Alexander Gil memorialized the event in invective elegaics, perpetuating its mythical aspects as well its now familiar facts. Gil was remarkable enough, incidentally, to earn the loyalty and "extravagant praise" (*DNB*) of John

Milton, and the unflagging enmity of Ben Jonson; but his verses on Blackfriars (*PARERGA, sive Poetici Conatus,* 1632) scarcely seem to merit either. The colonists in New England were kept posted by John Wilson, whose crudely versified *A Song or Story for the Lasting Remembrance of Divers Famous Works,* issued originally in 1626, reached the press of John Foster in Boston by 1680. And other cautionary compilations maintained the currency of the emblem at home. Anthony Munday and Henry Dyson in their revision of Stow's *Survey of London* (1633) reprinted W. C.'s account *verbatim.* The prolific and militant Rev. Samuel Clarke of Benet Fink cheerfully lifted Gouge's narrative word for word for his collection *England's Remembrancer* (1657). The raciness of Clarke's anthology carried it to three new editions in the reign of Charles II (1676, 1677, 1679), significantly thick in the period leading up to Titus Oates and the crystallized anti-Catholic xenophobia of the 'Popish Plot'; then, as in 1606 when Prosecutor Coke raised the ghost of the Squire plot to harass Fr. Henry Garnet, the interpretative content of the disaster was disinterred by every polemicist who recalled it, to reinforce a historical point made originally in 1588, again in 1605, and now once more with the enigmatic murder of a righteous examining magistrate. Apparently Gee's exemplary ten-year-old sensed the true nature of the disaster before any of her elders: "the scandal to our religion" survived, in the English press, long after the pathos of the natural "mis-accident" had evaporated, and more forcefully than any Catholic martyrological evaluation could counterweigh. Perhaps it is appropriate that the site of the fallen chapel, like that of most of the old Blackfriars precinct, is now occupied by the vast printing plant of London's hoariest daily newspaper.

In its own day, finally, the effect of the catastrophe clove its own politico-religious chasm for the victims. Thanks to its industrious exploiters, and the popular awakening to what seemed murmurs of revolt, a predictable furor ensued, and a sequence of measures calculated to snuff all possibility of a Catholic resurgence in the last years of James's reign. In swift succession, however tenuously related, came the collapse of the Spanish Marriage (1624), a last and most stringent edict banishing Jesuits and Seminary Priests, and following the shocking discovery of a domestic Jesuit educational installation as near London as the suburb of Clerkenwell (1627), an implementation of earlier anti-recusant laws unparalleled in recent history. With the tide of Puritanism fast rising, bearing men like Dr. Gouge to its crest in Commonwealth times, the disenfranchised and again disappointed English Catholics of 1623 could settle down in their precarious isolation for a long, a hazardous, and a winnowing wait.

CHAPTER III.

GAMALIEL RATSEY, THE ROUGH DIAMOND

"A FACE," SNEERS THE ALCHEMIST'S CAPTAIN FACE, OF HIS CONFEDERATE SUBTLE, "WORSE THAN GAMALIEL Ratsey's." And some forty-five years later Jonson's protégé Thomas Randolph warns us, of a painted lady,

> Take but the white-loam from this old mud-wall,
> And she will look worse than Gamaliel Ratsey.

As late as 1651, then, this highwayman, with his emblematically ugly face, still retained part of the notoriety he had acquired by 1605. No outlaw of the period so captured the popular imagination, and although now he seems no more than a folkloristic way station between Robin Hood in the thirteenth century and Macheath in the eighteenth, Ratsey himself and his legendary exploits, his methods, *milieu*, and celebrity, deserve exhumation. He is among other examples the very model of an Elizabethan rogue-hero, the embodiment of adventure, free enterprise, and anarchic revolt. His victims are popularly supposed to be rich "caterpillars of the realm"; he has a soft spot for the oppressed, a ready and engaging wit, a practical sense of humor, and a most reassuring streak of moral remorse. Every man could identify with him, delight in his prankish outrages, sorrow for his betrayal, and yet righteously concur in his inevitable end. Although most of the tales told of him no doubt are more fiction than history, outlines of a real life can just be discerned beneath the generalized portrait of contemporary accounts; and the real life is biographically intriguing.

Gamaliel Ratsey's criminal career belongs entirely to the first two years of the reign of James I, and earlier records of his life are understandably scant. He was born, probably in the late 1570's or early '80's, in the village of Market Deeping, a border-town of southernmost Lincolnshire on the river Welland. Travellers proceeding north from London often forded the river here, by ferry or the undependable bridge, and continued toward Lincoln via the ancient Roman Fosse Way.

To their right as they rode would lie the vast fens of "Holland" and East Lincolnshire; the land was low, watery, and thinly populated, the heath south of Lincoln a notorious haunt for highwaymen and inland equivalents of salvage-pirates. By Macheath's time, Dick Turpin and his band roamed Dunsby Heath near Sleaford to such effect that many eighteenth-century insurance policies specifically exempted themselves from recompensing losses incurred there.

In this small village, ninety miles north of London, forty-five south of Lincoln—a customary overnight inn-stop on the three-day journey—Gamaliel Ratsey grew up in comparatively easy circumstances. His father Richard, a gentleman "enriched, as well in the virtues of his wife, as in the qualities of his own condition . . . generous both by birth and other perfections of the mind," but, significantly, "more fortunate in the love of his neighbors than in the comfort of his children," determined on a scholarly career for Gamaliel. "His care was to bring [Gamaliel] up in learning and the knowledge of good letters"; he employed a tutor, in the dread of whose "awful correction," as in "the fear and reprehension of his parents," the boy lived as long as his youth compelled him to. But "growing more mature and ripe in years, and having that hand of restraint carried more loose and easy than he was accustomed," he "grew less duteous and more desirous to range abroad, and see strange countries, holding his hopes frustrated and himself disparaged by living at home." Throwing up scholarship, parental control, and the small-town life, he ran away to war.

At the outbreak of Tyrone's Irish rebellion early in 1599, and with the danger of Spanish intervention looming large, the Earl of Essex had promoted himself to the command of a formidable invasion army. With sixteen thousand foot and thirteen hundred horse he left London on 27 March, proceeded through Islington to Beaumaris, where he took ship; and by 15

April he was established in Dublin. According to *The Life and Death of Gamaliel Ratsey*, the more reliable of two contemporary printed accounts, Ratsey "ventured his fortunes" with Essex, "being at that time very young and unskillful in managing of any martial affairs." But the great Earl seemed scarcely more skillful: by July the infantry dwindled to four thousand, and by late October their embarrassed commander-in-chief had been summarily recalled to London, withered with royal disfavor, imprisoned, indicted, and left finally to the bitter reflections which would lead him to a last masterpiece of misjudgment—the wildcat insurrection of 1601. The English army now under Charles Blount, Lord Mountjoy—perhaps best known to us as the long-term lover of Penelope Devereux, Essex' sister and Sir Philip Sidney's beloved Stella, who bore him no less than three illegitimate children before their last, propitiatory marriage—fared far better. In December 1601 at Kinsale he defeated a combined army of Irish and four thousand Spaniards; by December 1602 he had compelled the unconditional surrender of Tyrone, and later in May, 1603, two years after the execution of his friend and prospective kinsman Essex, returned triumphantly to England, an earldom, marriage (1606), and death within months.

Ratsey's part in the campaign is a little obscure, but *The Life and Death* says he served under Captain [Roger] Langford, "spent much time in those wars," and earned promotion to Sergeant, a rank he retained until Blount's departure with most of the standing army. Langford's troop of a hundred foot probably formed part of the reinforcements sent from England in October 1601 to Carrickfergus, or Knockfergus, a strategically important seacoast town some ten miles from Belfast, in the extreme north-east of the island, and very possibly Ratsey's service began then, not earlier, thus missing the disastrous first months of Essex' incompetent command.

Carrickfergus in 1601-2 was strongly garrisoned by Sir Arthur Chichester, and a comparatively good place to pass the war, though in those skirmishes he experienced, young Ratsey "was not slack to show forwardness." Likewise, "in any private quarrel"—perhaps a more common form of conflict for the time—he was "very resolute to repel injuries," being "venturous and hot-spirited." Langford's foot remained at Carrickfergus over the summer of 1602, removed to a small neighboring town in October, and by 20 December received orders "to be discharged as they may have warning." Ratsey apparently returned to England with Lord Mountjoy at the beginning of the summer, while Langford stayed on in Carrickfergus, first as Captain of occupying troops, then, and until 1611, as Constable of the King's Castle—an office he had purchased in 1602, to the somewhat wistful admiration of Chichester, who could not afford it.

The young veteran came back to Lincolnshire between reigns. Elizabeth had died in March, and the coronation of James Stuart would be delayed until July. It was an unsettled time, not least because of the sudden superflux of cashiered soldiers now loitering aimlessly in London ·and the country round. Months of biscuit, cheese, and salt beef lay behind them, and severance pay in their purses; they had no employment in immediate prospect, and little respect for peacetime law; they were hardened and rowdy and soon drove the incumbent monarch to a proclamation. Whereas "rogues, vagabonds, idle and dissolute persons . . . have swarmed and abounded everywhere more frequently than in times past, which will grow to the great and imminent danger of the whole realm . . . his Highness' Privy Council . . . have by their order assigned places and parts beyond the seas, into which such incorrigible or dangerous rogues should according to the same law be banished and conveyed . . ." Transportation was, however, a comparatively mild corrective. Only ten years earlier the harsh Elizabethan statute against vagabonds whereby any shiftless person was to be burned in the ear for a first offence, and executed as a felon for the second or third, had been repealed; and celebrated poor laws of 1597 and 1601 had begun a new era in the judicial treatment of hardship. But in 1603 plague was sweeping the city of London, housing everywhere was overcrowded and unsanitary, and on the Scottish border lawlessness ran rampant; much of James's early legislation directed itself toward relieving these immediate crises.

Meanwhile in Market Deeping Gamaliel Ratsey cast about restlessly for some manner of excitement to replace skirmishes, private quarrels, and the "pranks" he had performed on the journey home. His "venturous and hot-blooded" spirit took him looking for trouble to the village of Spalding, a market town some ten miles up the river from his birthplace, where he found an inn and "insinuated himself into the league and love of a servant maid." From her by means of "pleasing speech"—"and with what else he pleased her I know not," adds the coy pamphleteer—he won the confidence of both maid and mistress, and was admitted the "privilege of the parlor," or free run of the house. Now according to *The Life and Death* all this formed part of a plan. Ratsey having "only made his mean to await some opportunity," but the opportunity itself, surely, was no more than a commonplace accident. A farmer came to town on market day with forty pounds in a bag, intended as payment of a due bond. Putting up at the inn, he asked the hostess to keep his money for him during the market. She accepted the charge and locked up the bag in a "press" or recessed cupboard of the parlor, but made the mistake of telling Ratsey about it. He in turn acquired the key, stole the money, and telling the credulous innspeople that "he would but walk into the market, and come again by and by," he went promptly home to Deeping and buried the spoils in his mother's orchard. This may seem a somewhat clumsy performance, as indeed it turned out to be; Ratsey remained brazenly at home until the Justice of the Peace of Spalding granted a warrant to the hostess and the farmer, who induced the Constable of Deeping to serve it. "Hundreds" or villages were still financially responsible, as they had been since the thirteenth century, for robberies committed within their boundaries, and zealous to prosecute offenders. Perhaps inexperience at law will account for Ratsey's naïveté: apprehended and brought before the Justice in Spalding, he "stood stiffly in the denial" of his crime, but was jailed on suspicion of felony until the next sessions. This could be a matter of months, and Elizabethan imprisonment, nearly always a private and profitable enterprise, was costly for the victim. Thus not long after his incarceration, drained of his means, Ratsey had no choice but to tap his hoard, and trusting blood above scruples, he revealed the hiding place to his long-suffering mother. She, however, "in a great perplexity" between natural bonds and "her reputation in the country," sought advice of Gamaliel's sister, who told her husband, who told another, and the story spread with remarkable accuracy until the Justice himself had heard precisely where the loot lay buried. Fortunately for Ratsey, news of the news also circulated, and leaked back to him, and he was able to escape "in his shirt," i.e., night-clothes, through a very narrow passageway out of the keep. Soon a chase by horse and foot was on, but the intrepid veteran led his pursuit to the banks of a "dangerous great water," presumably the choked river Welland, plunged in and swam across, "and after several bravadoes given them (for he knew none of them durst follow him) he went his way and outstripped them all." Borrowing a suit of clothes from a friend, and a little money, he set out on foot for London with all bridges behind him burnt.

One must realize that from now on Ratsey is beyond

penitence or redemption. The punishment for felony was unambiguous—death—and as much for a sheep as a goat. Ratsey now risked nothing but capture, and "well fleshed by his late escape," he was now "half armed to enterprise any exploit." Impersonating a gentleman, booted and spurred though horseless as he was, he gulled a servant on the London road of one fine gelding he was leading to his master, and the man's horse as well. Soon afterward he made two allies, one Shorthose, an old friend from Market Deeping who had been driven out of Lincolnshire by debt, the other Snell, a desperado "twice burnt in the hand in Newgate for his bad conditions." Snell was to prove the Judas of the group within two years, but for the present the three brigands settled on equal shares and common enterprise.

Despite all severity of punishment and all efforts of the authorities to suppress brigandage, the profession of highwayman must be said to have flourished in Ratsey's time. Not the least of its *raisons d'être* was the curious glamor which attached to these criminals, doomed though they appeared to be, the romantic aura of an almost chivalric calling, in which any number of the leaders were, or called themselves in the sessions records, "gentlemen." With the overdue improvement of highroads all over England, perhaps highwaymen seemed to the popular reader—particularly in cities—nearly anachronistic, survivors of the great race of knightly outlaws who had served in turn the interests of Celts, Saxons, Angevins and Plantagenets in past centuries. A folk-tale of the sixteenth century even brings the profession into a tenuous, if jesting league with piety: a certain parson is robbed by a band of Hampshire thieves and induced to preach them a sermon, which he accomplishes with such straight-faced eloquence that his money and two shillings to spare are restored him. "I marvel," he concludes, "that men can despise you thieves, whereas in all points almost you be like unto Christ himself:

for Christ had no dwelling place; no more have you. Christ was hated of all men, saving of his friends; and so are you. Christ was laid wait upon in many places; and so are you. Christ at the length was caught; and so shall you be. He was accused; and so shall you be. He was hanged; and so shall you be. He went down into Hell, and so shall you do. Marry, in this one thing you differ from Him, for He rose again and ascended into heaven; and so shall you never do, without God's great mercy, which God grant you! To whom, with the Father, and the Son, and Holy Ghost, be all honor and glory, for ever and ever. Amen!''

Evidence like this abounds of the popular appeal, at least in their fictional forms, enjoyed by the gentlemen of the road. Thus it is often difficult to separate folklore from fact in the accounts of Ratsey, particularly in the pamphlet *Ratsey's Ghost*, the spurious from real exploits—for example, a close analogue of the sermon story above is foisted on Ratsey's band in *The Life and Death*. And it is reasonable to suppose that such folklore had its effect on the highwaymen themselves, or at least on those who, like Ratsey, possessed imagination and perhaps learning as well. Quite possibly the precedent of Robin Hood, and the lovable bandits of past times suggested to these sixteenth and seventeenth century holdovers a modified program of the same sort of generosity: pure public relations might account for an occasional—and not very cost-ly—donation to a poor man, a widow, a parson. A band of renegades patterned on the Merry Men, with "characters" like Ratsey's Shorthose, playing Sancho Panza to his Quixote, a penchant for disguise, and a good sense of humor would go far to mitigate the embarrassingly ignominious realism of scrapes like Ratsey's in Spalding—scarcely a feat to measure with Earl Huntingdon's poaching the royal deer. Despite the occasional meanness of his work, it would seem that Ratsey at the top of his bent kept the image of his great predecessors somewhere in memory. Sorting history from tall tales will be all the more difficult in his case.

Having escaped trial at Spalding, and fled for greater safety out of Lincolnshire, Ratsey and his companions determined to divide their future operations among the various counties to the south of the Welland, keeping to the highroads between cities, the inns and hostelries where travellers would rest between days on a journey, and within areas where Ratsey could count on his own knowledge of the land, friends to conceal him, and intelligencers to spy out for him likely prospects. We first hear of the group at Helpsonheath in Northamptonshire, where Ratsey was "most skilful of the country," well south of Lincoln, and well on the way toward London; but after a successful *coup* against nine unarmed travellers—all Lincolnshire men, who knew Ratsey by his widening reputation—they apparently reversed their field and struck northward once more. The sophisticated capital with its crowded tempo and disproportionate cost of living remained for the three a resort, like Dodge City for outlaws of the American West, to spend rapidly what profits accrued on the road; but Ratsey himself kept mainly to his business as far from the comparatively efficient constabulary of the metropolis as practicable. Save for periodic recreational visits, the last of which proved disastrous, and one complex and unusually subtle robbery of an inn on the outskirts of London, Ratsey carried on mainly within an area of land no more than fifty miles from his abandoned home. No incidents—save one at Maidstone, which may be apocryphal—are recorded south or west of Bedford, east of Newmarket, or far north of the Welland. A favorite road of Ratsey's seems to have been the link between Huntingdon and Cambridge, where travelling scholars, priests, merchants, and even a conjurer could be isolated far from help; and many of his exploits are laid in and around the town of Stamford, no further west of Market

Deeping than Spalding is East, and like Market Deeping a ford and way-station on the journey north from London. Here apparently Ratsey enjoyed something like immunity and perhaps a considerable staff of spies and sympathizers. No doubt the occasional acts of gallantry and generosity he performed here earned him friends or at least minimized local antagonism, and if his crimes were committed chiefly against travellers from distant parts and unpopular landowners, the adverse effect upon those likely to know his whereabouts was not great. Prior to Ratsey's arrival the town had just suffered an interminable plague (October 1602—October 1603) which carried off 713 of a modest population, and confusion of administration following this paralytic blow may also account for Ratsey's choice of *venue*.

The qualities Ratsey brought to his work included intrepidity, wit, and a certain amount of good nature, or cheerful gallantry, when the situation provoked it. His original escapade on the London road exemplifies the first: nine men appeared on horseback; Ratsey discharged his two accomplices, and lay beside a hedge lazily cracking nuts. When the party reached him, he accosted them "roughly," and demanded money. Relying wholly on a bluff, that a band of desperadoes lay concealed behind the hedge who "upon a watchword will come forth," . . . and who, "if they stir, it is all things to nothing but some of you lose your lives and your limbs," he extracted two hundred pounds from the portmanteau of one luckless traveler. Near Stamford he was able single-handedly to fetch eighty pounds from a pair of woolmen on no more strength than the sound of "four words speaking: Stand, deliver your purse." But cunning and deception were perhaps more characteristic of Ratsey's performances than threats or brute force. His commonest technique was to isolate his victim on the road, some distance from a town or inn, sometimes by means of "befriending" him, and travelling in his company "for safety." A conjurer of Cambridge is quietly followed "till he came in Bawtrie Lane, where [Ratsey] intended this exploit, and which indeed is a very dangerous place for thieving," and there robbed of books, money, and a fine twenty-pound gelding, which was to serve Ratsey, like the fabulous steeds of romance, for all his remaining career. Upon innumerable occasions travelling victims are gulled into "lending" Ratsey a horse, or letting Ratsey's "man" (i.e., Shorthose) help with a little excess baggage. In an inn at Huntingdon Ratsey befriends a grazier, riding into Lincolnshire to buy cattle. The grazier however is providently armed, and so Ratsey induces him to discharge one pistol at a rabbit warren; when he misses the game Ratsey asks leave "to try what I can do with your other pistol." The outcome is predictable. "Ratsey did more by pranks and sleights than by power and strength," explains one pamphleteer. Near London, where silkier methods are required, he and his cohorts contrived to spend two days and two nights in a posting inn at Dartford, pretending to gamble feverishly. They bought a crown's worth of counters, or chips, obtained dice of the postmaster, shut themselves up in a room and "began to throw the counters upon the table, and shuffled them to and fro, and kept such swearing as if they had lost a thousand pounds a man. And with the noise they made, the servants would come and listen, and could hear them talk of nothing but of losing five pounds a cast and ten pounds a cast, and took them to be men of very great fashion." Ultimately Ratsey appeared to win all the money, and insist upon going, whereupon "the other two fell a swearing," promising to "send for an hundred pounds from London if he would but tarry till the next day." Not only would he not, but he will not pay the charges—five pounds—the three have run up in the bout. Host and accomplices join indignantly in upbraiding the ungenerous winner, who is supposedly forty-seven pounds to

101

the good. "'Surely', quoth the host, 'Sir, methinks that is but a small favor.'" "'Mine host,' quoth Ratsey, 'I grant it is. But it is not long since they won an hundredth pounds of me, and served me in like manner, and this is *Quid pro quo*' . . . and away went he with his bag of counters." The destitute losers now induce the host, with promise of discharging Ratsey's obligations as well as their own, to lend them a pair of horses and send his ostler with them to London on a third. Needless to say the ostler's horse is for Ratsey, who meets his companions on top of Shooter's Hill; and "how blank the postmaster looked when he saw his man return without horse or money let both hackneymen and others judge, that have been fleeced by such rank riders."

Disguise played its part in Ratsey's repertoire: he appears at an inn in one face, robs a victim in another, rejoins him in the first and helps him to pursue the thief, leads him into open country, and then of course serves him a second time. The clothes of a gentleman gain him admittance to aristocratic households; on other occasions he is a merchant-traveller, while Snell and Shorthose impersonate retainers. Spies, of which Ratsey seems to have had a private army, seek out appropriate objects for his group, and having led the party into the hands of thieves, may permit themselves for appearance's sake, to be robbed along with the victims. In Act II of *Henry IV, Part I,* Gadshill calls out the chamberlain of an inn,

> . . . for thou variest no more from picking of purses than giving direction doth from laboring: thou layest the plot how.
> CHAMBERLAIN. Good morrow, Master Gadshill. It holds current that I told you yesternight: there's a Franklin in the Wilds of Kent [i.e., an inn] hath brought three hundred marks with him in gold; I heard him tell it to one of his company last night at supper . . .

"Give me your hand," cries Gadshill, "thou shalt have a share in our purchase as I am a true man"—an oath the intelligencer is understandably wary of. "Certes," says

102

William Harrison in 1577, "I believe not that chapman or traveller in England is robbed by the way without the knowledge of some of them [tapsters, ostlers, and chamberlains], for when he cometh into the inn and alighteth from his horse, the ostler forthwith is very busy to take down his budget or capcase in the yard from his saddle bow, which he pieceth slyly in his hand to feel the weight thereof; or if he miss of this pitch, when the guest hath taken up his chamber, the chamberlain that looketh to the making of the beds will be sure to remove it from the place where the owner hath set it, as if it were to set it more conveniently somewhere else; whereby he getteth an inkling whether it be money or other short wares, and thereof giveth warning to such odd guests as haunt the house and are of his confederacy . . . Some [travellers] think it a gay matter to commit their budgets at their coming to the goodman of the house, but thereby they oft bewray themselves: for albeit their money be safe for the time that it is in his hands (for you shall not hear that a man is robbed in his inn) yet after their departure the host can make no warranty of the same, sith his protection extendeth no further than the gate of his own house—and there cannot be a surer token unto such as pry and watch for these booties than to see any guest deliver his capcase in such manner . . ."

By post-Elizabethan standards Ratsey's sense of humor may seem a trifle crude, but a contemporary readership recently exposed to the extravagant influx of James I's new Scottish knights could appreciate Ratsey's mock knighting of two fleeced wool merchants: "laying his weapon on one of them [he] bade him 'Rise up, Sir Walter Woolsack,' and the other, 'Rise up, Sir Samuel Sheepskin . . . if any ask you who hath bestowed that dignity upon you say you met with King Ratsey; and so farewell!'" Likewise a company of players who have shiftily been acting in one place under the patronage of a certain lord, and at another more distant disclaiming him, are given leave "to play under my protection for a sennights space, and I charge you do it, lest when I meet you again I cut you shorter by the hams," while the chief tragedian and sharer is "knighted" "Sir Simon Two-Shares-and-a-Half . . . the first knight that ever was player in England." Much of Ratsey's wit consists of paying knaves in their own coin, and a jest at the expense of the victimized generally betokens a deserving victim.

For the pamphleteers Ratsey, like Robin Hood, positively shone with generosity toward the poor or maltreated, gallantry and good-nature toward women and the rare man who could turn the tables of deception on Ratsey himself. Chivalry however more often than not linked up with profit: at an inn one evening in New Market he meets a poor farmer who owes "a gentleman not far from hence" two hundred pounds upon a bond due the next day, who laments "such losses and hindrances, that all I can make amounts to one hundred and fifty pounds, and I and mine are utterly undone unless I can take new order for payment of the other fifty pounds . . . which I am very doubtful of, he is reported to be so cruel and unconscionable."

"'If this be all' (says Ratsey) 'be of good cheer, for although myself am unknown unto him, yet I am sure he hath heard of my friends, for they are not dwelling far from him. And I will do so much for you to ride with you in the morning to him; and doubt not I will prevail that he shall forbear you till a further time, without forfeiture or advantage taken: for I presume one gentleman will not deny another such a request . . .' "

Now Ratsey is actually black-hearted enough to covet the farmer's hundred and fifty pounds regardless of his affecting tale, and would have robbed him as they rode were it not for "the continual coming to and from of passengers, who made Ratsey at that time *volens nolens* to play the true man."

Coming at last to the gentleman-banker's house, he does apply himself ("as well as he could, [he] played the rhetorician") to the farmer's cause. But the gentleman is a hard dealer, and excuses himself from obliging Ratsey because, as he says, he himself must pay out £300 elsewhere the next day. "'Nay, stay sir,' says Ratsey, 'I will once in my life play the merchant venturer and hazard fifty pounds upon a man I never saw before.'" Needless to say, Ratsey's hazard is repaid sixfold in the morning when his "man" (Shorthose) rides off blithely with the gentleman's spare horse and moneybags, Ratsey himself in feigned pursuit, and Snell bringing up the rear, until "at a convenient place of changing the way they reined their horses back toward the old gentleman (who followed likewise as fast as he could) and waved their hats over their heads as farewell for his 300 pound . . ." The farmer of course has satisfied his bond—for which he will be endlessly grateful to Ratsey—and is able to prove that he had no knowledge of the highwayman's identity, and so go free.

Selective generosity of this kind leads Ratsey to return two angels of his own money to a waylaid Cambridge scholar as payment for a half-hour sermon of repentance preached in the woods on Ratsey's request, who in parting "told him, if ever he came to be a Lord, he would make him his chaplain for his labor." It is indeed a penitent Ratsey who admits "I have been a long malefactor," and expresses hope—sincere, within bounds—that the scholar's sermon "may so prevail with me, that it may work me to some good deeds, after my many evils." And an admirable Ratsey who, encountering a poor man and his wife on the road between Huntingdon and Cambridge with no more than five nobles in his purse and in hers "one Edward shilling and a mill sixpence, which hath seen no sun these seven years"—money scraped together "to buy us one cow to keep me and my wife now we are old"—freely gives the pair forty shillings of his own to buy a second cow as well. Not, however, until he has searched them thoroughly, for "I have met with such as you that have said as much as you do, and yet I found more silver and gold in a russet hose than in velvet breeches." Finding no more, he offers his own generosity, for "while I live." he concludes, "the sermon in the wood must teach me to favor and pity them that are poor, and help them; for the rich can keep themselves." Countrymen (i.e., Lincolnshiremen) in distress merit the same aid: a purse maker of Stamford, returning from London, is robbed of the proceeds of his trip—three pounds—by his own companions near Stangate Hold. Collapsing in grief by a roadside beer-booth (where "it fortuned that Ratsey at the same time was [inside], dallying and sporting with the wench of the house") he attracts Ratsey's attention, sympathy, and finally a free gift of four pounds for his missing three. Is Ratsey perhaps embarrassed by the unscrupulous rapacity of his ilk? Again, however, he is on guard against hypocrites: "Take heed thou hast not presented any false matter into my hearing, for therein (although I spare not them that are rich) thou wilt but give me cause to hold back my hand, and refrain that willingness to others that I do to thee; and to wrong thee too, if ever I meet thee hereafter." Reassured, Ratsey bids the grateful purse-maker farewell with a concern for his reputation characteristic of the trade, and which seems as well to have run in the Ratsey family—we remember Richard "more fortunate in the love of his neighbours than in the comfort of his children," and Gamaliel's mother weighing "her reputation in the country" against the ties of kin—"When thou hearest my name spoken of, report well of me amongst my countrymen."

Gallantry too has its own rewards, and when near Stamford Ratsey adds three angels of his purse ("to buy her a petticoat also") to the forty shillings a parson's daughter has saved toward a new gown ("If you take that away from me," she assures him, "I am utterly undone, for God knows I shall not get another of [my father] these seven years") he earns her "joyful thanks," her esteem, and the gratitude later of her brother and his friends; "and if there passed any other kindness between the parson's daughter and him," adds the disingenuous pamphleteer, "that is more than I am able to affirm." And on at least one occasion Ratsey is able to accept gracefully being himself outwitted by a prospective victim, much as Robin Hood can cheerfully own up to a dunking by Friar Tuck. Here a traveller whom Ratsey would rob casts his purse with feigned furtiveness over a hedge. "Ratsey espied him, and told him that should not serve his turn. So made over the other side of the hedge to fetch the gold: in the mean space the fellow got upon Ratsey's horse, having a portmanteau behind him, and an hundredth marks in it, and rode away. But when Ratsey saw that he called to the fellow, 'Come again, Sirrah, come again, I am but in jest.' 'I mean it not, Sirrah,' says the other, 'for I am in earnest: *fallere fallentem non fraus*, and so farewell.'" And when Ratsey was finally brought captive to Newgate, a friend of the trickster paid him a visit "to know whether any such matter passed upon him at any time."

"'Yes, marry, did there,' says Ratsey, and told him how, where, and when. 'And if I could see the man himself,' quoth Ratsey, 'I would give him a gallon of wine—there is all the ill I owe him; for in my life I never had such a prank passed upon me, nor did I ever receive such foil at mine own weapon before.'"

Like all heroic rogues of fable, moreover, and in fact like the "rufflers" or "upright men" among Elizabethan vagabondry who acted as self-constituted magistrates of their own profession, one of Ratsey's tasks seems to have been—or is so reported—the control of his kind. As an aristocrat among criminals who would not stoop to rob a poor man ("he had too high a mind to look upon so low a matter'') he is properly contemptuous of those rogues who violate his personal principles, and quite willing himself to redress the iniquities of others. He appears frequently in this guise of controller or commentator upon such lesser poachers of his proper domain, deceiving the deceiver, outwitting the rogue or malefactor, showing up the sleights or shifts of unselective coneycatchers and hypocrites. Normally Elizabethan prejudices about individual professions are born out by Ratsey's findings: lawyers, preachers, players, tapsters, and usurers yield up their ill-gotten gains to the more clean-cut highwayman like taxpayers to an inexorable collector.

One such small operator was a pick-lock who toured the countryside posing as a footpost, or mailman, with a leather bag full not of letters in fact but keys. "In every alehouse where he lodged all night," says the pamphleteer, "he paid the hostess with her own money, and carried somewhat away besides too, for there was not a cupboard or chest that he could come near but he would pick open and if there were no money in it, then moneyworth should walk with him;" nor would he scruple to rob milk-maids or servants when occasion arose, "if they had not above sixpence in their purses." Clearly this was a low rogue, and when Ratsey at last caught up with him at Stilton in northwest Huntingdonshire, he served him with a device out of *Hamlet,* sending him as a supposed letter-carrier to the jailor of Cambridge with a sealed message. The pick-lock in hope of a second reward did deliver the *mittimus,* which of course directed the authorities to seize its bearer; and a bag full of lock-picking equipment was more than this victim could explain easily away.

In London an annoying "makeshift" or moocher is crudely gulled by Ratsey into expecting a loan from a barber-surgeon, who in turn made to believe the victim is sick of the pox. The makeshift is shamed. A preacher near New Market.

suspiciously affluent, is robbed "by persuasion," tricked by his own logic and protestations of Christian charity into turning over ten pounds. And a tapster of Maidstone, a sly charlatan who "will mix lime with ale to make it mighty," who "will cozen the King's liege people for their drink by fobbing them off with your slender-waisted black pots and cans," "will put small beer into your bottle ale, and gunpowder into your bottles while the ale is new, to make it fly up to the top of the house at the first opening; then, by stopping it close, make folks believe it is the strength of the ale, when in truth it is nothing else but the strength of gunpowder"—a formidable array of sleights—finds himself justly gulled and gulled again by Ratsey, in two disguises, for his sins.

Lawyers perhaps above all other professionals were anathematized, for good reason, by Elizabethan pamphleteers; and we are not surprised to hear a suddenly passionate Ratsey harangue, with something like missionary zeal, an attorney he has robbed at Stangate Hole: "'Faith,' saith Ratsey, 'there is no pity to be had of you, nor of such as thou art; thou art worse than I, that take it by the highway, for let me meet with a poor man and take his money, if I perceive him indigent and needy I give it him again, and somewhat back to boot; but you pick every poor man's pocket with your tricks and quillets, like vultures preying upon your client's purses, till you leave them never a penny to bless themselves; and when money is gone, you shape the copy of your counsel and countenance accordingly.'"

Ratsey's disposition of the original case, however, tempers his judgment, as faint praise tempers calumny, and the writer behind him has it both ways: "I must needs say," he relents, "'there are some among you very upright and of good conscience, that will not take fees on both sides . . . and it may be that you thou art one amongst them few. Therefore tell me: What is the usual fee that you do take at a time?' 'Faith, sir,' saith he, 'our ordinary fee is ten shillings, and a many fees will not get so much money as you have taken from me,' 'Well, well,' saith Ratsey, 'you will lie apace till you fetch up then your losses again. But hold, here's a brace of angels back, and that is a double fee to carry thee home withall; and I would give it all again, and a great deal more too, upon condition that lying were as little used in England amongst lawyers, as the eating of swine's flesh was amongst the Jews.'" So much the last word.

Perhaps the most curious single episode recounted in these rambling biographies concerns Ratsey's run-in with a company of travelling players. The passage, which makes rogues of the actors and depicts Ratsey again as vigilante-controller, may indeed be apocryphal—we must take most of the matter of *Ratsey's Ghost* with a grain of salt—but the light it casts glancingly on Elizabethan theatrical conditions remains valuable and intriguing.

The roguery of the players indeed is no more than nominal disloyalty to a patron. On their first evening's meeting with Ratsey, in his *persona* of gentleman, they have alleged that "they served such an honorable Personage;" whereas a week later and at a distance from the first inn they disown their former allegiance—"for like chameleons they had changed that color"—and play "in the name of another, whose indeed they were, although," we are told, "afterwards when he heard of their abuse he discharged them and took away their warrant. For, being far off, for their more countenance they would pretend to be protected by such an honorable man, denying their lord and master; and coming within ten or twenty miles of him again, they would shroud themselves under their own lord's favor."

Now at the first inn Ratsey commands a performance of the company, and its details, as well as the highwayman's remarks, are interesting: "'I pray you,' quoth Ratsey, 'let me hear your music, for I have often gone to plays more for music sake than for action.'" Indeed, as the decade progressed, orchestral and vocal *entr'acte* music—as employed particularly in the performances of the juvenile company at Blackfriars Theatre, Rosencranz's "aerie of children, little eyases," who with their sudden popularity "are most tyrannically clapped for," and drive forth adult companies like these to travel the countryside—gained more and more of a hold on all London's theatrical proclivities. Acting itself, Ratsey tells the company players, seems now to please less, "for some of you, not content to do well, but striving to over-do and go beyond yourselves, oftentimes—by St. George—mar all; yet your poets take great pains to make your parts fit your mouths, though you gape never so wide." "Suit the action to the word, the word to the action," urges Hamlet in the same vein, "with this special observance, that you o'erstep not the modesty of nature; for anything so o'erdone is from the purpose of playing . . . [and], though it makes the unskilful laugh, cannot but make the judicious grieve." Has the turn of the century seen a new vogue of the bombastic style of acting, thus to call forth such censure? More probably we are being confronted with Jacobean critical refinement in its earliest, dissatisfied state, a new sophistication common, suddenly, to such disparate personalities as Shakespeare's and a jesting felon's.

There are competent players, of course, "very well deserving both for true action and fair delivery of speech," and yet wages are not always commensurate with talent: "I warrant you the very best have sometimes been content to go home at night with fifteen pence share apiece." Whereas, adds Ratsey scornfully, "others there are whom fortune hath so well favored, that what by penny-sparing and long practice of playing, are grown so wealthy, that they have expected to be

111

knighted, or at least to be conjunct in authority, and to sit with men of great worship on the Bench of Justice.''

Such new affluence among players seems a bee in Ratsey's bonnet. He commissions the company's revelry, singing and dancing ''as if Lord Prodigal had been there in his ruins of excess,'' and pays them all handsomely in the morning; but when a week later, ''disguised . . . with a false head of hair and beard,'' he discovers their shift of patronage, he seizes the opportunity to rob them and lecture them once more. For performance on their second occasion, he gave them ''very liberally'' forty shillings—''with which they held themselves very richly satisfied, for they scarce had but twenty shillings audience at any time for a play in the country.'' (Forty shillings is incidentally what Sir Gelly Meyrick, a retainer of Essex, paid over to the manager of Shakespeare's own company, to enact the outmoded play of *Richard II* on the eve of the 1601 insurrection. The analogies—weak monarch, strong rebel—came clear the next day; Meyrick paid for it with his life; and the unwitting acting personnel were lucky to escape with theirs.) Ratsey, at any rate, overtakes the company in the morning and strips them of their profit, now chiding them for ''an idle profession that brings in much profit,'' in which ''every night where you come, your playing bears your charges, and somewhat into purses besides,'' where ''you have fiddler's fare, meat, drink, and money.'' ''If the worst be,'' he assures them, ''it is but pawning your apparel, for as good actors and stalkers as you are have done it, though now they scorn it''—more evidence of the untoward self-aggrandizement of the profession.

Turning from economics to art, Ratsey singles out one actor who it appears is wasting his talent on the road: '' 'And for you, sirrah,' says he to the chiefest of them, 'thou hast a good presence on the stage; methinks thou darkenst thy merit by playing in the country. Get thee to London; for if one man were dead, they will have much need of such a one as thou art. There would be none, in my opinion, better than thyself to play his parts: my conceit is such of thee, that I durst venture all the money in my purse on thy head, to play Hamlet with him for a wager.'" Again an interesting constellation of allusions—first to Richard Burbage, who is certainly the "one man" pre-eminent on the London stage, second to *Hamlet*, presumably Shakespeare's new version (1600-1) of the old tragedy, and third to the obscure tradition of playing "for a wager"—a kind of acting competition which seems to have been in current use, or at least consideration, as a means of settling which player was the best in a part, since 1589.

In London, continues Ratsey, still harping on the same string, and with a bitterness which bespeaks somebody's personal experience, "thou shalt learn to be frugal (for players were never so thrifty as they are now about London), and to feed upon all men, to let none feed upon thee; to make thy hand a stranger to thy pocket, thy heart slow to perform thy tongue's promise; and when thou feelest thy purse well lined, buy thee some place or lordship in the country, that growing weary of playing, thy money may there bring thee to dignity and reputation: then thou needest care for no man, nor not for them that before made thee proud, with speaking their words upon the stage."

It is possible of course that the "lordship in the country" is a satirical hit at playwright-actor Shakespeare, who in 1597 with his company share-profits had purchased the manor house of his home town and obtained a grant of arms for his father—that he himself might be the second armiger of his family. Indeed at least one playwright-satirist, John Marston, seems to have selected the new Shakespeare motto ("Non Sans Droict," i.e., "not without right") to lampoon, as his Geoffrey Balurdo (*Antonio and Mellida*, 1599) commissions a coat of arms quartering mutton and ham, with the blazon "Not

113

without mustard." But here apparently the chronicler, or rather artificer of Ratsey's polemic takes the part of the playwrights who "before, made thee proud,"—and playwrights often turned pamphleteers in lean or plague years like 1605—against non-literary but shareholding players. If indeed Shakespeare is one of the intended butts of these reflections it is fascinating to speculate about the extent of his aristocratic ambitions: did he in fact harbor hopes of a knighthood, or a place in the judicature? If not he, who may Ratsey be signalizing? It is a brief but tantalizing glimpse of theatrical life he affords us.

To what extent did exploits like these broadcast the name and reputation of Ratsey during the short twenty-two months of his highroad career? We have unfortunately little to guide us: the two extant pamphlets and two lost ballads only issued from the press after his execution, and no record of his notoriety before that date is now known to us. But from the printed accounts we can establish some of the details of what led up to Ratsey's fatal last felony, and how, faced with the inevitable end, he finally behaved.

No formal national or even county-wide constabulary existed in the early 1600's, a fact which perhaps extended Ratsey's otherwise doomed career. But outlaws as exuberant as he must eventually face some sort of concerted opposition, in the form at least of local pursuit; and the first indication we have of a tightening net comes in Lincolnshire, Ratsey's home county, after "the many robberies" he had committed there, causing the combined officialry of the area "to make search and watch to be laid in every place for him." Disguise for a while sufficed the band—Shorthose wore a rich livery of green velvet—but their activities were by now considerably restricted. It became inadvisable to work before moonrise, despite their outlay on elegant clothing, and robbery by night turned out a relatively unprofitable substitute for the customary bold daylight strokes. Faced finally with the need for retreat, or more simply escape, Ratsey and his group passed surreptitiously out of Lincolnshire into Norfolk via the castellated outpost of Wisbech, but not without hazard and not without the usual ingenuity on Ratsey's part.

In Norfolk, indeed, the three were beyond local jurisdiction of such towns where warrants had been served for them; extradition was a cumbersome and inefficient business at best for the forces of law in this period. But more and more the closing-off of exits for Ratsey's group becomes a matter of time, and the remaining free pasture smaller and drier. Either diminished returns, warmer pursuit, or plain country boredom may account for the separation, which we now first hear about, of the companions, Snell and Shorthose to London, and a comparatively lower order of crime—small theft in the disguise of footmen, cozening merchants with unredeemable orders, stripping drunken country-bumpkins, and a little primitive pocket-picking—and Ratsey apparently left to shift for himself in the provinces. Snell in particular, "a thief of longer continuance, though not of the note that Ratsey was," seems to have returned to his old conditions, working the various coneycatching tricks which could reap heavy rewards in the crowded city. With a partner named Collins he haunted taverns and ordinaries, both posing as gentlemen, willing on occasion to outface some accusation with indignation and a challenge for the injury. So Collins once, after clumsily clipping a gentleman's purse, must carry through his threat to cross swords with his victim, and in the fields "hurt the gentleman very sore;" but such violent characters as Collins come swiftly, his chronicler assures us, to the gallows.

Violence indeed has not characterized any of the known exploits of Ratsey, as it would seem the appearance of his unmistakably ugly face was enough to terrify even nine travellers at a time into humble submission. Failing the

115

appearance, a word or two in the voice of command might suffice; none of his flock turns against the shearsmen in the preserved anecdotes, save one; and that, Ratsey's fatal last robbery, is significantly a matter of assault and resistance. As long as he fleeces the willing with a jest or the license of "control," shares out his gains with the unfortunate, and combines cautionary instruction with personal profit, folklore's Ratsey leads a charmed life; when the fair image blurs, however, fair play palls, and the victim—suddenly sympathetic—strikes back, we sense the end of his invincibility. A serious Ratsey is a doomed man.

The last exploit finds the hero reunited for the occasion with Snell and Shorthose, as far west and south of his original haunts as Bedford. A major opportunity confronts them, a gentleman and his brother with nearly £200 between them, alone on a highroad six miles from the city. The place of assault is fixed somewhat hazardously a mere half-mile from the gentleman's dwelling, and at a signal the three descend upon the pair with their demands. But for once they meet opposition, in the person of the gentleman "known in his country to be very stout and valiant." He draws on Ratsey; they fight; "and had not his sword broken, it is thought that Ratsey and Snell both could not have robbed him (for Shorthose never came in)." Before this mishap the swordsman drew blood, however, wounding the hitherto unscathed highwayman "very dangerously," and was himself stabbed in the leg not by his opponent, but, scurrilously, "by Snell coming in." The whole performance, though ultimately some money changed hands, was a butchery, and the three thieves escaped the raised hue and cry only with difficulty. They lay concealed for a time at Saffron Waldon, and then fled to London where at an inn in Southwark they shared out their profits. Ratsey received half the loot, by consent, "in respect of his hurts received."

116

But the damage was done, damage to the self-esteem of the leader, perhaps to the solidarity of the group. Possibly Snell, who takes now the part of informer, was at heart not so agreeable to the last concession as he professed to be; at all events luck had run out. Captured in Duck Lane for a wholly unrelated theft of a horse from Gravesend, Snell turned state's evidence in hopes to lighten his sentence. The hypocritical accord of the judge (promising "his lawful favor") duly given, Snell volunteered all he knew. By his directions Ratsey was taken near Doctor's Commons and committed to Newgate, where he and Snell remained without trial for the space of two or three sessions.

Shorthose meanwhile remained at liberty away from London; but unwisely after a time of wandering "he unfolded his mind to one Walter Skillington, a countryman of his" who turned him in to Newgate authorities; he was apprehended in Long Lane, in the London liberty of Great Saint Bartholomew. The two now confronted their betrayer, and Snell lost no time appealing for transfer to King's Bench Prison. Severally the band cooled their heels until Spring Assize time at Bedford, when they were all remanded under strong guard to a jail in that city.

Ratsey was by no means yet resigned to his fate, however. Soon he had managed to cut through his leg irons with an acid he had somehow procured, and nearly effected a last-minute escape. When time for judgment came, the three defendants struggled at the very bar, "thrust twelve men in a corner," and required forceful restraint while the magistrate passed sentence, concluding with his formulaic "Lord have mercy upon you." On the twenty-seventh of March, 1605, Ratsey, Snell and the hapless Shorthose were reunited for the last time on the gallows.

Perhaps Ratsey's last hour passed in the exemplary fashion so admired by Elizabethans, in resignation and remorse,

117

self-loathing and contempt for the life he would soon abandon. Little about his recorded conduct suggests so, but there are hints—in the episodes of the gulled preacher, at the scholar's sermon in the wood—of a character subject to the claims of conscience, and an imagination capable of the poem fostered on Ratsey by the author of *The Life and Death*: "Ratsey's Repentance, which he wrote with his own hand when he was in Newgate." Like the convicted assassin Chidiock Tychborne, whose famous renunciatory elegy ("My Prime of Youth is but a Frost of Cares") occupied his last night in the Tower, like Walter Ralegh, whose similar vigil is supposedly responsible for "On the Snuff of a Candle" and "Even Such is Time," we are asked to believe that Ratsey in his penitence turned to verse, and the sentiments which came crowding down upon him yielded forty-one hexaines of doleful apology:

> I that of late did live a soldier's life,
> And spent my service in my country's good,
> Now captive lie, where none but cares are rife,
> Where is no hope but loss of dearest blood,
>   This is befall'n me, 'cause I did mis-spend
>   That time which God to better use did lend.

> Sigh, for my music is a siren's song,
> A fair deceit, to shadow men in grief:
> Did I say fair? Alas, I called it wrong . . .

Is this our devil-may-care hero, our jaunty rogue? Is his remorse so profound, his transformation so complete?

> Confounding sadness, like a load of lead,
> Chills all my blood and makes my sinews shrink,
> "Revenge," quoth Wrong, "let rigour stand in stead."
> Death fills the cup, and says that I must drink.
>   This make me plead, this makes me call and cry

118

To Heaven's great King for mercy ere I die.

Shall we account this ringing declamation sincere?

> Villains, avaunt! You bastards are by kind
> That do perturb the country's quiet state.
> Shame to offend, shun a corrupted mind,
> And learn by me your former life to hate.
> > Live of your own, and brave it not with brags.
> > Least Law condemn you in your proudest rags.

And above all his piety—shall we accept its profession?

> This little remnant of my life so poor
> I'll teach to shun all sin, and vices all.
> Giver of grace, grant grace I sin no more,
> Establish me, that I may never fall,
> > To Thee my heart, my life and soul I give,
> > Who after death eternally makes live.
>
> Direct my paths even for thy mercy's sake,
> Guide thou my steps to keep repentant ways,
> Keep me from sleep, in thee still let me wake,
> To laud thy name, during these earthly days,
> > And when from earth I shall dissolve to dust,
> > Grant that my soul may live among the just.
> FINIS.   Gamaliel Ratsey.

Now is the author of these lines the swashbuckler who at the very dock "thrust twelve men in a corner," and in fact passed a major portion of "the little remnant of my life" treating his fetters with strong water? Such a likelihood is not altogether remote. The cheerful mutability of an Elizabethan conscience remains attractively characteristic of that versatile culture, and we need not account those all bald hypocrites who flaunted their own spirituality with the conventional insincerity of poets, who may indeed have burned, like poets, with the conviction of the moment, as if enthusiasm could compensate where consistency faltered. The pleasurable catharsis of penitance does not of itself render more painful anyone's natural inclination to backslide; no more than passion made literate is by those means less likely to decay. It is perfectly possible to imagine an Elizabethan like Ratsey writing in such a vein, with all the intensity of an immediate confrontation with death, all the sincerity words themselves whip up in their speaker, and yet carrying on simultaneously and afterward with the same old unregenerate obstinacy a life the world makes necessary. There is a time to repent, a time to protest, and a time, finally, to die—die *well*, above all, and like More at the block, with a capping jest.

Mounted on the scaffold Ratsey spies "a great storm and tempest coming on . . . an extreme tempest of thunder and rain." He pleads for time with the sheriff, first extracting a promise "that I might see the others die before me, especially that villain Snell who betrayed me," then promising to reveal a certain secret "in private," and thus is suffered to descend—"but all he uttered was to little purpose." The rains come and the whole party is drenched; when they cease, Ratsey admits he only temporized, "that he might see them all well washed before he died." Of himself, then, he mounted the ladder again "and showed an end of courage even to the resolution of his death. Confession he made none," save an equivocal one, of complicity in a certain unsolved robbery near Tyburn Hill. "More could not be gotten from him," says the pamphleteer, "but as he lived so he died, careless and resolved, yet very patient for his sins"—a concession, we are pleased to record, "which the standers-by were very glad to see and behold."

CHAPTER IV.

DAREDEVILS AND SHOWMEN

BANKS AND MOROCCO

"WE HAVE DAILY HERE MANY NEW EXPERIMENTS MADE," WROTE JOHN CHAMBERLAIN ON 3 FEBruary 1601, "as the last week one came hopping from Charing Cross into Paul's bound in a sack, and this morning another carried up a horse and rode upon him on the top of Paul's steeple."

The choice of St. Paul's Cathedral for "experiments" by two zanies in one week need not wholly surprise us. For a century or more the great church of London, with its vast interior, its walks, and crowded courtyard, had served, among more appropriate functions, as a traditional nexus for exhibitionism of all kinds, for impromptu and spectacular performances like these as well as the institutionalized sermons and masses, for gatherings of gallants, sightseers, *littérateurs* and thieves, indiscriminately mingled, as well as state, city, and parish officials in ceremonious conclave. As early as 1546 an intrepid Spaniard gained the admiration of young King Edward VI by sliding headfirst, "as if it had been an arrow out of a bow," down a rope stretched from the battlements of Paul's to the ground, then tumbled, danced, and hung by one leg from the taut cable; and in the reign of Queen Mary another perhaps less skillful performer repeated the trick—successfully once, but which "shortly after cost him his life." "From the top of the spire," declares a pamphleteer of 1563, "at coronations or other solemn triumphs, some for vain glory used to throw themselves down by a rope, and so killed themselves vainly to please other men's eyes . . ." Coronations indeed inspired the most elaborate exploits. For Mary's

123

(1553) a Dutchman named Peter scaled the steeple and "stood upon the weathercock . . . holding a streamer in his hands of five yards long, and waving thereof." He balanced on one foot, knelt, and attempted to wave torches as well, but the wind was so high that none would remain burning. Peter duly received £16 3s. 4d. from the grateful city "for his costs and pains, and for all his stuff." The weathercock incidentally, then gilt-plated copper, was actually once stolen—according to Thomas Deloney—by a clever and evidently acrobatic cripple.

Perhaps casting oneself off the battlements with or without guide-ropes remained a sport in Elizabeth's day, at least for the "Kit Woodruff" who Dekker (1609) tells us "durst vault over" the railings to the courtyard below; but most gallants at loose ends in London preferred less arduous forms of showing-off. Taking your "Paul's walk" down the Mediterranean Aisle of the Church, among "main shoals of islanders," sumptuously attired and on the look-out for new wrinkles, you are advised to "bend your course directly in the middle line, that the whole body of the Church may appear to be yours; where, in view of all, you may publish your suit in what manner you affect most, either with the slide of your cloak from the one shoulder—and then you must (as 'twere in anger) suddenly snatch at the middle of the inside (if it be taffeta at the least) and so by that means your costly lining is betrayed—or else by the pretty advantage of Compliment [i.e., a deep bow]." And if you seek new fashions, be ready to steal them: "warn your tailor to attend you in Paul's, who, with his hat in his hand, shall like a spy discover the stuff, color, and fashion of any doublet or hose that dare be seen there, and stepping behind a pillar to fill his table-books with those notes, will presently send you into the world an accomplished man; by which means you shall wear your clothes in print with the first edition." Tiring of the company

124

indoors, and never, for fashion's sake, paying any heed to the service (save on occasion to tip a choirboy or two ostentatiously *during* their performance), the model gallant or gull takes himself outside to the packed courtyard. There, among the bookstalls, tailors, seamsters, and "the new tobacco office" lay the heart of London's low and lively society, at once bookish and ignorant, pretentious and elegant, and above all eager for novelties. To these came "one hopping from Charing Cross . . . bound in a sack"; and for this audience William Banks led his dancing horse up the narrow and interminable stairs to the rickety roof of St. Paul's.

Among all such showmen, private and public, Banks and his miraculous horse Morocco have managed to survive the longest in English memory. And for good reason: in an age which had begun to value artistry in the most primitive forms of its entertainment, the pair raised one brand of vaudeville to an unprecedented level. Their celebrated ascent of Paul's was perhaps the high point of a distinguished career, but by no means the sum of it. "If Banks had lived in older times," Ralegh assures us, "he would have shamed all the enchanters of the world; for whosoever was most famous among them could never master or instruct any beast as he did." Over sixty allusions, principally laudatory, to Banks and Morocco can be gathered from English and French authors before 1675, including Shakespeare, Jonson, Dekker, Nashe, Donne, Middleton, Webster, and Sir John Davies; no showman or theatrical figure, save possibly Tarleton the clown, can claim, in this era of Shakespeare, Burbage, Alleyn and Kempe, the popularity, the universality, and indeed the familiar affection Banks seems to have elicited during and beyond his playing days. Yet the full history of his career has gone curiously unremarked.

Banks was probably a native of Staffordshire, although one Frenchman describes him dubiously as "Ecossais." A

Scottish witness, on the other hand, *ca.* 1596, calls him unequivocally English. We first hear of him as a performer in Shrewsbury, where he visited on 16 September 1591 bringing "a white horse which would do wonderful and strange things." The act comprised counting, identifying men by the color of their coat, or the character Banks gave of them, and curtseying to a bailiff who had treated Banks with especial civility. The horse could tap out with his hoof the number of coins in a designated purse, and locate with his nose "any man, being never so secret in the company," described orally by his master, for instance, as "the veriest rogue" present. The performance was impressive enough to gain space in a chronicle history of Shrewsbury written after 1603, and so baffled the audience "that many people judged that it were impossible to be done except he [Banks] had a familiar, or done by the art of magic."

We may note that the horse here is white. Morocco, the little bay gelding whose name is inextricably linked with Banks's in later years, was apparently then not the first of his master's teaching, unless the chronicler has erred. We hear definitely of the bay no earlier than 1594, when Thomas Nashe explains that Banks wisely "made his juggling horse a cut [i.e., cut-tail, or curtal] for fear if at any time he should foist, the stink sticking in his thick bushy tail might be noisome to his auditors." Morocco is characterized as "a young nag" by the title of a lost ballad of 1595, but the same undependable French witness who called Banks a Scot describes the horse as "de moyenne taille, bay, guilledin d'Angleterre, âgé d'environ douze ans," this in 1601, which would set Morocco's birthdate near 1589. About the color and size of the horse there is some dispute: "bay" is the commonest description, but the Scots annalist gives "chestain colored," and one probably second-hand allusion of 1601 makes it "black." Middle or small size seems necessary in consideration of the stairway to St. Paul's roof, and the limitations of space on the stages of the Bel Savage and Cross Keys inns. Nashe, Dekker, one "E.S.," and Gervase Markham (1607) agree that Morocco was cut-tailed. No indication of his life-span can be gathered from extant allusions, but by the time of Markham's *Cavelarice*, and Dekker's *Seven Deadly Sins of London* (1606) he is being mentioned in the past tense. Perhaps it was after his triumphs of 1601, at Paul's and on the continental tour, that his prosperous master had him shod with silver. "Goldsmiths did shoe me, not the *Ferri-Fabers,/* One nail of mine was worth their whole week's labors," Morocco is made to tell Don Quixote's Rosinante many years after, and other contemporaries attest to this curious but surely appropriate extravagance.

In the mid-nineties Banks and Morocco seem to have codified their performance, as they held forth steadily at small tavern-theatres near Ludgate Hill. Dancing and counting were the mainstays of the act: "How easy it is to put 'years' to the word 'three', the dancing horse will tell you," says Moth to his master Don Armado in *Love's Labour's Lost*. Banks could "borrow from twenty or thirty of the spectators a piece of gold or silver, put all in a purse and shuffle them together; thereafter he would bid the horse give every gentleman his own piece of money again." And he "would cause him tell by so many pats with his foot how many shillings the piece of money was worth." Identification of course remained another featured detail. One possibly apocryphal anecdote concerns Richard Tarleton, the most famous clown of his age, and Banks, then holding forth at the Cross Keys Inn in Gracious Street. "Tarleton then, with his fellows, playing at the Bell by, came into the Cross Keys, amongst many people, to see fashions; which Banks perceiving, to make the people laugh says 'Signior,' to his horse, 'Go fetch me the veriest fool in the company.' The jade comes immediately and with his mouth draws Tarleton forth. Tarleton, with merry words, said nothing but 'God a mercy, horse.' In the end Tarleton, seeing the people laugh so, was angry inwardly, and said, 'Sir, had I power of your horse, as you have, I would do more than that,' 'What e'er it be,' said Banks to please him, 'I will charge him to do it.' 'Then,' says Tarleton, 'charge him to bring me the veriest whoremaster in the company.' The horse leads his master to him. Then, 'God a mercy horse, indeed,' says Tarleton. The people had much ado to keep peace; but Banks and Tarleton had like to have squared, and the horse by to give aim. But ever after it was a byword thorow London, 'God a mercy, horse,' and is to this day.'' The expression indeed became proverbial in the early seventeenth century; but Tarleton died in 1588, and so either this admittedly circumstantial jest is fabricated or foisted on Tarleton, or the horse is not likely to have been Morocco.

There were other specialities in Morocco's routine: at a word he would kneel, or lie down and play dead; at another he would rise and "most daintily hackney, amble, and ride apace, and trot, and play the jade." Furthermore he would drink great draughts of water whenever and as often as Banks commanded, and piss as well upon direction—a detail of the repertoire seemingly eliminated from some more elegant showings. A particular favorite called for the horse to bow submissively "for the Queen," but when asked to stoop "for the King of Spain" instead to bite, paw, and furiously resist anyone's handling, or simply refuse to perform. This latter trick was popular enough to be duplicated by dogs, and by "a well-educated ape," which *ca.* 1614 will "come over the chain for a king of England, and back again for the prince, and shall sit on his arse for the pope and the king of Spain." Even the elephant, Morocco's chief rival perhaps among trained animals in London, seems to have mastered the idea: Donne satirically characterizes "a grave man" as one who

doth move no more
Than the wise politic horse would heretofore,
Or thou, O elephant, or ape wilt do,
When any names the King of Spain to you.

How did Banks manage these tricks which drove his bewildered contemporaries to suspect witchcraft? According to Markham, there is nothing whatever miraculous about the necessary training, only great patience, care, and a formidably strict routine. One chapter of his *Cavelarice, or the English Horseman* reveals "how a horse may be taught to do any trick done by Banks his curtall." The secret, says Markham, lies in training the horse from his infancy to the most stringent obedience, and in keying his obedience to a few well-chosen—but for the audience, misleading—words, like "be wise" for "no," "so, boy," for approval, and "up" for lifting the hoof, and to the motion of the trainer's eyes: "whosoever did note Banks his curtall might see that his eye did never part from the eye of his master." By systematic application of reward and punishment, by withholding food and allowing no other man to feed or handle the horse, a relationship of complete dependence and fidelity can be established. What the trainer makes of this is limited only by the capacities of the horse and the extent of his own patience. Markham suggests that stamping the hoof be linked with a slight downward motion of the trainer's hand, all following upon the appropriate code-word, in this case, "up"; thus the trainer can have his horse tap out any number desired. "Deliver" evokes a different but also programmed response, here causing the horse to accept a glove or other small article in his mouth, and follow the master's eye to an indicated recipient. The code-word for "piss" is simply "piss," apparently. Thus what Banks must have done, according to Markham, was merely to insert a key command somewhere among his patter for each trick, thereby alerting Morocco to

129

the matter next at hand. Banks's "spiel" would have been formal indeed, and repetitive: Sir John Davies remarks of "some prose speeches," tedious in a contemporary poetaster,

> The man that keeps the *Elephant* hath one,
> Wherein he tells the wonders of the beast,
> Another *Banks* pronounced long a-gon,
> When he his curtall's qualities exprest.

Markham gives as well—reluctantly—directions for making a trained horse lie down, seem to kick and bite, dance, trot, and other "superficial toys," the burden of which he thinks hardly consonant with the natural dignity of a horse. These frivolous activities, he objects, "more properly do belong to dogs, apes, monkeys and baboons," but if educated to such uses, the horse by native intelligence is quite able "to do any other action as well as any dog or ape whatsoever, except it be leaping upon your shoulders, climbing up houses, or untying knots, all which are contrary to the shape and strength of his great body."

The popularity of Banks's act may be gauged from contemporary literary response. By late 1595 both a ballad (lost) and a satirical pamphlet had celebrated Morocco's "strange qualities." *Maroccus Extaticus, or Banks' Bay Horse in a Trance*, "by John Dando, the wire-drawer of Hadley, and Harry Runt, head ostler of Besom's Inn"—probably pseudonymous Oxonians—professes to record a spoken dialogue after hours at the Bel Savage between master and horse, thereby "anatomizing some abuses and bad tricks of this age." Banks and Morocco are the pretext, rather than the subject of the pamphlet, but the very absence of specific description gives some indication of their familiarity to the light-reading public; and a frequently-reproduced woodcut remains our only known illustration of the act—Morocco on his haunches with forelegs raised, a stick in his mouth, and dice at his feet; Banks with a pole or cudgel,

130

and four witnesses looking on from beyond a low railing. Morocco incidentally *has* a tail in the woodcut.

Perhaps London alone could not always sustain the same pair in a fairly set performance, or else a widening reputation made the prospects of a road-trip enticing; for about 1596 they appear in Edinburgh. Earlier, as we have seen, Banks has been in Shrewsbury, and Morocco has probably played at Oxford, where Dando and Runt jest that he learned his Latin. For Edinburgh Banks added James VI to Queen Elizabeth as a name for whom Morocco would duly "beck"; and the performance again was considered miraculous, "such as never horse was observed to do the like before in this land." Apparently there were few more worlds for Banks and his beast to conquer, at least within the borders of the United Kingdoms.

Meanwhile, in London, a whole legion of animal acts had risen to challenge the pre-eminence of the pair. Not that Banks was the earliest exhibitor of a trained animal—tumbling apes, dogs, and dancing bears had preceded him, and in the baiting rings mastiffs had long "performed" cruelly against chained bears and bulls, and apes ("jackanapes") rode on horseback and bearback for enthusiastic audiences before 1572—but Banks and Morocco were probably responsible for the new wave of such exhibits from the mid-nineties onward. The elephant was one, evidently, and another was a certain Mr. Holden's dancing camel, exhibited on London Bridge. All three are associated in passing by the satirist Joseph Hall (1599), as "strange Morocco," "the young elephant," and "the ridg'd camel," along with an otherwise unknown "two-tailed steer." Donne, Davies, Webster, Basse, and Jonson are acquainted with the elephant; Davies, John Taylor, and the author of *The Return from Parnassus* with Holden's "old, unwieldy camel." Davies as well knows of a "western hog" on show. Jonson in 1614 mentions "dogs that dance the morris," and a hare who can beat on a tabor—and we have a fourteenth-century illustration of a similar prodigy—while in 1610 three showmen procured a license from Sir George Buc to "show a strange lion, brought to do strange things, as turning an ox to be roasted, &c. . . ."

Faced with such formidable competition, Banks on his return to London would have been hard pressed to maintain his wonted supremacy among theatrical animal trainers. Perhaps the need for new *éclat*, an unprecedented *pièce de résistance* to reassert his claims, inspired him to the crowning single achievement of his career, the feat for which he is most widely memorialized. At any event, the ascent of St. Paul's assured Banks and Morocco of fame far outreaching the unwieldy camel's and the ponderous elephant's; it seized the popular imagination much as Drake's piratical marauding had, and Thomas Stukely's mercenary adventuring, as Robin Hood's exploits did, and Gamaliel Ratsey's would, and for similar reasons—a feat of extraordinary audacity and skill, a "first," a bold stoke, an Englishman (who else?) on the pinnacle, literally, of an improbable success. Eccentric or not, it was a purely English triumph, and instantaneously endeared its perpetrators to a public eager for fresh heroes. Perhaps half of the early allusions to Banks are solely to this celebrated climb.

Now the ascent was by no means easy. St. Paul's Cathedral as Banks knew it burned to the ground, of course, in the Great Fire of 1666, but its dimensions and appearance have come down to us with some accuracy. The stone body of the church to the base of the square, untapering spire, was 260′ high, and the spire itself rose another 260′ to its projecting battlements. A staircase of what well may have numbered a thousand steps—probably circular, within the stone walls, and cramped—led to the summit, where Dekker advises you above all if you lean out to lean cautiously, "for the rails are as rotten as your great-grandfather." The fee for the climb was a penny in 1609, and a penny still after the Great Fire. No separate schedule for livestock has come down to us; but perhaps Banks paid double.

The climb, at any rate, and the equestrian pose at the top had their hazards; and one wonders if the descent were not more hazardous yet. Rewards of notoriety followed swiftly, however. "I have heard of the horse's walking a'th' top of Paul's," remarks Horace hard on the event in Dekker and Webster's *Satiromastix* (1601-02); while Samuel Rowley remarks archly on the "transforming of the top of Paul's into a stable," and Dekker again urges his fashionable gallant (1609) "to talk about the horse that went up, and strive, if you can, to know his keeper." "Let us compare our feats," offers Morocco, in Edward Gayton's doggerel, to Don Quixote's Rosinante in 1654.

> thou top of knolls
> Of hills hast often been seen, I top of *Paul's*.
> To Smithfield horses I stood there the wonder;
> I only was at top, more have been under.
> Thou like a *Spanish jennet*, got i'th' wind,
> Wert hoisted by a windmill: 'twas in kind.
> But never yet was seen in *Spain* or *France*
> A horse like *Banks* his, that to th' pipe would dance,
> Tell money with his feet; a thing which you,
> Good *Rosinante*, nor *Quixote* e'er could do.

The only possible encore was a triumphant continental tour. Morocco and Banks appeared in Paris in March, 1601, at the Lion d'Argent in Rue St. Jacques, and a remarkably full account of their performance there, from a French observer, has come down to us. It is the best surviving résumé of the act in detail, and finds the pair at the height of their powers, showmanship and skill wonderfully mingled in a true *tour de force*, winning the French as they had won the English before.

133

. . . He fetched whatever anyone threw on the stage, and brought it back like a spaniel. He jumped and capered like a monkey. He stood on two legs, walked forward and backward, and then knelt, extending his hooves straight out in back of him.

His master threw up a glove, commanded him to fetch it and carry it to whoever in the company wore (for example) spectacles. Morocco did so, approaching the wearer unerringly.

He asked him to carry the same glove to someone in the company who wore a cloak lined with such and such a material (plush, for example: I swear I saw him do this). Morocco chose among more than two hundred persons the one his master had designated, by some mark of appearance, and brought him the glove. To demonstrate that Morocco knew colors (or rather the dexterity of his master's art, which no one yet could penetrate), if he told him to bring the glove to a lady who had (by chance) a muff of green velvet, or some other color, he went to her unhesitatingly from one end of the room to the other. We saw him do this with two muffs at once, one green, the other violet, with other details too numerous to mention.

His master covered his eyes with a cloak, then asked three of the audience for three different coins of gold or silver. We saw him given a sol, a quarter ecu, and an écu, then put them in a glove, remove the blindfold, and ask Morocco how many coins were in the glove. The horse struck the floor three times with his hoof to indicate three. Then his master asked how many were gold, and Morocco stamped only once, to say one. Then, asked how many francs an écu is worth, Morocco stamped three times. But stranger still, because the gold écu was worth a little more than three francs in March, 1601, the Scotsman asked how many sols this écu was worth beyond the francs, and Morocco struck four blows, to designate the extra four sols. The Scotsman brought out a deck of cards, shuffled them well, and had one selected by a member of the audience, then commanded his horse to rap as many times as the number of the card, and if it was red, with the right foot, if black, with the left. We saw this done with the five of spades.

He commanded him to walk as he would if he had to carry a

134

lady. Morocco took two or three turns around the room, ambling very gently. That he walk as if carrying a valet; he went on a brisk impatient trot. Then he commanded, as if a riding master were mounted upon him. The animal began then to bow and scrape like no other horse imaginable, bounded, made passades, and all other leaps of a trick horse.

If his master scolded him for being lazy, and threatened to give him to some carter who would work him to death, and give him more thrashing than hay, Morocco, as if he understood his speech, lowered his head and by other gestures made known that he was unhappy. He fell on the earth as if sick, stiffened his legs, and remained a long time in his posture, counterfeiting so well that many thought him actually dead. We saw his master trample on him, and promise nevertheless to pardon him if someone in the audience asked the pardon for him. "Pardon him," cried one of the spectators at the back of the room, "he will do his duty well." So the Scotsman commanded him to rise, and go thank the one who had asked and obtained his pardon. Morocco went and chose a man with red hair, the one who had actually interceded, and for a sign of gratitude put his head in his cloak, caressing him and making much demonstration of recognition. After that "I will send you," said his master, "into the postal service, to warm up your legs, since you wish to do nothing." Morocco, to show that he would be useless for such service, raised up one leg and pretended to be lame, cantering on three only.

He commanded that he sneeze three times. He did it at once. That he laugh: he did likewise, showing his teeth and pricking up his ears.

He gave a glove to someone in the troupe, and commanded Morocco to lead by the cloak the man to whom he had given it. The horse took him by the cloak, and pulled so strongly with his teeth that the man was obliged to follow; and led likewise all those his master wanted, indicating them by some mark, such as a black, white, or red plume, to see someone who carried under his arm a bag of papers, or even still if he hid them: we have seen all this done . . .

A certain magistrate, thinking that such things could not be

135

accomplished without magic, had somewhat earlier imprisoned the master and sequestered the horse; but having been manifestly shown that it was only by art and by signs that all this was done, he freed him and permitted him to go on exhibiting. The Scotsman asserted that he could train any horse to do the same within one year . . .

Comic though it may now seem, the allegations of magic in connection with his act gave Banks considerable trouble. Even Isaac Casaubon, among the most learned humanists of his day, took seriously the possibility of a supernatural agency, until Banks with understandable readiness explained precisely how each trick was accomplished. But the stigma followed him to Orleans, in Capuchin jurisdiction, where, says Bishop Morton, "he was brought into suspicion of magic, because of the strange feats which his horse Morocco played . . . where he to redeem his credit promised to manifest to the world" that his horse was not a devil. "To this end he commanded his horse to seek out one in the press of people, who had a crucifix on his hat; which done, he bade him kneel down unto it, and not only this, but to rise up again and to kiss it. 'And now, gentlemen,' quoth he, 'I think my horse hath acquitted both me and himself'; and so his adversaries rested satisfied, conceiving, as it might seem, that the devil had no power to come near the cross." Indeed, there was nothing new about the Capuchins' and Casaubon's suspicions: as early as 1591 at Shrewsbury he had been judged to have a "familiar" or demoniac assistant, and after his Edinburgh performance the Scots chronicler recounts that "the report went . . . that [Morocco] devoured his master, because he was thought to be a spirit and naught else." "May not the Devil, I pray you, walk in Paul's," inquires Middleton's Lucifer in *The Black Book* (1604), "as well as the horse go a top of Paul's? For I am sure I was not far from his keeper." And Dekker directs his credulous gallant to "take the day of the month, and the number of the steps, and suffer yourself to believe verily that it was not a horse, but something else in the likeness of one: which wonders you may publish, when you return into the country, to the great amazement of all farmers' daughters, that will almost swound at the report, and never recover till their banns be asked twice in the Church."

The supreme whimsy, however, was Ben Jonson's, who went so far as to versify the report of a continental *auto-da-fé* involving horse and master.

> both which,
> Being beyond sea, burned for one witch:
> Their spirits transmigrated to a cat . . .

and a marginal note in the romance *Don Zara del Fogo* (1656) places the unhappy event at Rome. But Banks as we shall see was alive well into the late 1630's, and these facetious allusions can thus be discounted.

Paris and Orleans, then, were visited by the pair, possibly Rome, and evidently Frankfurt, where Banks told Bishop Morton of his escape from the Capuchins. We know no date for their return to England, nor do we hear more of the act in London or elsewhere after 1601. Silver shoes and all, Morocco was probably retired or dead by 1606, when his age would have been sixteen. No replacement is known to have succeeded him, belying perhaps, the easy one year his master had once claimed for training.

Banks, however, had reaped from his immense celebrity a signal benefit, an *entrée* into the fringes of court and high households, and no better example of the new ameliorated social status of entertainers, the "rise of the common player," by which Shakespeare, Jonson, and their contemporaries set likewise great store, can be gathered from the sparse records of such personal careers. Already in 1604 King James was well aware of Morocco's excellence in dancing, for he jested of it

137

on New Year's Eve with the French Ambassador during a festive masque; and in 1608 we find two considerable payments from Prince Henry's privy purse "to Banks, for teaching of a little nag to vault, by His Highness' command." Perhaps the old trouper remained within the royal household through the decade following, for the aging King's favorite in 1622-25, George Villiers, Duke of Buckingham, is also on record employing Banks to "teach" a bay horse of his own. And the last heard of Banks, some ten years beyond this, speaks still of a little influence at court. Not unlike other veteran showmen, he ventured to open a tavern, obtaining for it not the franchise of the Vintners's Company, with its strictly limited membership, but—straight from the top—a royal or Great Seal license. The significance of such a license perhaps lies in its rarity: in November, 1633, there were 203 taverns in the city and liberties (of which less than sixty lay in the city itself) licensed by the Vintners' Company, and six only by His Majesty. Banks moreover chose to set up shop at a very elegant address, in Cheapside, the mercantile main street of London, what the annoyed Lord Mayor and Court of Aldermen of London called an "inconvenient place." In spite of the anxiety of municipal authorities, who were concerned to reduce the number of such resorts for "loose persons, bankrupts, and such as are otherwise obnoxious," Banks under his royal warrant won through and established himself, apparently the unique tippling house there, in crowded Cheapside. His sign was "not yet up" on 8 October 1633.

Less than a year later we find him petitioning the King—always the King—for permission to serve food in his tavern, that privilege lately having been withdrawn by the city officials, who thought it a good way to control the popularity of alehouses. Apparently Banks again was successful, for a satirical squib of 1637 jests at the "rare delicacies" one might consume, with one's drink, at his now famous establishment.

138

Nothing is heard of Banks personally after 1637, but as late as 1662 a pamphleteer can say, "I shall never forget my fellow humorist Banks, the vintner in Cheapside, who taught his horse to dance, and shooed him with silver." A year earlier another writer had apostrophized "Banks his horse, that rare master of the caballistic art, whose memory is not forgotten in England." In a few seasons St. Paul's would exchange its square turret for a great circular dome, and no animal will ever be able to duplicate Morocco's crowning achievement. And it is dubious to this day, by the testimony of all the enthralled witnesses, if any horse-trainer has surpassed William Banks's eccentric but no less praiseworthy technique, or the above all amiable partnership of his human art with his animal's somewhat more than equine response.

THE GREAT EATER
OF KENT

"Who, I sir? I am GLUTTONY: my parents are
all dead; and the devil a penny they have left
me but a bare pension, and that is thirty meals
a day and ten bevers [i.e., snacks between meals],
a small trifle to suffice nature."

Doctor Faustus.

FROM DIAMOND JIM BRADY TO JACK'S HOST AT THE SUMMIT OF THE BEAN-STALK, PRIDE IN APPETITE AND CAPACITY have long been some men's meat. Boswell and his esteemed "six-bottle men"—i.e., those capable of draining off three quarts of port wine at a sitting—Milo of Crotona

139

at his celebrated feasts, Maecenas, Lucullus, Britain's Queen Anne, even trim athletes have plumed themselves forever on how much they could comfortably eat and drink. Throwing comfort to the winds, competitive or even professional gluttons still race through watermelons, pies and upon occasion alcohol, but curiously now concentrating upon one single pre-arranged species of edible or drinkable at a time, and by state-fair standards, with an often almost ritual decorum. No gastronome with respect for nineteenth-century tradition can pass over without deference Thackeray's or Abraham Hayward's or Saintsbury's stupendous bills-of-fare, running generally to seven courses or more, soup, *relève, hors d'oeuvres, entrée,* roast(s), *relève,* and a dessert or two, with interval between *entrée* and roast, and a fresh wine with each new platter, but it is worth recalling that among prodigies, Mr. Daniel Lambert in 1807, weight 704 and apparently both healthy and energetic, "eats with moderation and of one dish only at a time," and "never drinks any other beverage than water." What contemporaries of Shakespeare called "surfeits" or overeating, and what we may now suspect as at least in part poisoning by bad pewter or lead for tableware, and inadequate refrigeration, carried off Robert Greene in 1592 ("a surfeit of pickled herrings"), King John (1216, in the Catholic version, a surfeit of peaches and beer) and even Shakespeare according to local tradition, by a surfeit of toasts for old times' sake. In a less delicate age, less delicate members of the competitive fellowship flourished as well: gorging the body remained an activity popular in Stuart as in Tudor England, and among amateurs there were champions.

An early exemplar, the quasi-mythical "great eater" of Henry VIII's reign, had been one Woolner, a "singing man of Windsor"; his name alone stood for indiscriminate gluttony well into the next century, but no extant court or local record appears to name him. One anecdote survives, in a popular chapbook, *The Life of Long Meg of Westminster*, of which the earliest surviving edition is dated 1620, although almost certainly earlier printings have perished. Long Meg was an archetypal jesting virago, tavernkeeper, brawler, railer, "roaring girl," her specialty being to beat men at their own game—even war, when she followed Henry to France and fought at Boulogne (1544) in male attire. She is perhaps more a figment of folklore than a subject for strict biography, but her name, like Woolner's, held currency for years through jestbooks like *The Life of Long Meg* and sporting allusions by later playwrights, poets, and prose journalists. In the tale in question Woolner visits her inn at the instigation of certain gentlemen, practical jokers, and as he is not recognized by Long Meg, asks innocently about the price of a breakfast. The table has been laid for ten, explains Meg, food, ale and all, but Woolner is the first arrival; it is "all you can eat" for sixpence. She goes about her business and leaves her guest to the groaning board.

In an hour Woolner had consumed the entire breakfast—ten generous portions of what was, in his era, the main meal of the day. Rising at Long Meg's return, he solemnly pays over the promised sixpence, and shrugs off her protests by reminding her of the terms she herself had set. But Long Meg is never easily put by. Systematically she lays the table once more for ten with fresh food and ale, and offers the Great Eater three choices: repeat the achievement at once, pay for the ten breakfasts, or go three pikestaff bouts with his hostess for the true reckoning. Presumably a little heavy from dining, Woolner prudently declines the latter chance, after refusing the first two on principle; whereupon Meg bolts the exits and beats him over the head unmercifully until his outcries bring the "merry gentlemen" who had chartered the charade in the first place to break in, explain, and pay up in full.

But if Woolner dwells in the hazy half-world where myth

meets history, and popular tradition feeds on exaggeration—like the exploit of Aulus Vitellius, solemnly retailed by Suetonius and Josephus, of being served at one supper with at least two thousand different sorts of fishes and seven hundred fowl, clearly a zoological improbability—his seventeenth-century successor Nicholas Wood is a more substantial champion of gluttony, perhaps in two senses. "Woolner of Windsor was not worthy to be his footman," claims Wood's contemporary biographer John Taylor.

The source of nearly all our knowledge of this prodigy is Taylor's pamphlet of 1630, *The Great Eater of Kent, or Part of the Admirable Teeth and Stomach's Exploits of Nicholas Wood, of Harrisom in the County of Kent. His Excessive Way of Eating without Manners, in Strange and True Manner Described.* Taylor dedicates this slim volume magnanimously to Wood himself, "the most famous, infamous, high and mighty feeder, Nicholas Wood, great and grand gourmandizer," swearing meanwhile to his readership to "write plain truth, bare and threadbare and even stark naked truth," even though "that which is only true is too much [i.e., for belief]" Wood's birthplace and parentage were unknown to Taylor, and modern research can add nothing to his information. In all probability Wood was Kentish by origin, of the hamlet of Harrietsham, seven miles south-east of Maidstone, about forty-five miles from London. Exploits take him to the nearby settlement of Lenham, and for a major exhibition, ten miles to the larger town of Ashford, a route now traced by the A20. Evidently he was in service, for at one point Taylor records Wood's fear that "his Grace (I guess who he meant) should hear of one that ate so much and could work so little," and thereby "would come a command to hang him." Punishment in the provinces was, to say the least, a matter of prerogative.

When Taylor met Wood personally in or about 1630, the Great Eater was apparently in the twilight of a long career, but

142

some particularly energetic displays of earlier days are recalled. As a matter of course, the champion could consume "a whole sheep of sixteen shillings' price, raw, at one meal," leaving only skin, wool, horns and bones; he has eaten a whole hog at a sitting and topped it off with three pecks of damson plums. Raw ducks are another specialty, although he "abhors the swinish vice of drinking," a weakness which nicked him for at least one gourmandizing defeat. Local reputation led to command performances: he once dined spectacularly, downing "as much as would well have served and sufficed thirty men," at Leeds Castle, the Kentish seat of Sir Warham St. Leger, a knight who had seen Guiana with Ralegh, and again in similar form at Romney Marsh or Southfleet with Sir William Sedley (= Sidley), elder brother of the dramatist and erotic poet Sir Charles. Here, however, Wood so gorged himself "that his belly was like to turn bankrupt and break, but that the servingmen turned him to the fire and anointed his paunch with grease and butter, to make it stretch and hold"; afterward, having been carried to bed, he slept fasting for eight hours, which when found out caused Sedley to put him in the stocks, "there to endure as long time as he had lain bedrid with eating." At Baron Wotton's in Boughton Malherbe, he accounted for seven dozen rabbits; but his great setback came locally, at Lenham one fair-day, when a certain John Dale laid odds he could fill Wood's belly for no more than two shillings—which he accomplished by soaking twelve one-penny loaves of bread in six pots of strong ale, the fumes of which alone put the Great Eater soundly to sleep for nine hours, before finishing.

Presumably the meeting between Wood and Taylor occurred during one of the latter's country expeditions (see Part IV below), and the waterman-poet was so impressed with the first breakfast he saw wolfed by the eater that he offered him "down" a pound to come north into London to his "house"

143

on the Bankside for ten days, all he could eat plus five shillings a day while he stayed, and a pound more at the end of the visit; in addition, he offered to pay Wood's close friend Jeremy Robinson half wages to accompany them. An experienced showman, Taylor's "plot," as he freely admits, was to exhibit the Great Eater at the amphitheatrical Bear Garden on the Bankside to a paying audience, feeding him one day a wheelbarrow-full of tripe, the next "as many puddings as would reach over the Thames"—which canny Taylor intended to measure at the narrowest stretch between London and Richmond—next a fat calf or twenty-shillings sheep, and, on the fourth day, thirty sheep's "gathers" [i.e., heart, liver, kidneys, etc.].

But stage fright and inertia kept Nicholas Wood an amateur to the end. Suppose before all London he were to fail, he asked himself? His hard-won reputation in Kent would vanish overnight. Furthermore, his long-suffering employer might hear of the business, question his utility, and sack him. And lastly, he pleaded, age, infirmity, and a certain inevitable queasiness had reduced him to the state recently of attempting no more than a whole fat sheep, but "tenderly boiled" now, and no longer raw, especially since he had apparently lost all but one of his teeth at Ashford by chewing and not choking on a quarter of mutton, *bones and all.* All things considered he begged off, and slipped his contract.

Taylor bore him no grudge, evidently. His panegyric pamphlet history, larded with wit and discursion, of this ultimately bashful champion piles so much praise upon praise, that one may distinguish a certain unfeigned admiration in the old showman alongside the obvious literary hack's job of whipping up the same in his reading public, the plain awe for all natural prodigies he accorded such a kindred figure as the champion valetudinarian, 152-year-old Mr. Thomas Parr, in 1635. "Thou," concludes Taylor of Wood, in verse at last,

Thou that putst down the malt below the wheat,
That dost not eat to live, but live to eat,
Thou that the sea-whale and land-wolf excells,
A foe to Bacchus, champion of god Bael's:
I wish if any foreign foes intend
Our famous isle of Britain to offend,
That each of them had stomachs like to thee,
That of each other they devoured might be . . .
Though *Maximus*, Rome's great emperor
Did forty pound of flesh each day devour,
Albinus th' emperor did him surpass:
Five hundred figs by him down swallowed was,
Of peaches he consumed one hundred more,
Of great muskmellons also half a score,
One hundred birds, all at one meal he cast
Into his paunch, at breaking of his fast.
Pago surpassed both these two together,
A boar, a hundred loaves, a pig, a weather [sheep],
All this the rascal swallowed at a meal
(If writers in their writing true do deal).
But sure I am, that what of thee is writ
Is sure (although not all the truth, nor half of it):
Thou dost exceed all that our age e'er saw,
Thou potent, high, and mighty man of maw.

THE VANISHING ACT

O N SATURDAY 6 NOVEMBER 1602, FOR A PRICE RANGING FROM ONE SHILLING AND SIXPENCE upward, one might have been enticed to the Swan Theatre in the Paris Garden pleasure haunts of London's Bankside for a

145

remarkable performance. A flyer, a broadside "program"—and the earliest printed example, unique, now surviving—would have let a spectator know what to expect. "England's Joy" is the name of the pageant, a kind of court masque with all the elaborateness associated with those costly spectacles, short on plot but pleasing to the eye and ear. By way of "induct, by show and in action," all the civil wars of England from Edward III to Bloody Mary, "with the overthrow of Usurpation," will be presented. The grand entrance of ENGLAND'S JOY herself follows, namely Elizabeth the Queen, symbolically attended at her dramatized coronation by "Peace, Plenty, and Civil Policy," a prelate of the reformed Church at her right hand, Justice at her left, and at her royal feet, War, "with a scarlet robe of peace upon his armor, a wreath of bays about his temples, and a branch of palm in his hand." One might anticipate a pause to let all this sink in, before three furies, representing dissension, famine, and bloodshed are herded in and cast roughly "down into hell," probably an open trap in the floor of the stage. More topical politics follow these generalized goods and evils: Spanish soldiers drag forward a beautiful lady, personifying the Low Countries, "whom they mangle and wound, tearing her garments and jewels from off her, and so leave her bloody, with her hair about her shoulders, lying on the ground." England's aid is solicited, and somebody descends from the royal dais to bind up the victim's wounds, load her with money, and present her with a small army of her own, who escort her, comforted, from the stage. A fifth "scene" depicts the Spanish tyrant, "more enraged," sending forth letters, spies, and "secret underminers," all bound by oaths and paid handsomely; if we need a key, "these signify Lopez," the doctor who attended and attempted to poison the Queen in 1594, and may have afforded Shakespeare a prototype for

Shylock, "and certain Jesuits, who afterward, when the tyrant looks for an answer from them, are showed to him in a glass with halters about their necks, which makes him mad with fury." Retro-chronistically, the tyrant sends off the Armada of 1588, which is defeated. Seventh, he aids Tyrone's Irish, and is driven home again by Charles Blount, Lord Mountjoy—an event as recent as the Battle of Kinsale on 24 December 1601, and its aftermath. To wind up the festivities, "a great triumph is made with fighting of twelve gentlemen at barriers, and sundry rewards sent from the throne of England," while at last the Nine Worthies and various seraphim re-crown the Queen, and she in her throne is pulled up into heaven, where she reappears surrounded by "blessed souls"; "and beneath under the stage," a piece of elegant theatrical craft dating back to the mystery cycles, "set forth with strange fire-works, divers black and damned souls, wonderfully described in their several torments." A fit conclusion.

Had you paid your money and assumed your seat, warm with expectation, the results might have left you furious enough for riotous violence. As John Chamberlain retails the story to Sir Dudley Carleton, a Mr. Richard Vennard of Lincoln's Inn, Gentleman, the sponsor of this much-puffed extravaganza, "when he had gotten most part of the money into his hands, he would have showed them a fair pair of heels," but being "not so nimble to get up on horseback," took to the water. He was pursued and apprehended, and brought before the Lord Chief Justice, who luckily for Vennard treated the whole matter as a prank, "a jest and a merriment," binding the culprit over at only £5 to the next sessions. Unluckily for the theatre, however, "in the mean time the common people, when they saw themselves deluded, revenged themselves upon the hangings, curtains, chairs, stools, walls, and whatsoever came in their way, very outrageously, and made great spoil." Finally, says Chamberlain, "there was great store of good company, and many noblemen"—the entrepreneur had drawn a whole flock of gulls.

As we shall see, Vennard himself provides a somewhat different version of the events, insisting that he really had meant to offer some sort of show, but that bailiffs had carried him off during the very prologue. Whether or not he was absolutely culpable—and the autobiography he composed in his own defense in 1614 is so studded with inaccuracies and improbabilities that we must employ it with extreme caution—it is certainly true that the show was never intended to be all it claimed to be, that Vennard was in fact the "grand coneycatcher" John Manningham calls him, and among theatrical dadaists one of the very earliest.

His cozening trick was remembered in England well into the 1650's, and the nick-name "England's Joy" clung to Vennard for the rest of his life. But the perpetrator of the hoax itself, and Vennard's life on either side of his most famous exploit have some of the qualities of nightmare and ambiguity which raise an "unworthy" from ignominy to the *DNB*. Part charlatan, part philanthropist, fake showman, bad poet, toady, courtier *manqué*, liar and talebearer, but evidently a charmer and "a man of reach," perhaps nearly as much sinned against as sinning, and certainly the victim of "the insolence of office and the law's delay," we can add to his lightly sketched portrait in *DNB* and *The Elizabethan Stage* a few strokes which may leave the reader as puzzled about his true nature as Chambers was certain of his "impudence."

The first problem we must face, however, as often before, is that Vennard's life as Vennard writes of it, in *An Apology written by Richard Vennar of Lincoln's Inn, abusively called England's Joy* (London, by Nicholas Oakes, 1614), is often at considerable variance with extant records, and that other assertions cannot any more be verified; hence that the whole autobiography calls for salt, and fragmentary documentary evidence must be set against it or reconciled with it as economically as possible. His origins, however, are beyond dispute. He was the younger of two sons of John Vennard, a Justice of the Peace and relatively well-to-do merchant in the cathedral town of Salisbury. Vennard tells us he received his first communion from John Jewell, the eminent Bishop of Salisbury (*d.* 1571), in the presence of the Earls of Bedford and Pembroke, as befits even the cadet of an important local house. Dates in his later career lead one to estimate Richard's birth at approximately 1555. He was educated first by Jewell's protégé Adam Hill, a Balliol B.A. (1569) and M.A. (1571), later B.D., D.D., Prebendary and Succentor at Salisbury Cathedral; then, according to the autobiographer, at Balliol as well. He may of course have accompanied Hill back to Oxford about 1571 or 1572, but no record of Vennard's matriculation at any college survives, from registers usually thought fairly complete. But Vennard claims he was a fellow commoner for two years at Balliol, when, afflicted by "the windy humor of travel," he left school and with his father's suffrance, an Italian guide, a servingman, and a page—something of a young aristocrat's *entourage*, if we are to believe him—visited first the court of Henri III at Paris, ingratiated himself, and then with the French King's own letters of introduction, the court of Emperor Maximilian II (*d.* 1576.), his extended tour wound back through Germany, but Vennard had already acquired the taste for court life and its expensive accoutrements which would lead him to spend the rest of his days shifting between debtors' jails and the seats of Queen Elizabeth and King James. "Forthwith" on his return, says Vennard, he entered Lincoln's Inn, during Lord Ellesmere's readership (Lent 1582, but perhaps earlier as well), and in fact on 10 June 1581 the Inn registers record the admission of

"Richard Venarde, of Wilts., of Barnard's Inn." For the first time Vennard's chronology and assertions may be checked, and found, here, to be true.

If he studied his law hard he nevertheless gathered enough wool in the next six years to require a new "special admission" for continued residence on 25 July 1587, an indication, later to be confirmed, that he had not yet been called to the bar. Perhaps these long and expensive sojourns in Oxford, London, and abroad, while his elder brother married, sired four children, and continued to dwell in Salisbury, affected some kind of estrangement between Richard and his father, but we must hold fire, for now and hereafter the accounts of complex and confusing financial affairs in the Vennard family become irreconcilably contradictory. Taking first Richard's version, the elder brother, John Junior, predeceased his father, leaving a widow who shortly thereafter remarried herself to a lawyer, a real barrister of Lincoln's Inn (entered 1574) as well. The living father, claims Richard, who had intended "to leave his lands to her children," now in annoyance "made a deed of gift to me of all his goods, to the value of many thousand pounds," and promptly died. But the dispossessed widow's new husband in Richard's absence, "by a supposed will . . . possessed himself of the estate before given unto me . . . laying supposed forgery of that deed to my charge." From now on it is the deed of gift against the will, and according to Richard, the litigatious brother-in-law "in malice. to weaken my estate," drew the case into Star Chamber, where lawsuits could malinger for years. Meanwhile, Richard, deprived of patrimony or allowance, got himself convicted for debt at King's Bench, and incarcerated in Fleet Prison. Finally, faced with an interminable suit and insoluble debts, he accepted a "composition" of £150, presumably a quittance from his antagonist, and an end, temporary at least, to his hopes for the family estate. Nor did his troubles now cease with his quittance, for, says Vennard, knowing that his own reputation was at least tainted in the matter of forgery, a young man "in the shape of a gentleman of the Lord Admiral's" counterfeited Charles Howard's hand and seal on a draft for £40 payable at the Deptford Storehouse, took rooms near Lincoln's Inn on Chancery Lane, cultivated Vennard's acquaintance, feigned sickness, and persuaded Vennard to collect the cash "as I passed that way to my house at Lewisham, in Kent. Which project carried thus much safety to himself, that if the sum were delivered, it was easily earned, if it miscarried, it was easily answered; where my avowing was to be avoided by his denial, which falling on me, with some amazement, brought full astonishment in his confident abjuring: here was the proverb verified: *An ill name, half hanged.*" In other words, Vennard was seized, held, and would again have been victimized if "the free language of [his] heart" had not moved Lord Burleigh's compassion, to the end that the true malefactor was examined, found culpable, and Vennard exonerated; a narrow escape.

So far we have been following Vennard's swift account, witty and readable, but unfortunately at considerable variance with the damning records still preserved among the Privy Council Papers, the Domestic State papers, and at Somerset House. To begin with, the affair of the forged forty-pound receipt appears to have *preceded* the rival claims to the Vennard estate, thus casting an apparently retrospective pall on the proverb and Vennard's elaborate explanation of his non-accomplice's motives in choosing him out—a rather long way to go, one might think, for forty pounds. But the contested will, the questioned deed of gift, and the barrister antagonist must first be brought into the history.

John Vennard, Jr., died in Salisbury in 1588, a year after Richard's "special admission" to Lincoln's Inn, leaving a wife and four children, the eldest son John III. His father, John the elder, has left a will dated 7 July 1589 "making all other wills before this frustrate and void," the copy of which only is at Somerset House, and which no doubt was the testament Richard calls "supposed." It is a curious document. After various charitable bequests, it begins by demanding that Richard, the testator's younger son, "deliver up . . . a counterfeit or forged writing which he calleth a deed of gift," and enter into a £1000 bond that he will no more "vex, molest, or trouble" the executors and assigns of the parental estate, all on pain of getting no part of it. The bulk of the estate is then left in trust for young John III, several relatives are bequeathed token sums, but nothing more specific is said about what Richard is to receive if he complies with the initial conditions. John Senior was dead by 15 August of the same year, when the will was proved in the Prerogative Court of Canterbury.

Clearly, then, either the "deed of gift" or the will *in extremis* is a forgery, or at least one lies. As both have vanished, and as no contemporary court was able easily to decide between them, our evidence is entirely inferential. Against Richard we may hold simply (a) that the will as quoted above did pass probate, (b) that he himself, whether as he says unjustly or truly was to be charged more than once in his mixed career with documentary forgery, and (c) that deathbed reversals of wills, with Richard "away" and the sister-in-law no doubt attending, are by no means rare; a barrister husband might have come in handy for drafting such a repudiatory will.

In Richard's behalf, we may point once more to certain oddnesses in Vennard Senior's alleged last testament. First, there is the question of what Richard was supposed to gain by complying with the requirements made of him. Second, there is the invective tone and insistent preliminary placement of the conditions concerning him, and the emphasis on not vexing or molesting the true executors, something which might truly imply an *ex post facto* demand based on the antagonists' experience if it were not so conventional a legal phrase. Third, and most telling, is the very logic of the father's supposed repudiation and Richard's own sensible strategy: if John Junior died in 1588 and Richard had in fact forged a deed of gift during the next year, is he likely to have revealed this forgery or claim to his father in the interim? Is he not more likely to have saved the deed quietly until after the old man's death, and then to have produced it in court? For the testator to have known about a deed of gift at all we must assume one of three things: (1) Richard the forger or somebody privy to it—say a money-lender or accomplice—told the elder Vennard about it, a piece of catastrophic strategy or bad luck, (2) the deed was genuine, but the testator suffered or was induced to suffer a change of heart, hence to renounce it in the only way possible, as a forgery, or (3) that the Vennard will was made or forged after the death of the testator, and with full subsequent knowledge of Richard's means of claiming the estate.

In my opinion the latter two alternatives are the more probable. One may consider also that Richard in his *Apology* freely admits that his father *had* intended to bequeath his estate to his primary grandchildren, bypassing Richard, before John Junior's widow remarried; and that nowhere in the extant copy of the will—a most curious omission—is the name of the new husband, Richard Lowe, to be found. He is not even among the several executors of the trust-fund for his own stepson. Does this perhaps point to a deliberate self-effacement? If one were forging a will ultimately in one's own behalf, might he not think it a sly maneuver to omit his own name altogether from among the beneficiaries, even of token bequests?

But no real case can be constructed from these surmises, although we imagine the courts over the ensuing years painfully sifting such hypotheses as these above. There remain the traces of what actions they in fact took. Sometime after his father's death in the summer of 1589 Richard is claimed to have entered, presumably forcibly, the premises at Salisbury he now claimed as his own, and presumably he was ejected. This must have occurred before 21 September 1590, when investigation of the Howard forgery affair began; contrary to Richard's own chronology, a Privy Council warrant went out for his arrest "to bring him before my Lord Admiral with all such writings and instruments as my Lord's hand is at." By 30 November both he and his colleague—surely the instigator Vennard himself accuses, one Garrett Swift—were in Marshalsea prison awaiting examination. Apparently more than one counterfeit document of the Lord Admiral's had turned up in their possession, and a carefully forged silver seal with Howard's arms on it is spoken of.

Now three days after Christmas the name of Richard Lowe first enters the records of the Privy Council. Writing to the Master of Requests, Richard Rokeby, the Solicitor General, Thomas Egerton, and factotum William Waad, they seem now belatedly to have been informed that it was by "the suggestion" of Lowe, Mrs. John Vennard's new husband, that Richard was apprehended in the first place. A rather strongly worded letter calls attention to the commissioners' delay of examination in the Howard case, apparently credits Richard's claims to the goods "which the said Lowe detaineth in his hands notwithstanding an assurance thereof made to the said Richard Vennard from his deceased father," mentions the "great hindrance and impoverishment of the said Richard Vennard, his wife and children," calls for an immediate hearing and for the authorities "to take some extraordinary pains for the relief of the poor gentleman in prison."

But 1590 dragged into 1591, and on 9 January the Privy Council once more directed its officers the Lord Keeper Sir

John Puckering, Egerton, and the Admiralty Judge, in language almost identical to that quoted above, to see to the matter "with all expedition." Lowe had made his appearance before them three days earlier, and had been indemnified to remain within call. Apparently, however, he had meanwhile managed to have Richard charged with felony in Wiltshire, for entering his deceased father's house, and on 10 January the Privy Council was obliged to explain to the Mayor of Salisbury that Richard was not yet available for extradition. On February 1 they called for Lowe, on February 7 they heard him, and again bound him to remain nearby. A month passed, and on March 9 Lowe was permitted to go back to Salisbury, on the condition that he make himself available to the Council "from time to time."

Now it is April 6, and still both the inheritance and the felony charge in Salisbury hang fire, and Richard has spent about five months in the Marshalsea. Apparently, however, their examination of Lowe has given the Privy Council second thoughts about "the poor gentleman in prison" and this "very intricate" cause, because having noted that Richard is now lining up witnesses in his own behalf to be examined in the High Court of Chancery, and their depositions taken, which "might greatly carry the arbitrators in favor of Vennard," while Lowe has not taken such steps, they feel that both parties should be accorded similar treatment, and so direct Puckering. In spite of such opportunity, Lowe has done nothing by 24 May, and the Privy Council think it a matter for Chancery to try, if the Attorney General will agree. On 30 May they dictated a short but extremely strong note to Puckering and Egerton, having been advised by Vennard's deprived wife that "notwithstanding our letters . . . you refuse to take pains therein," adding perhaps wryly "which we do not believe," and calling for a reply forthwith.

Alas, it is June 27 before the examinations are concluded,

and the profound findings of Puckering and Egerton were that the case might well be tried at common law, most swiftly in Wiltshire. Acting only slightly more rapidly, on 25 July the Privy Council requested the Mayor, Dean, and Bailiff of Salisbury to take back their own litigants and handle the case in a Salisbury court.

Perhaps now the Council considered its hands washed of the matter, but Lowe's ingenuity and the compliance perhaps of officials in Salisbury turned it all back to London once more. After the new assignation of venue, presumably through Burleigh's personal intercession, as *The Apology* claims, Richard had at least been released from prison on the first forgery charge, but his freedom was brief: on 1 December 1591 a warrant went out from Star Chamber to apprehend him "on a commission of rebellion," a catch-all charge; had Lowe managed, as Vennard says, to "draw the case into Star Chamber," where the wait would be crippling to an already undermined personal estate? It would appear so. Nor were Vennard's fellows in Lincoln's Inn a great stay in troubled times. During his enforced absence they had taken away his chambers, and the Privy Council, perhaps wearily, was obliged (30 January) to request the benchers to restore them. Months passed, and on 7 May 1592 for the last time Vennard's name appears in the minutes of the Privy Council: Lowe continually "makes delays in pleading," and the Council, recalling its past recommendations of the case to common law, perhaps unaware or uninformed by Vennard of Lowe's designs for a Star Chamber hearing, upon Vennard's "humble suit" requests the Judges of Her Majesty's Bench to bring about a trial during the next term, "not doubting of the performance with effect."

Only a fraction of the Star Chamber records survive, and if Vennard vs. Lowe ever came to trial at all we cannot now tell. The next documents concerning Richard find him in debt in

Fleet Prison and angling about for an escape. Perhaps, as he later states, it was the long litigation which had broken him, but in his duplicate supplications of 25 February 1596 to Attorney General Coke and Lord Burleigh he takes a rather different line of explanation. As he tells it, a year and a half earlier he had informed on certain recusants for treasonable remarks, and in revenge they have (a) gotten him imprisoned for debt, (b) bribed his long-suffering wife, now living with her father in Holborn, neither to visit him nor intercede for him, and (c) promised "to pay my creditors if I may be continued in prison." Vennard encloses an account of inflammatory opinions expressed to him by one Tristram Cotterell and one Thomas Dymoke in Hampshire on 20 September 1594, as he passed through the countryside on horseback. But little notice apparently was taken of Cotterell and Dymoke, and perhaps Richard's letter was put down mainly to spite and guile. Cotterell, at any rate, was to effect an equivalent revenge, after nine years.

As for Vennard, the appeal went flat. On December 16, 1599, he was still imprisoned "at the suit of Richard Lowe," and applied once more for release to the "new man" Robert Cecil, whose powerful father, Lord Treasurer Burleigh, had died and bequeathed him in effect a political empire. Richard enclosed certain "Verses upon my late Lord Treasurer's Death," his first known essay at panegyric poetry, complained of the "intolerable wrongs" done him by the Lord Keeper in neglecting to hear the case in spite of the pressure of both Council and Queen, and hints darkly at "matters as are not fit to be concealed from the Queen," which he would tell Cecil of were he free to attend him—perhaps an echo of the recusant accusations levied in 1596. As Lord Keeper Thomas Egerton, Lord Ellesmere, had succeeded Puckering on the latter's death in May, 1596, and if we recall the Privy Council's persistent reminders and reiterations to both during 1590-92 and

157

extrapolate, we may easily find matter for consideration in Richard's complaint.

At all events, Vennard did get out of jail fairly soon, perhaps by Cecil's intercession, perhaps by allowing his lawsuit to elapse with the quittance or "composition" he speaks of in *The Apology*. Let us suppose that he was now about 45 years old, possessed only of "a younger brother's patrimony, my limbs and my wits," and "that to add to my wants I had the remembrance of former plenty," and we may find it remarkable that his spirits are unbroken. Bitter, perhaps, but persistent, "I put new wings to my dull hopes," and with a combination of apparently compulsive ill-advisedness and the homing instinct to foreign courts, took horse for Scotland to procure letters, if he could, from King James to the Council urging "a hearing of my cause, the former agreement notwithstanding." Vennard's naïveté seems to have been in balance with his foresight.

He arrived in Scotland on 7 August 1600, precisely in time for the celebrations attending James's narrow escape from the Gowrie plot. Overwhelmed by the festivities, the widespread liberality and popular joy "did so stir up my affection that it moved me to a passion," and a new poem of praise was the outcome. Richard wrote his "Prayer of Thanksgiving" while still in his bed the next morning, and promptly it was passed along—its author modestly suggesting by little more than accident—to the poet-King himself by one Master Duncan Moore, giving Richard his *entrée*. He kissed the Royal hand, and formed part of the courtly group which accompanied James to Faulkland, where he remained for a time in attendance.

These fawning verses and others like them, composed mainly in the automatic decasyllabic hexaines (ababcc) so popularized by Shakespeare's *Venus and Adonis*, were published by Vennard in a little collection called *The True*

Testimony of a Faithful Subject (n.d., but probably late 1605) after the Scottish monarch had assumed the English throne as James I. Like all other of Vennard's verses they are mediocre, hortatory, political in the extreme (those on the Gowrie plot, for example, include a discursion on the King's favorite hobby-horse, witchcraft), pious, rousing, and about as concerned with imagery or lyric movement as the sub-average broadside ballad. Ramsay, the King's rescuer, comes in for extravagant praise, as Lord Mountjoy soon would; Vennard worked as many living heroes into his panegyrics as could possibly fit, possibly with an eye to patronage; his villains tend to be abstract (popery, the Spanish), distant (Tyrone, Don John of Aquila), or dead, like Gowrie.

Upon his return to Edinburgh, however, Richard found himself in some international hot water. George Nicholson, the English agent, questioned him closely about his loyalty. When he finally backtracked to London, later in the same year, and seemingly followed Elizabeth's court to Richmond, he was, he says, apprehended, examined, and committed as a "dangerous member to the State." The new imprisonment was brief, but on his release he felt too poor even to trump up enough finery to revisit the more hospitable Scottish court. No more is spoken of his lawsuit; only literature and legal practice remained to him, and perhaps the shadow of a patron or two. To Attorney General Sir Edward Coke and Sir Christopher Yelverton he applied with a formal request to be called to the bar—at last, one may say, twenty years after his first installation at Lincoln's Inn—and took the precaution of begging a personal letter from the Queen to the Lincoln's Inn benchers in support of his motion. The request and its bearer were passed along by Yelverton and Coke to Sir Robert Cecil on 28 January 1601, who evidently exerted himself in the matter, for shortly thereafter Richard gratefully presented Cecil with the manuscript of a "small volume . . . very

159

needful to be published in print." Another Council member, he explained, had already seen and allowed it, but he wished Cecil also to have a pre-publication glimpse in gratitude for his "late motion in my behalf to the Queen."

This "small volume" of verse hexaines, prose exhortations, characters and homilies, and two appropriately incompetent acrostics, dedicated to the Queen, appeared in 1601, printed by Thomas Este, as *The Right Way to Heaven: and the True Testimony of a Faithful and Loyal Subject.* A second edition was entered on 19 November, adding "a good precedent for lawyers," and printed in 1602, as was a separate issue of the prose portion, Vennard's *True Testimony.* In the 1601 edition the penultimate poem is a versified prayer for the success of the English forces in Ireland, likening Charles Blount, Lord Mountjoy, to Saint George, exhorting him to slay a contemporary dragon, to "quell that Hell's shape of proud devilish Tyrone,/And cover with the dust his stubborn crest." Now Mountjoy did in fact quell Tyrone and put the small Spanish supporting forces to flight at Kinsale on 26 December of the same year, a crowning achievement which Vennard immediately celebrated in 20 more six-line stanzas of victory verse, with a new "Elizabetha Regina" acrostic, and more puns on "mount" and "joy"—a *separatim* signed "R.V." and often rather stupidly attributed to Richard Rowlands, *alias* Verstegan (see *STC* 21358), the exiled recusant antiquarian and religious poet whose sympathies lay quite elsewhere. This short and characteristic panegyric, printed again by Thomas Este presumably in 1602, is titled, coincidentally, *England's Joy.*

Now either law practice was slow or literature, as usual, was unremunerative, for by November of 1602 Richard is once again skint. Begging was not out of the question, but charity seemed as hard to come by as earnings or inheritance, and envy of more successful entrepreneurs drove Richard to the exploit which even he cannot quite justify, though sophistically he reminds us victims "at the highest rate, you lent me but an afternoon's hearing, the expectation being worth the money; since Philosophers say that the sweetness of hope is beyond the enjoying." Seeing, as he says, "a daily offering to the God of Pleasure, resident at the Globe on the Bankside"—pleasure which might have included among other experiences the premieres and original-cast performances of *Hamlet, Henry V, As You Like It, The Merchant of Venice, Twelfth Night, Every Man Out of his Humor,* and *The Merry Wives of Windsor*—Vennard "noted every man's hand ready to feed the luxury of his eye, that pulled down his hat to stop the sight of his charity," and "concluded to make a friend of Mammon, and to give them sound for words." Apparently Vennard then rented the Swan Theatre for the night of November 6, circulated his advertisements for *England's Joy,* and let curiosity come to him instead. He claims, as we have mentioned above, actually to have had something to show—in his words "divers chorus to be spoken by men of good birth, scholars by profession," before the bailiffs, for a misdemeanor which Richard does not specify, interrupted his prologue and put an end to the whole action. And there is indeed evidence that a pageant of the same name, presumably picking up Vennard's pieces, was in fact offered, as a *soi-disant* impromptu recitation, by a court rhymer named William Fennor sometime later. A doggerelists' flyting-match of 1615 finds the Water Poet John Taylor accusing Fennor of just such a "cover":

Thou bray'st what fame thou got'st upon the stage,
Indeed, thou set'st the people in a rage
In playing *England's Joy,* that every man
Did judge it worse than that was done at Swan.
I never saw poor fellow so behist;
T'applaud thee, few or none lent half a fist.

Some of the ignorant did applaud, concedes Taylor, but only because Fennor was supposed to be "extemporizing," and Taylor asserts contemptuously that the Royal Rhymer had been practicing for a month, and had stolen "the best conceits . . . from another wit," presumably Vennard, who evidently was ghost-writing for Fennor again in 1614-15. Further, there is evidence that Vennard was neither disgraced nor discomfited greatly by the failure to produce, that he in fact went on to plan at least one other such spectacle, and possibly stage something more modest in London and the countryside in the ensuing years. But one almost would prefer *England's Joy* to have been an out-and-out hoax, suggested perhaps, as E. K. Chambers has pointed out, by a jest-book tradition at least fifty years old—the empty theatre and the gulled audience. For its scope and undeniable bravado, however, Vennard's hoax far exceeds George Peele's at Bristol or the prototypical jesters he may have emulated. It is a kind of high-water mark of non-theatre in England, a *Fichtes Nachtsong* or *Emperor's New Sonnet* of the stage, perhaps worthy now to be revived by some popular cultist with feet nimbler than Vennard's. And in its negative way it proves again how uncritically magnetized the Elizabethan audience remained, high prices and all, by pomp, circumstance, and publicity, as much as by plot or the playwright's reputation.

After *England's Joy* Vennard's career follows familiar patterns, and the record can be briefly set down. No repercussions in the lawcourts are indicated, as the inclination of the first magistrate to treat the whole matter as a practical joke would nearly ensure. At Court itself, where Vennard rather cheekily ventured to put in an appearance within days, he was observed wearing a black suit, without rapier, but with golden spurs on his boots—and, as one wit observed, a brazen face which clashed for color; hence another's *bon mot:* "It seems," punned an unidentified "R. R.," "he hath some

162

mettle in him." Vennard himself would have us believe, perhaps audaciously, that "no man of my degree in this kingdom hath with more danger of his person and adventure of his estate brought equal benefit to his country," and that "never man of my rank, considering the late lightness of my purse and now weakness of my friends, waded deeper to reach the general good of my country." Reform is the new hobby-horse.

Richard's self-recorded philanthropies, however, are scarcely of an extraordinary number or nature. Close acquaintance with the iniquities of prison, and an undoubtedly genuine conviction that jail was no place for a debtor to do anything constructive about his conditions, had led him in Elizabeth's reign to ally himself with two activist countesses, Margaret of Cumberland and Anne of Warwick, as a fellow-traveller if not member of the Queen's "commission for speedy enlargement of all unable debtors" in King's Bench Prison and the Fleet; the Commission were encouraged or manned by a number of distinguished Londoners, and won a promise of "mercy" from the Queen. This "mercy" having been "stopped" by a severe judge, Vennard says, he himself re-opened the case to the new King after 1603, who re-granted clemency. Vennard then volunteered to be "Register of the Commission" and solicitor of the debtors' causes, and with the aid of the Countess of Warwick—or she with his aid—procured the release subsequently of thirty-four penniless prisoners. About the same time—the early months of James's reign—he embarked on an undetailed program of protection for his own countrymen, bumpkins from Wiltshire who had streamed to the city for the coronation, and stood in grave fiscal danger of the wiles of the London slickers and confidence-men Vennard could warn them about. He may be draining the lees of his memory to point out that he once won a case "before the late Earl of Northampton" (Henry Howard, *d.* 1614), for an "unnaturally dispossessed mother," in a mere two weeks, after years of delay had nearly ruined her, but the analogy it offered to his own cause could not have escaped him. And finally he claims in 1614 to have recently drawn up proposals for a hospital at Bath consecrated to the memory of the Gunpowder Plot, which he still hopes will be carried into effect.

Vennard seems to have viewed his own writing as well as a kind of philanthropy, and indeed there is little else but evangelism to remark in his verse. He wrote a book, he informs us (no doubt the 1605 re-issue of *True Testimony* which is about half lifted from *The Right Way to Heaven,* substituting only "King" for "Queen" among the "God saves"). on the Gunpowder Treason, and distributed it personally through Surrey, Sussex, Kent, Essex, and Hertfordshire. It remains excessively rare, like all of Vennard's printed work, regardless. And he presented "my more public device in picture and verse, describing *a Papist Dormant, a Papist Couchant, a Papist Levant, a Papist Passant, a Papist Rampant,* and *a Papist Pendant,*" as also "the Portraitures of my Sovereign, the majestic Queen, and the memorable Prince, with a true subject's prayer inserted under it [in verse]" to Richard Vaughan, when Bishop of London (1604-07), who provided "letters of ample commendation to *publish* them" (my italics: is Vennard speaking of broadsides or *tableaux vivants,* semi-theatrical performances?) both in London and in his other dioceses.

On the other side of the ledger, in 1603 a deposition by Richard Woodward, based on information donated by Tristram Cotterell—the Hampshire recusant of 1594 striking back—accused Vennard once more of tampering with a document, of inserting matter in a deed of gift between the bottom of the writing and the seal. And late in 1606 a new project for an elaborate show (one must wonder at Vennard's persistence in this occupation) fell very much afoul of a powerful and ruthless antagonist. According to Vennard, he had undertaken, upon somebody else's suggestion, to present a masque "by the citizens" at court on Christmas, at the marriage of Lord Hayes to the daughter of Lord Denny. First, he says, he sought and acquired a small contribution from the King himself, then assured the project of £1000 from the Lord Mayor, Sir John Watts, if a matching sum could be raised privately. He landed a promise for half of that from Sir Stephen Soame, a colleague on the debtors' commission, and former Sheriff of London. The remaining £500 he attempted to extract from Sir John Spencer.

This proved another downfall. In presenting his credentials to Spencer he freely admits he went "beyond [his] commission" in using "an honorable person's name to him"—and indeed Richard always gives the impression of name-dropping a little in excess of his true right. Because "my name carried doubt enough in it," but also because Lord John Spencer was as bad a choice as could have occurred to Vennard—a stingy, truculent, cruel and very wealthy self-made man—he was checked out and promptly apprehended on a charge of fraud. Despite the clearing evidence of Soame, and the forgiveness of "the honorable person . . . for that boldness," and despite a final verdict of not guilty, Vennard again suffered interim incarceration. Writing in 1614 he says his name is so muddied in London that he lives now, single and "in years sufficiently aged to carry my sight to the grave," in Kent and Essex, where the hospitality of the honorable natives makes up in part for the hostility of vulgar London.

Of his late years we know little, save that he penned an *Apology*, bitterly dedicated half "to the purblind multitude that feed with spectacles to make their meat seem bigger," and half, a trifle snobbishly, "to all generous persons, whose births and qualities are the same." John Taylor tells one

165

relevant anecdote in his assault on Fennor to show that
Vennard was still a rhymer in 1615:

> Upon Saint George's Day last, Sir, you gave
> To eight Knights of the Garter (like a knave)
> Eight manuscripts (or books) all fairly writ,
> Informing them, they were your mother wit;
> And you compiled them; then were you regarded,
> And for another's wit was well rewarded.
> All this is true, and this I dare maintain:
> The matter came out from a learned brain;
> And poor old *Venner*, that plain-dealing man,
> Who acted *England's Joy* first at the Swan,
> Paid eight crowns for the writing of these things,
> Besides the covers and the silken strings:
> Which money back he never yet received,
> So the deceiver is by thee deceived.

And Fennor himself, in a quite different context, tells us both
of an exploit of Vennard's in prison and the melancholy end of
"England's Joy." The first tale, possibly from an earlier time,
shows us Vennard in the Woodstreet Counter, a particularly
unsavory London prison, where, as "an old hand," he flatly
refused to pay upon entry the customary but unsanctioned
"fees and garnish" to the Chief Chamberlain. The latter in
revenge appropriated Vennard's cloak, but Vennard, legalist
to the end, smuggled out a writ of complaint, and upon being
indicted for theft, the astonished Chamberlain begged Vennard
to accept his cloak back, with a remission of all unnecessary
fees, and to drop the charges; which Vennard magnanimously
agreed to.

But perhaps one jailor's memory proved Vennard's final
undoing—although after a life spent so largely in close
keeping it seems somehow inevitable that he should perish in
jail. He was alive, presumably, in 1614, but dead by 1617, the
publication date of Fennor's chilling compendium of abuses in

166

Woodstreet, *The Counter's Commonwealth*. As Fennor tells us, the sexagenarian Vennard "died here in misery, plagued by the Keepers, being more guilty of his death than his cruel adversaries, for after he began to tell them of that they were loath to hear of, they thrust him into the Hole, being in winter, where, lying without a bed, he caught such an extreme cold in his legs that it was not long before he departed this life."

IMPROBABLE JOURNEYS

WHEN ELIZABETH II OF ENGLAND LAID SIR FRANCIS DRAKE'S OLD SWORD UPON THE SHOULDERS OF Francis Chichester, at Greenwich on 7 July 1967, knighting a mariner for circumnavigating the world alone, she was recognizing and even canonizing beyond the imaginable expectations of earlier dreadnoughts a tradition of "dare" journeys, self-imposed tasks and travels, which her earlier namesake might well have similarly admired, if not so formally rewarded. Within weeks an airplane pilot had claimed a new women's solo Capetown to London flight record, although even the Guinness Book appears not to have noted any standard in that particular category to break; a like-minded lady challenged authority to swim naked, or at least topless, if greased, across the English Channel, and a man set out to circle the globe, in Chichester's wake, but in a powerless glider. Three comparable attempts may be chronicled here, each idiotic in its own way, but pointing curiously toward the growing professionalization the entertainment

167

value of exhibitionism thrust on its participants, the development of stunting from pure sportsmanship to calculated profit and career.

1. London to Bristol, 1590

Richard Ferris (Ferrour, Ferres, Ferrers, Ferrours, Feryr, Ferrar) had long led an adventurous and often hazardous existence in royal livery as one of five or six named "Messengers of the Queen's Chamber," a kind of cross between secret police, errand boy and bailiff, for the particular use of the Privy Council, which exposed him to uncertain receptions and sent him posting on horseback to nearly all parts of the kingdom. Often the work at hand was merely to turn over an official copy of a Privy Council letter, a demand for a loan, or a troop levy, to the appropriate mayor or sheriff; on other occasions his job was specifically to "attach" or forcibly summon a man or whole group to the Council's examination in London. Thus in 1581 he found himself "very violently used" as he attempted to take into custody certain "obstinate recusants" in Staffordshire; but the methodical Council tracked down his tormenters as well as the resisting parties, and punished them.

Born in Westminster, Ferris is first heard of in London circles in 1579 or 1580, and during the next decade his services were called upon with regularity by the Council. He visited the stately home of William Paston in Norfolk, he travelled north, south, east, and westward to Wales, and on 7 March 1590 he delivered in Dorset, Devonshire, Cornwall and Somerset a certain directive to "mariners, gunners, fishermen and other seafaring men" which amounted to restrictions on their movements and a requirement to keep better import-export and logbook records. Perhaps this not unusual mission, thrusting Ferris as it happened into the company of seamen all over the south and west coasts, put him first in mind of the expedition for which he is best remembered; no more, at any rate, is heard of him in any official capacity until over a year had passed.

Ferris himself has conveniently left us a record of his hazardous voyage, in "a small wherry boat"—little more than a large dory with a single sail—from London down the Thames, along the entire south coast, and well up the west to Bristol, a passage under normal conditions of about six hundred sea-miles. *The most Dangerous and Memorable Adventure of Richard Ferris* (London, by John Wolfe, 1590) is his personal account of the exploit, undertaken in sport, pure sport, and rewarded, as the original Olympic competitors were rewarded, with no more apparently than a rousing welcome and the fame gained.

Nothing is especially easy about the task Ferris had volunteered for, despite the constant proximity of a coastline, in the period when Drake and Cavendish in larger craft left all land behind as they nosed into the unfamiliar Atlantic. Currents run oddly in the bays, the weather whips up unpredictably from calm to gale, shoals and reefs surround the whole chalky or rockbound coasts to Land's End, and in the western reaches even close to the shore piracy was no stranger to the waters. No less a captain than Cavendish, at the climax of his triumphant circumnavigation, had nearly wrecked his experienced vessel on the treacherous Lizard, England's southernmost peninsula and Ptolemy's "Promontory of Demons." Added to this was, as the zaniness of similar experiments often inspires, Ferris' personal and apparently pure ignorance of seamanship and the sea. "I was never trained up on the water," he explains to his dedicatee, Vice-Chamberlain and Privy Councillor Sir Thomas Heneage; hence we may better appreciate the reluctance and persuasion of his intimates as he set out "rashly," against the advice of

169

"sundry my good friends, but especially full sore against my aged father's consent."

Prudently, he included in his "crew" of two assistants one William Thomas, an experienced mariner who more than once, in all probability, saved the lives of all three, and a perhaps unskilled companion, Andrew Hill. Their "new-built" boat, painted a fresh bright green, with green oars and a green sail, and a red cross for England upon it, was launched from below Tower Bridge on midsummer day, 24 June 1590, to a tumultuous popular send-off. For more solemn blessings the trio rowed downstream to Greenwich, where a departure party of well-wishers included Heneage, Chancellor Burleigh, and the Lord Admiral himself, Charles Howard, for good measure. Feted and fed, they set sail to Gravesend, their first overnight port of call.

Thence the long journey began in earnest. In twenty-two stages, some as long as fifty or sixty sea-miles, some of necessity short or even retrograde, their voyage totalling precisely a suggestive forty days was to conclude at Bristol on 3 August. At each major *étape* they did not neglect to acquire certificates attesting to their arrival and departure, a precaution, like Kempe's "umpire" (below), to offset the inevitable backlash of popular skepticism or "detraction"; nor, save for one weatherbound sojourn, did they ordinarily remain at a landfall more than overnight, or, as in the case of Dover, a mere six hours before sailing again.

Out of Gravesend they navigated the Thames to its mouth at Margate, called, turned the cape to the Small Downs and Sandwich, Dover, and Newhaven, enjoying good holiday weather for the entire south-eastern stretch. In the Solent Passage between the Isle of Wight and the mainland, however, a storm overtook them and forced them to cut short a day's sailing at Portsmouth. With clear skies they rounded the Bill of Portland into Lyme Bay, and put in at the village of

Abbotsbury in Dorset; another day's passage took them onward to Lyme Regis.

They were now beginning to enter an area of rougher water, and bad weather burst on them at Seaton, presumably off Beer Head, some eight miles only from Lyme, forcing a landing. By Teignmouth to anchorage near Dartmouth, then, where they remained two days, only to encounter another storm and a stopover at "Sancome" (? Salcombe) before pulling safely into Plymouth harbor. All this while the seamanship of Thomas was sustaining the venture, but the landlubbers were learning, and the charterer himself was obeying orders smartly. At Plymouth they received "good entertainment" and godspeed from naval captains Fenner (Edward, William, or George, all masters against the Armada, but not Vice-Admiral Thomas, killed off Lisbon the year before) and Wilkinson (probably George, boatswain, if not a captain at least, of the Cygnet in '88). Now for the inevitable Lizard, where the half-moon of the Spanish Armada had first been sighted two years before, which they skirted "God be thanked . . . in the current of the tide with great swiftness, but with wonderful danger," to anchor safely at Looe, East or West. A long haul to the Cornish village of St. Mawes, and another milestone—Penzance—where they revictualed and prepared to turn Land's End.

Only a short sail out of Penzance harbor Ferris and his mates met up with the conventional hazard these waters connote even to the time of Gilbert and Sullivan. A pirate sloop sighted them, gave chase, and their narrow escape was due only to coursing so close to the stony shore in their shallow-bottomed wherry that the deep-drawing pirate could not follow to board. Thus rounding the most westerly spit of Cornwall, *Ultima Thule* in its time, they drew briefly into the harbor of St. Ives, their first west-coast port of call. Presumably they neglected to revictual, for at nearby Godrevy—a steep headland facing a

171

small rocky island—long-suffering William Thomas was obliged to scale a forty-fathom cliff which neither Hill nor Ferris, the latter cheerfully admits, would dare attempt, in search of food. About here, apparently, the first really violent weather set in, and the party laid up for two days in one house, and a full seventeen more at the hospitality of one Master Hynder of Bottrick's Castle; thus nearly half the trip saw them weatherbound ashore, awaiting a sea safe to navigate, tantalizingly close to their destination.

On regaining the water, understandably, their pace reflected both rest and impatience. Long hauls took them by stages to Padstow, a village in a little estuary, Hartland Point, the last corner of the voyage now all eastward, Clovelly in Bideford Bay, and Ilfracombe. Nor were all circumstances again perfectly benign, for between Hartland Point and Clovelly Hill fell over-board—presumably in a squall—but clung onto a piece of sail and was hauled back to safety "although he were a very weighty man." By the time of their arrival at Ilfracombe on 1 August, Ferris was so thirsty for Bristol that he importuned his doubtful companions to set sail at night. This ill-advised action nearly cost them disaster at the threshold of triumph. Winds arose sharply, and while Thomas desperately struggled with the rudder and one oar, Ferris had to man the larboard oar alone for four hours, and Hill constantly to bail the boat. They found haven at last at Mineshead, and from there made finally without incident into the designated port.

Forewarned no doubt, Bristol gave the trio a heroes' welcome. Mayor and Aldermen came down to the docks, and the people carried the wherry off by hand to lie in state overnight in City Hall. The next morning the battered wherry was borne all about the city with a great entourage, flags, fifes, trumpets and drums, while Ferris, Hill, and Commander

172

Thomas feasted with the officialdom of Bristol, Mayor, Aldermen, and Sheriff.

The celebrities now made their way back to London by land, rearriving to acclaim and festivity on 8 August, having left their instructions for the matchless boat to be carted overland after them. The news of their success had in fact outrun them, a hastily-concocted broadside ballad account (lost) being entered at Stationers' Hall on 7 August, and a similar evocation of the festivities of 4 August at Bristol entered on the tenth. Possibly the first ballad, the work of James Sargent, is the poem annexed to Ferris' own highly unliterary report which John Wolfe published in the same year; its conventional hexaines thump out the tale smartly:

Good *Andrew Hill*, thy pains were great,
And *William Thomas'*, in this wherry,
And honor, *Ferris* sure doth get:
He doubtless means to make you merry.
    Your fame is such, through travail's toil,
    You win the spur within our soil.

Shall I prefer this to your skill?
No, no, 'twas *God* that did you guide,
For this, be sure, without His will
You could not pass each bitter tide.
    But pray you did, no doubt, each hour,
    Whereby *God* blessed you by His power.

O gallant minds and venturous bold
That took in hand a thing most rare:
'Twill make the Spaniards' hearts wax cold
If that this news to them repair,
    That three men hath this voyage done
    And thereby wagers great have won.

But now we may behold and view
That English hearts are not afraid
Their sovereign's foes for to subdue.
No tempest can make us dismayed,
   Let monstrous Papists spit their fill:
   Their force is full against *God's* will . . .

Well, *Ferris*, now the game is thine;
No loss thou hast (thank Him above);
From thy two mates do not decline,
But still in heart do thou them love.
   So shall thy store increase, no doubt,
   Through Him that brought thy boat about.

"Why did you do it?" we can imagine some primal journalist in a mob reception interrogating the victorious daredevil, who obliges the public and Sir Thomas Heneage with a reply worthy of any latter-day celebrity at his blandest: my example, he says, will aid others "the better to daunt the enemies of this nation, who in such flaws and frets at sea dare not hazard their galleys to go forth, though they be of far greater force to brook the seas."

Perhaps this clarion-call to patriotism for a while lent Ferris some extra dignity in his resumed duties. The next August the Council granted him an open warrant against personal debtors which "his daily attendance in Her Majesty's Service" made difficult to pursue. But more likely he was simply back at work. All through the nineties he went about the Council's business, being "assailed and hurt" in October 1591 in the course of a routine arrest, apprehending "divers beerbrewers" of London in March, 1597, a suspect in Worcester in 1600, and perhaps as a cultural high-spot, a visit to Thomas Nashe, a delivery to the Council of matter pertinent to his scandalous satirical play, *The Isle of Dogs*, on 15 August 1597—"Such

174

papers as were found in Nashe his lodging" relating to the "lewd play that was played in one of the playhouses on the Bankside." Through 1601 he was still similarly employed, but the eleven-year gap in Privy Council minutes leaves us only one chance mention of Ferris, in the same service, in 1606. After 1613 he is no longer there.

2. Twelve Days' Wonder, 1600

With William Kempe, a new professionalism enters the business of "dare-journeys," and a true professional to bring it in. At the time of his contribution to this sport, Kempe had for at least fifteen years performed as a highly successful actor, dancer, even singer and instrumentalist, an all-around entertainer and without doubt the second most famous sixteenth-century clown. "Vice-gerant [i.e., substitute] general to the ghost of Dick Tarleton [*d.* 1588]," Thomas Nashe calls him, and with Leicester's Men in the eighties and Shakespeare's and Burbage's Chamberlain's Men in the nineties Kempe carved out a supremacy among clowns: to him fell the parts of Peter in the original production of *Romeo and Juliet*, and of Dogberry in *Much Ado about Nothing*. More widely travelled than most of his contemporaries, he had exhibited himself in Venice, the Low Countries, and in Denmark before Shakespeare was twenty-five, and in his heyday published at least four "jigs" (all now lost) of his own composition—the madcap song-and-dance numbers, some with slight plots, which Elizabethan producers tended to tag onto their plays, however tragic or self-sustained. His speciality indeed, apart from "merriments" or general cavorting, was the morris-dance, especially applicable to the jig, and as Kempe was to demonstrate, no man alive could match him, for endurance, certainly, in his speciality.

For some reason, early in 1599 Kempe seems to have severed his connections with the powerful and successful Chamberlain's Company, and shortly after February 21 sold out his share in the Globe Theatre to Shakespeare and three fellow stockholders; "I have danced myself out of the world," he puns wryly, and without Kempe's good help it is interesting—if perhaps coincidental—that henceforth Shakespeare's own attention turned more and more from comedy to tragic drama. But Kempe was at loose ends during 1599, it would seem, until the notion of an improbable journey struck him early the next year. He would morris-dance, he advertised, the entire distance from London to Norwich in nine one-day stages—a "nine days' wonder"—and to forestall reproach or doubt he would be accompanied throughout by an overseer or umpire to enforce the strict steps of the dance and attest to the satisfaction of the terms.

The morris, originally "morisco," a Spanish dance much altered in its French and English adaptations, can be performed by anywhere from one to a dozen or more participants. In formal village morrises, some of which may still be witnessed on feast days, various characters from British legend are represented, in costume or symbol—Robin Hood, Little John, Friar Tuck and Maid Marian, *alias* the Lady of the May, as well as the Fool, a piper, a drummer or taborer, and odd animals like the Dragon and the Hobby-horse, whose disappearance from this ensemble Hamlet needlessly laments, for the figure even now survives, a man with a *papier-mâché* horse head, a similar bustle, and a covering footcloth. As many others as wished could include themselves under no ritual names, but merely as "the morris dancers." In 1609 in Hertford, for example, one extravagant performance involved eighteen exceptional dancers, each one over ninety years old and half over a hundred, their composite age 1837. "Maid Marian," Meg Goodwin of Erdestand, was

120, and if not strictly a maiden, she claimed to have been chaste for the preceding sixty years.

The conventional costume for the soloist, like Kempe, included twenty to forty bells on one's wrists and calves, high-laced buskins, and a kind of divided cape which flaps when the arms wave. The steps vary, but resemble generally high hopping to a piped melody in the following rhythm, incessantly repeated: tum tum tum tum, *thump*; tum tum tum tum, *thump, thump*; tum tum tum tum tum tum tum tum tum tum tum, *thump, thump*—with "tum"'s for quarter-notes and "thump"'s for halves or wholes. One hops forward and back in a closed area, stamping hard on the *thumps*, but in a straight line like Kempe's, obviously, one moves forward only.

From London to Norwich by rail in our time is a journey north-east of 114 miles. Road travel of course makes for less of a direct line, and Kempe seems to have covered about 134 miles, including a rather odd detour west which impassable highways may have necessitated. For a part of the journey the Roman road "Ermine Street" may have provided good footing, but for long stretches, as Kempe himself complains, the high-road was little more than a ditch with great pot-holes full of mud and water. Given an average of nearly fourteen miles a day—in fact the pace varies from about six to eighteen-and-a-half—Kempe's marathon seems truly a remarkable one. Certainly no successor has ever attempted to duplicate or surpass it.

Before seven a.m. on a clear day, the first Monday in Lent, 11 February 1600, the clown set forth from the Lord Mayor's house with a retinue of three—Thomas Sly, his taborer, to keep time and march before, clearing the often obstructive congregations of the curious, William Bee, his servant, and George Sprat, the "overseer," to bear constant witness. A small early-morning audience showered them with small

177

change as they began, but by the time they had passed the north-east gate of Whitechapel the accompanying throng had grown to "many a thousand" Londoners keeping Kempe encouraging company; and indeed scarcely ever afterward was he alone on his journey—often, he complains, to his considerable discomfiture. To their importuning he halted at Stratford-le-Bow, three miles east of St. Paul's, for rest, but firmly refused to drink the "full cups" offered. Like an athlete he is in strict training for the duration.

Thence on to Stratford proper, where a bear-baiting—his favorite spectacle—had been arranged in his honor, but which the great press of admirers prevented him from actually viewing. Seven miles from London, at Ilford, he prudently declined once more the offer of "carowses" out of a traditional "great spoon" or ladle holding over a quart, and pressed on via the Roman road until nightfall caught him three miles from the village of Romford. Weary with jostling and halting, and perhaps not yet into his second wind, only nine miles out of London he marked his advance and rode horseback forward to his inn. During the next two days he remained to rest while Londoners "came hourly" to see him, impossibly crowding the small town, determined to keep company with Kempe.

By Thursday he was ready to continue, and scrupulously returned to the mark three miles behind, passed Romford, and advanced "merrily" to Brentwood, a nine-mile stint in all, "yet now I remember it well," he recalls, "I had no great cause of mirth, for at Romford Town's end I strained my hip, and for a time endured exceeding pain." Great multitudes met him at Brentwood, and the persistent Londoners continued to follow him, among them two enterprising cutpurses who were apprehended there in the act. Trying to slip away unnoticed, or so he claims, Kempe waited for moonlight and proceeded thence to Ingatestone, nevertheless still tailed by fifty of his

Londoners. The day's journey, hip, crowds, and all, had been a satisfactory fourteen and a half miles. He rested overnight only, perhaps an error of exuberance.

On Friday the total crowd had diminished to a new daytime low of two hundred, but at the bridge over the river Wid a great mob lay in wait. Kempe paused at Moulsham Hill to present Sir Thomas Mildmay, who met him at the fence of the estate, with a symbolic pair of garters, together with gloves and points of which he had provided himself a supply for hand-outs. But the pace told on Kempe and his resilience expired at Chelmsford early in the day, only six miles from the morning's start.

Now it is apparent that Kempe's contract was specifically for a nine-day performance, because rather sophistically he "reclaimed" the lost part of Friday with a three-mile stint the next morning, and counted that as part of the third day. Here he marked, and returned to Chelmsford to gather strength over the weekend.

On the by now technical "fourth" day, Monday the 18th, Kempe rode the three miles to his mark and struggled eight miles further to Braintree. He had left the Roman road and suffered greatly because "the way were rotten"—thick woods on either side, and the lane perforated with puddles and holes. The average pace may now have begun to perturb him, for he exercised once more the curious liberty, perhaps established by his Chelmsford precedent, of proceeding three miles Tuesday morning "to ease my Wednesday's journey," and then rested.

The next stage, passing from County Essex into Suffolk, proved more encouraging. Kempe reached Sudbury with time to spare, once more insisted on temperance, and concluded a fourteen-mile lap at Long Melford, where one Master Colts was kind enough to put him up until Saturday. Occasional partners had turned out—a butcher for half-a-mile in the evening, and a fat cheerful girl with the old-fashioned morrising kerchief "a long mile" between Sudbury and Long Melford. On Saturday, the "sixth" day, Kempe set what may be a one-day distance record for the morris of over eighteen miles. He detoured sharply west six and a half miles to Clare, perhaps because of the "deep and troublesome" roads William Camden remarked on in this area in 1607, and then managed to reach Bury St. Edmunds—twelve miles as the crow flies, probably more for Kempe—by nightfall. It was a great leg, and the Lord Chief Justice with another wild throng fittingly met him at the gate of the city.

Here Kempe was delayed by an unexpected "great snow" from Saturday night to Friday of the third week, the first of March. Passing now into Norfolk with the new energy of an uncaged beast, Kempe covered the distance to Thetford—ten miles, he says, but it would appear to be nearer fourteen—in no more than three hours, from seven a.m. to ten. "It was no great wonder," he explains modestly, "for I fared like one that had escaped the stocks and tried the use of his legs to outrun the constable: so light was my heels that I counted the ten mile no better than a leap." Over the weekend his host was Sir Edwin Rich, a veteran of the Cadiz expedition of 1596, and a liberal and likeable man; again a great crowd, due partly to the assizes then being in session, thronged Kempe at Thetford on arrival.

The "eighth" day, Monday, with time running out, took Kempe a most difficult and heroic seventeen miles, detouring from what is now the A11 to Rockland All Saints (fourteen miles) whence his fat and convivial host accompanied him dancing the space of two fields toward Hingham. But he was troubled all day with "a foul way" and throngs—twenty, forty, even a hundred—at each mile-end, confusingly urging him to pass through *their* villages, as the most direct or easiest route to Norwich.

The official last day's dance took place on Wednesday 6 March. Kempe footed eight miles to Barford Bridge over the river Yare, but with Norwich "in view," and taking into account the probable crowd in wait, while wishing to dance in freshly, he halted "a little above St. Giles his gate," another seven or eight miles, perhaps, and rode into the city instead. When Mayor Weld learned of the delayed climax he himself visited the weary clown at his inn, and induced him to postpone his final entry until Saturday so that "divers knights and gentlemen" among all those who had expected him, might have sufficient warning to be present.

We are now in a kind of official overtime, but Kempe waited, and on Saturday 9 March returned to the gate and danced in, to the most tumultuous welcome, naturally, of all. Police cordoned his passage while one Thomas Gilbert recited a celebratory acrostic ("WELCOME WIL KEMP"), but the press so overflowed its boundaries that Kempe's "overseer" lost him in the crowd, and evidently for strict legality required him to repeat the climactic stage on Tuesday next. In the market place a dense throng so surrounded Kempe that he tripped (by accident, he protests) over the new-fangled petticoat of a girl fastened with only one point before, and exposed, to her horror, her smock—which, however, "though coarse, it were cleanly." After Tuesday's re-run, Kempe's buskins were ceremonially nailed to the wall of Norwich Guildhall, and the Lord Mayor granted the dancer a £5 honorarium, plus £2 a year pension for life.

We do not know how long Kempe took to accomplish his return, but the journey concluded on March 12, and by 22 April was entered at Stationers' Hall the clown's own account of it, purportedly to counterweigh the "malicious and lying ballads" (all now lost) which had circulated, accusing him of rigging the escapade. Let no man, he prays in his *Nine Days' Wonder, Performed in a Dance from London to Norwich,* believe the "lying ballets and rumors" that "ways were laid open for me, or that I delivered gifts to Her Majesty [i.e., bribed]." "True it is," he admits, "I put out some money to have three-fold gain at my return," i.e., he had laid three-to-one bets at the outset; but less than half the wagers had been successfully collected—perhaps on the technicality of a nine-day wonder which required actually twelve days or thirteen. John Taylor would raise the same complaint later, on more than one occasion.

What else had Kempe gained from the sporting venture? Five pounds and pension from the Mayor of Norwich, five pounds more as a parting gift from Sir Edwin Rich, and notoriety to match Banks's. Playwrights and poets from Jonson onward touch in passing on the act for nearly a century. No doubt fame eased his journey of 1600-1601 to Italy and Germany, during which it is possible that he morris-danced across the Alps. On his return, apparently needy, he re-entered the theater, playing with Worcester's Men for at least two years. Nothing is heard of him in person during the reign of James; after 1603 he vanishes from record. Richard Brathwaite has left a charming epitaph:

> Welcome from Norwich, Kempe: all joy to see
> Thy safe return, moriscoed lustily!
> But out, alas! How soon's thy morris done,
> When pipe and tabor, all thy friends be gone,
> And leave thee now to dance the second part
> With feeble nature, not with nimble art.
> Then all thy triumphs, fraught with strains of mirth,
> Shall be caged up within a chest of earth.
> Shall be? They are. Thou danced thee out of breath,
> And now must take thy parting dance with Death.

3. London to Queenborough, 1619

John Taylor "the Water Poet" has crossed our path before, as entrepreneur and biographer in the case of the Great Eater, and as apologist for Richard Vennard. Part showman, waterman (i.e., manager of a barge crossing or navigating the Thames up or downstream from Greenwich to Richmond), and extemporizing poet, he could flyte, apparently, with his chosen rivals—Fennor, Thomas Coryate, even Ben Jonson—as easily in oral rhymed couplets as in versified pamphlets, of which he cranked out an astonishing quantity. Although he lived to be seventy-five and died in an unwelcome interregnum in 1653, by 1630 a folio *Works* had presumptuously been issued, with full sixty-three *individua*, and earlier octavo collections had been assembled by his enterprising publishers. Little survives of literary worth in the vast output of his verse, but as an entertainer he well deserves the entertaining notice Wallace Notestein has provided in *Four Worthies* (London, 1956), no less than the elaborate and still unpublished bio-bibliographical study by R. B. Dow (Harvard Ph.D. thesis, 1931). As a dare-traveller he perhaps represents the apogee of the new professionalism. Professor Notestein describes his "routine":

> He would announce a proposed journey: he was going to travel from London to Edinburgh and back without a penny of money, neither borrowing nor stealing on the way; he was going to scull in a paper boat from London to Queenborough on the Kentish coast; he was to proceed through Germany to Prague, and that during the wars. As soon as he had determined his itinerary he caused to be printed bills describing the coming adventure: he urged readers to subscribe a sum of any amount they pleased, but not less than sixpence, to be paid to Taylor if the journey came off. This scheme proved rewarding. It called for no great outlay of money, and yet it appealed to the eagerness of men to share in a popular project. At the end of the trip subscribers received

183

Taylor's account of his adventures, set forth in prose and verse, with enough flings at those he had found cause to dislike to satisfy the taste of his clientele.

Not always was the outcome perfectly satisfactory, for Taylor was "forced to hound his debtors from lodging to lodging, into the back alleys of Alsatia between Fleet Street and the river, and even into suburban villages. Indeed after he found his debtors he was sometimes defied. So great was his disgust on his return from Edinburgh, when 750 of his debtors defaulted, that he wrote a pamphlet, *A Kicksey-Winsey, or a Larry-Come-Twang*, in which all his powers of denunciation were exhibited. If the debtors did not pay up at once, he promised to bring out a new edition, wherein he would satirize, cauterize and stigmatize all the whole kennel of curs." And bets laid out on the side, like Kempe's, at the start of a journey, proved no easier to collect upon completion.

As perhaps the least likely and most hazardous of all the improbable journeys Taylor undertook or we have earlier remarked, let us consider his voyage of 1619, in a small boat made entirely of brown paper, from London to Queenborough, a Kentish port on the Isle of Sheppey at the Thames' mouth about two miles before Sheerness, nearly fifty miles rowing on the widening river. His account of it, in facile doggerel with glosses, is wedged between a general praise of hemp-seed and its products, an attack on Coryate, and "the commendations of the famous River of Thames" in a sixteen-part 48-page pamphlet of 1620 (entered 22 May) entitled *The Praise of Hemp-Seed, with the Voyage of Mr Roger Bird and the Writer hereof, in a Boat of Brown Paper.*

Sometime in the early spring of 1619 Taylor built his boat and picked his shipmate, a vintner named Roger Bird, "a man whom fortune never yet could tame," who "dwelleth now at the Hope on the Bankside," among the bears, bulls, mastiffs and Henslowe's players. Perhaps Taylor knew him from a

184

melancholy experience of his own at the Hope five years earlier—an advertised slanging-match in verse with Fennor, which, like *England's Joy*, failed to materialize as Fennor failed to appear.

On the eve of St. James, Saturday 24 July, Bird and Taylor took to the river in the unparalleled vessel, with oars made of local stockfish (dried cod) "bound fast to two canes with packthread," both fortified solidly for the occasion—"liquored to the calves." The boat began to leak almost at once, a not unexpected contingency, and in a half hour was full to the half-staffs of the "most liberal" Thames, and fast rotting apart. Facing maritime disaster so short a pull from port, Taylor "thought it fit/ To put in use a stratagem of wit," namely eight inflated bulls' bladders "bound fast and taut." But the breath in these bladders was by no means ordinary or uniform, for each had been blown up, at Taylor's whim, by a different species of rogue: a usurer, a drunken bagpiper, a whore, a pimp, a cutpurse, a "post-knight" or sharking bail-bondsman, an informer, and "a swearing roister/ That would cut throats as soon as eat an oyster"—Taylor explaining that such persons never meet death by drowning, but always high and dry on a scaffold, and hence their several breaths might best preserve the waterbound. Bird and Taylor strapped four bladders to each outward side of the sinking ship, and thus buoyed, proceeded. But the water still rose, "in three miles going almost to our knees," and the bottom fell off completely; henceforth they were sustained entirely by the bare sides and the bladders, "with these wicked winds encompassed round."

By good luck and now effectively swimming in a framework, the half-salt water six inches from the brim of the sides, they passed Gravesend with a convoy of Saint's day scullers and bargees, the shores lined with "thousands." All day they struggled onward, losing their stockfish paddles, and

185

found themselves at last in pitch dark with the canes only to propel them, a skeleton of a craft, in the four-mile-wide estuary where the water roughens considerably. "Twixt doubt and fear, hope and despair,/ I fell to work and Roger Bird to prayer" recalls Taylor, perhaps with a touch of irony, but by morning, and a vigil of heroic scrambling, they sighted the imposing ramparts of Queenborough Castle. Wherever they had originally intended to put in, Bird and Taylor now settled on Queenborough, and Monday morning early managed to haul what was left of the vessel ashore. They happened, it seems, to have reached the town precisely on an annual feast-day, when bread, beer, and oysters are distributed free in the streets, and a thousand or so countrymen flock to the celebrations. "'Twas our luck to come in all this rout," claims Taylor, but one half suspects the showman in him had planned every detail. To the Mayor, who welcomed them grandly, they attempted to present their boat—"He meant to hang [it] up for a monument," like Kempe's shoes—but while eating and drinking heedlessly, the crowd in the streets "tore our tattered wherry/ In mammocks [i.e., shreds] piecemeal, in a thousand scraps,/ Wearing the relics in their hats and caps"—perhaps a more fitting end to the affair. The Mayor "took patient what he could not remedy," the carousing wound up, and Tuesday Bird and Taylor posted home on horseback. Bird seems to have laid a few bets around, but, Taylor complains—not for himself, but good Hodge Bird—is still struggling to bring them in. Taylor concludes with a severe malediction on all defaulters save "those that are poor and cannot, let them be/ Both from the debt and malediction free."

Less than thirty years lie between Ferris' sporting voyage in the spirit of post-Armada bravado and Taylor's near parody in the reign of the "wisest fool in Christendom." Between the apparent altruism of the first, and the bookmaking and literary commitments of the second, between grave enterprise and farce, between the green sail with a red cross for England and the stockfish and bladders of bad breath lies a time of professionalizing and sophistication in stunting, amazingly rapid in its growth, quite paralleling the motion of the English drama, domestic and foreign policy, and the contemporary personality itself. The kindred exploits of Ferris and Taylor stand for alien eras.

CHAPTER V.

THE ROARING GIRL

"MOST WOMEN HAVE NO CHARACTERS AT ALL," OFFERS ALEXANDER POPE IN 1735—AND ALTHOUGH WE torture Pope's meaning by ignoring his context, and over-simplify our earlier context with so characteristically Augustan a generalization, yet we well might begin our examination of the career of one renegade seventeenth-century English lady with that provocative, if second-hand, dictum in mind. For despite Long Meg, shrewish Kate, Bess of Hardwick, the Wife of Bath, and Elizabeth herself, there can be little doubt that contemporaries of Shakespeare leaned as reluctantly to the individuation and selective esteem of the majority of women as they inclined to suffer them lives of their own in a stratified and only partially franchised society of men. Not simply that woman was the Tennysonian "lesser man," nor that her company stifled the magnanimous mind, as Bacon proposed, but that all she was and could do must then have been measured by men's standards, and evaluated by prescriptions and regiments not very much more modern than those of John Knox and the strait ages past. The Duke of Württemberg in 1602 remarked that in England "the women have much more liberty than perhaps in any other place"; but the crux of the assertion for the era, and for the student of its social culture, is most probably "liberty to do what"?

In London, one suspects, the Duke's "liberty" meant walking the streets and speaking out in mixed gatherings—which was freedom indeed, of a sort, especially in comparison with the conventions of southern Europe—but London was not all England, and the prerequisite for most such freedom was the renunciation of a freedom more fundamental. From birth Elizabethan women were trained, even educated, toward the unquestioned objective of an early marriage; from marriage to motherhood, domestic administration, and a schedule of leisure, entertainment, and self-cultivation entirely dependent on the demands of the husband

and his station. Widowhood came when it came, but the virtuous widow, in John Webster's "character," "is the palm tree that thrives not after the supplanting of her husband," who "marries no more . . . receives but one impression . . . is wrought into works of charity . . ." [note the passive constructions], "an ancient pyramid . . . a relique." No such demands would be made of a widower; indeed, such posthumous fidelity might coast close to Hamlet's "unmanly grief."

One must not however insist that marriage was in Elizabethan times a captivity, but rather that most aspects of personal or intellectual development in a wedded woman came down ultimately to matters of permission. The cultivation of letters, crafts, music, even embroidery, might serve for leisure hours; but no more than a courtier could a woman seek print or a public, and in effectively no case fame, or a fortune of her own making. Not all household duties were especially onerous, at least in London, and pastimes, by consent, were available to the wife whose husband could afford them. Intrigues were apparently rare; piety widespread. Among the moneyed or aristocratic classes, subsidized spinsterhood or Court attendance offered alternatives, but their conventional regulations seemed scarcely less constricting than the obligations of matrimony.

What, then, of the unmarried, the undesired, or the abandoned? What careers lay open for a seventeenth-century woman with or without verve and ambition, whose principal distinction was the lack of a husband, or the lack of desire for one? The paths were few and each in its own way frustrating, for the lower and middle classes in particular, and the risks and penalties for failure disproportionately great. Menial service, an essentially "honest" occupation for a young girl, could conceivably lead into service of a more responsible nature—the governance of a household or inn, the management

192

of a shop—but the opportunities ended with minor mercantilism or domestic promotion, selling fish, groceries, cloth and dry goods, or superintending a new cadre of servants from whose position the clever servant had risen. Ruled out, for example, were positions in major commerce, adventure, capitalistic investment, the law, the military, humanistic or hack-literary pursuits, entertainment (the first actress on an English public stage, partaking in a visiting French company's performance, was pelted with oranges by a relatively sophisticated audience in 1629), clerical or secretarial work, teaching, medicine, any skilled profession with a guild at its back, and even the Church, save for small eclectic groups like Nicholas Ferrar's at Little Gidding, and Catholic convents overseas. What remained, practically, were careers in prostitution—these, at least, at all levels, from courtesan or mistress to barfly or a brothel's "nun." It is curious that the most recent and authoritative account of Elizabethan womanhood refers only to this profession in terms of its costume and cosmetics. Among its advantages, for the single woman, were its compatibility with other activities, its temporary nature, and the possibility—often remote—of a move upward in class, like the Dark Lady's or Fanny Hill's.

Morality of course was against the working girl in this almost exclusively "free" profession, and the thunder of preachers and playwrights alike is fashionably directed at the perfidiousness, the turpitude, and the contagious corruption of even an "honest" whore: the writers who set out to justify in some measure prostitution inevitably conclude by evading its implications, as all whore-heroines in the early seventeenth century seem to repent and give over, or, worse, seem never to have been guilty as named. Nor were the lawcourts more generous, when pressed to a decision. One might wish that Montaigne had considered the matter, but it is refreshing to read in Edward Sharpham's ironic comedy *The Fleire* (1607) a discussion between two sisters, former princesses of Florence, now self-established courtesans in London:

FLORIDA. Sister, what think you of this trade of ours?

FELICIA. 'Tis base to be a whore.

FLORIDA. 'Tis base to abuse great place, or baseness to deceive great trust.

FELICIA. And is't not baseness to abuse great birth?

FLORIDA. . . . You'll say we are forbid to live by sin; and yet we are commanded 'seek to live'. The letter-law express forbids to kill, and yet the sense permits it, rather than be killed; and, since of two extremities the least is to be chosen, you know we have no other means to live—but had we, yet we are fair by nature, scorning art, and was not beauty made to be enjoyed? Do we not exclaim on those who have abundant store of coin, and yet, for want, suffer the needy perish at their door? So might all do on us, having so much beauty, if we should suffer men for love of us to die. Shall we, in whom beauty keeps her court, be curbed and tied to one man's benevolence? No, no, not I: rather than in virtue to live poor, in sin I'll die.

FELICIA. Your resolutions hath confirmed my doubts . . .

No matter if eventually they repent, are spurned, avenge themselves merrily, and miraculously turn out chaste for the *dénouement*. At least some perspective has been exercised by the dramatist.

These, then, were the true possible careers for an Elizabethan woman, a woman who thought, as few did, in terms of choices and vocations. In the midst of so intractable a society with such unappealing alternatives and limitations of scope, we find the equally intractable presence of Mistress Mary Frith, "Moll Cutpurse," "a prodigy of those times she lived in," thrust into London and literature with notions of conduct as original as her costume. Such a square peg claims unquestionable place in any breviary of eccentricity, and her story is so uncommonly well-illustrated, although generally unfamiliar, that I choose it to terminate my sequence of miniatures. Crime will again be the matter of the career, but crime which paid: and "what's a play," as Hieronimo says, "without a woman in it?"

Mary Frith was born about 1589 into a modestly well-to-do working family. Her father, a sociable and good-natured shoemaker—or more properly a cordwainer, practitioner of that "gentle craft" celebrated by Deloney and Dekker—dwelt in the Barbican, an area not far from the north-east of St. Paul's and the City, formerly occupied by an ancient watchtower, at the very limits of London proper. His house lay between Aldersgate Street and Redcross Street, alongside Garterhouse, a mansion owned by the Wriothsleys, opposite the old park called Jews' Garden and the almshouses eastward. One might care to imagine infant Mary catching an occasional glimpse of Henry Wriothsley, the splendid young Earl of Southampton, passing in or out of Garterhouse, accompanied, let us assume, by his somewhat older, "dutiful," and "devoted" protégé Shakespeare.

If Mary were baptized it was not in the nearest church, St. Giles without Cripplegate, nor in the three next closest to the Barbican. We are told that her paternal uncle was a jovial and eccentric pastor, who "had a whimsy . . . that is, he refused to take tithes of his parishioners, but received his maintenance from them under the notion of contribution; and yet a jolly fat fellow he was, and would take off his cup merrily"; doubtless her parents were not poor, but they died before her twenty-first birthday and left her little if any legacy. We hear nothing of sisters and brothers, and Mary's age at the death of her parents is not known. What is certain, however, is that the unspecified "friends" who inherited the upbringing of this recalcitrant orphan found more on their hands than they bargained for.

For Mary's character was cast early, and it ran counter and cross to all the good notions of feminine behavior any family or friends might predictably avouch. Before dying, her parents had despairingly observed "her boistrous and masculine spirit" become "predominant above all breeding and instruction."

"A very *tomrig* or *rumpscuttle* she was, and delighted and sported only in boys' play and pastime, not minding or companying with the girls: many a bang and blow this hoyting procured her, but she was not so to be tamed or taken off from her rude inclinations; she could not endure the sedentary life of sewing or stitching; a sampler was as grievous as a winding-sheet; her needle, bodkin, and thimble she could not look on quietly, wishing them changed into sword and dagger for a bout at cudgels . . . she would fight with boys and courageously beat them, run, jump, leap or hop with any of them, or any other play whatsoever. In this she delighted; this was all she cared for." Furthermore, although she had indeed learned to read and write "perfectly" when not brawling with boys, simultaneously she had developed appalling habits of speech, "of profane dissolute language, which in her old days amounted to downright swearing," and "was not for mincing obscenity, but would talk freely whatever came uppermost." And the usual company of ladies and babies was not Mary's: 'she could not endure the bake-house, nor that magpie chat of the wenches . . . but above all she had a natural [sic] abhorrence to the tending of children, to whom she ever had an averseness in mind—equal," adds the pamphleteer tendentiously, "to the sterility and barrenness in her womb, never being made a mother to our best information." Sex itself she shied from, apparently, "whether the virility and manliness of her face and aspect took off any man's desire that way (which may be very rational and probable) or that . . . she herself also from the more importunate and prevailing sway of her inclinations, which were masculine and robust, could not intend those venereal impurities and pleasures . . ." Whatever her reasons, they were buttressed with self-knowledge, above all of her own physical unattractiveness. "No doubt," in the biographer's opinion, "Moll's converse with herself (whose dis-inviting eyes and look sank inwards to her breast, when they could have no regard abroad) informed her of her defects, and that she was not made for the pleasure or delight of man"; in fact, taking that handicap for granted and advantage, Moll deliberately dressed the part from an early age, in a man's costume, complete with doublet and trousers, "so that by this odd dress it came that no man can say or affirm that ever she had a sweetheart, or any such fond thing to dally with her . . . she was not wooed or solicited by any man, and therefore she was honest."

The psychological implications of Moll's early aversions and compensating eccentricities are almost too obvious to a post-Freudian readership, but they bear continuing inspection, open-minded and particular if possible, while she attains fully to womanhood—as it were—in spite of herself. For the parents had died vainly trusting to the proverb "*that an unhappy girl may make a good woman*," in which expectation family and "friends" were apparently deceived. By now "a lusty and sturdy wench, and fit to be put out to service," Mary kicked against the goad and the grain: "she was too great a libertine, and lived too much in common," explains the biographer, "to be enclosed [note the land-management pun] in the limits of a domestic life." In despair, perhaps, the responsible guardians turned to the plantations and marriage for the unmanageable, to America, where "some Jack as good as myself"—Moll is now speaking—"whose dominion over me might subdue that violence of my spirit, or else I should be so broke by hard labor that I would of my own accord return to a womanly and civil behavior."

She was scarcely twenty, she tells us, when by conspiracy the deportation was arranged: tricked aboard a vessel bound

197

for New England with supplies and potential frontier wives, plied with "strong waters," she was suddenly seized and cast in the hold as the crew prepared to hoist anchor. Only by hectoring the Captain himself "with a submissive gesture . . . and with many a briny tear," with protestations of innocence and injury, and bribery to the full extent of her resources, did Moll win her escape from what seemed to her no less than ignominious exile. One cannot but wonder what effect on the history of North America Moll might have achieved, now or later, and remark how close to the test she once came. But most probably the "settlements" involved were those of an abortive colony, the first in New England, established at the mouth of the Kennebec River in 1607 and abandoned by spring, 1608. Moll's exile would have been short.

Penniless now, and brooding on vengeance or defense against "such desperate and dangerous enemies," given over wholly to "Hot-spur meditations, to which I was very prone," Moll settled for self-maintenance on a life of petty crime: whether by default or choice she never makes clear, but remorse and apology are not among Moll's characteristic extravagances. The chronology of her early career in the low echelons of felony is confusing, but she may have begun with the traditional lowest, the practice of pick-pocketing. Allying herself with the inconsequential "*divers* or *file-clyers*" in London, she prospered by means of nimble hands and "a long middle finger," learning rapidly the nuances of the trade, the functions of a "bulk" (a brawler who distracts the victim), a "whipster" who cuts the purse, and a "rub," or conveyer, who carries the booty away with him, leaving the principal malefactors for the instant "clean." Perhaps such apprenticeship led to Moll's participation in a cabal of female fences or receivers, although along the way she appears to have familiarized herself with fortune-telling. For the latter occupation she exhibited little respect, and for the former little talent, at first. Some sort of "gang" had coalesced about her, for she already was demonstrably a leader of thieves and outlaws, but when of her associates "most . . . were either hanged or run away," she cast about for "a civiller life . . . a mean between the strokes of justice and the torments of poverty." From this time hence Moll clung to her materialistic ideal of "safe" lawlessness, and her criminal pattern now follows the path of least hazard while serving, as her experience and ingenuity suggested, the needs of a more desperate community of offenders. The career was established; variations remained to be assayed; and the personality, in comparative security, allowed itself latitude for expression.

Eccentricity of costume had been Moll's first departure from a plausible lady's life and manners, but before one labels her categorically transvestite, some understanding of the contemporary confusion about proper dress must be attempted. Long before 1431 and the Anglo-Burgundian trial of Jeanne d'Arc at Rouen, a major accusation concerning the wearing of men's clothes, ecclesiastical and civil authorities had laid heavy hands on sumptuary offenders, especially those of either sex who affected the dress of the other. By 1620 the English pulpit and press rang with denunciation, apparently ineffectual, against the novel and degenerate manner—short hair, French doublets, breeches and boots. Clearly in most cases inclination preceded crime. Leaving to historical sociology the reason why, we can at least agree that some women in the early seventeenth century were drawn to masculine costume, regardless of its legal and even popular opprobrium, and that equivalent aberrations existed among men. The vogue for long hair, for example, and "lovelocks"—i.e., abbreviated and crisped pigtails, twined in silk—with pistol, pipe, garters, and short sword worn as ornaments (1620) rather than as functional arms or apparel, drew fire from the same puritans who viewed with increasing alarm female defection toward male accoutrements and demeanor. And perhaps it is impertinent to accuse puritans alone, for the popular sentiment, as measured by literature and gossip, lay against such exchanges, and popular reaction offered its chauvinistic support. Liberty of dress, like liberty of profession, galled authorities and the unauthorized alike.

Moll wore alternatively a petticoat and skirt, or breeches or trousers, with a severe, thick, and buttoned doublet above. One mid-seventeenth century engraving shows her from the waist up with a wide-brimmed sugarloaf hat, a strict clerical bib, slit sleeves, short hair, and the hilt of a broadsword: "Here's no attraction that your fancy greets," the legend prompts. Her full-length woodcut portrait on the title-page of Dekker and Middleton's *The Roaring Girl* (1611) offers a more elaborate ruff and cuffs, loose pantaloons, shoes with daisy-shaped buckles, a mannish hat, a heavy cloak, again the stout brandished sword, and, prominently, a lit pipe of tobacco. Tobacco was one of Moll's most ostentatious affections. "No woman before me ever smoked any," she boasts, "though I had a great many to follow my example"; indeed, no earlier *habituée* is recorded in literature, although we may assume less notorious ladies tried out the vice in comparative privacy. One of Moll's inadvertent discoveries appears to have been the original exploding smoke—in this case a pipe filled with gunpowder covered by a thin layer of tobacco, foisted on her by "an unlucky knave" at a grocer's shop. Moll brained the culprit, a servant boy, with the shattered apparatus, and characteristically resolved on "no less satisfaction than *blowing up* both of master and man by *engines* and *devices* in convenient time."

Moll's sense of humor seemed generally in keeping with the harsh, often cruel manner of jest perpetuated by books of anecdotes since early in the sixteenth century. Among

200

countless and often pointless illustrations of her quick wit is a long, tedious account of her quitting the keeper of the Globe Tavern, her local, for watering his white wine. Intransigent as always, she begins by exposing the sharper—much as Gamaliel Ratsey had—but concludes sourly by forsaking "utterly . . . the fellow and his drink," despite years of patronage.

Moll seems to have been personally a close woman. Her most intimate friends included in considerable number tame animals; from an early age she patronized bear-baitings, bull-baitings, and kept pets. "A good mastiff was the only thing she then [when young] affected and joyed in," the biographer asserts, and her affinity for dogs is memorialized in *The Witch of Edmonton* (1621), although Gifford's suggestion that some were named after her is extravagant. At her home in Fleet Street she kept parrots and as many as nine elegant bulldogs or "shocks," of whom she was both solicitous and proud, training them to a fine edge. A tame eagle and a lion have been added to her zoo by certain imaginative commentators, but in later life she apparently did house such disparate beasts as baboons, apes, squirrels, and "a strange cat," whatever such might be. Beside animals, her house was full of painted pictures, and—curiously—mirrors, "looking glasses, so that I could see my sweet self all over in any part of my rooms."

Did narcissism, perhaps of a self-deprecatory and ironic sort, underly Moll's personality, at once flamboyant and withdrawn? Certainly her sexual life, as she or the mask of the autobiographer records it, was by any definition odd. We have observed her defiance, from an early age, of the conventional demands men make upon women. What male friends she maintained were either harmless or pitiable: the earliest on record, a shoemaker like her father, wasted her money and drove her to discard him. Years passed, apparently, while

Moll's acquaintances among men remained professional or perverse, despite one piquant line in *The Roaring Girl*: "Thou hadst a suitor once, Jack [i.e., Moll, in disguise]; when wilt marry?" In mid-career a certain "hermaphrodite" contemptuously styled "Aniseed-water Robin" emulated Moll's dress and clung to her company, until in embarrassment she cut him off. To her shame he had been popularly called "Moll's husband."

But despite such persecutive incidents, and Nat. Field's derisive nickname of "Madam *Hic* and *Haec*," one must not easily term Mary a lesbian, unconscious or determined. The seventeenth-century biographer, curiously passionate, inveighs against the trappings of homosexuality at length and in vehement terms, and exonerates his own subject with a fervor which approaches too much protest:

Several romances there are of many knights who carried their ladies away in disguise from their parents and native countries, most commonly in the habits of a page or some such man-servant: certainly it must be a stupified and far advanced affection which can admire, or fancy, or but admit the view of so unnatural a shape—the reverse of sexes in the most famed beauties, to whose excellencies and lustre the world were devoted. How unsightly and dreadful is the hinder region of air in the sable breeches of a dropping cloud! What an uncomely mantle is that heap of waters which covers the ground, and deluges and invades the dry land! That which so much offends us in the boisterousness of the elements cannot but be disgustful to mankind in the immodesty of either sex's attire and dress.

Hercules, Nero, and Sardanapalus: how they are laughed at and exploded for their effeminacy and degenerated dissoluteness in this extravagant debauchery! The first is portraited with a distaff in his hand; the other recorded to be married as a wife, with all the conjugal and matrimonial rites performed at the solemnity of the marriage; the other lacks the luxury of a pen as loose as his female riots to describe them. These were all monsters or monster-killers, and have no parallels either in old or modern histories, till such time as our Moll Cutpurse approached this example; but her heroic impudence hath quite undone every romance—for never was any woman so like her in her clothes.

A similar indignation is voiced by Moll herself, later in life, against "a shameless jade . . . called Abigail," a "stinking slut" who assaulted Moll as if she were a client, by clapping her on the back and kissing her as she turned, "by somebody's setting her on to affront me." With extraordinary violence Moll dragged the joker to the Conduit, London's gutter and aqueduct, "washed her polluted lips for her," stripped her, soaked her, "and had her soundly kicked to boot."

We verge here, but verge only, on sadistic reaction, and Moll declares herself in no sympathy with five "woman-shavers in Drury Lane," whose vicious revenge in the thirties against a demonstrably loose lady is decried by Moll, and the retribution (pillory, self-exile, family ruin) warmly applauded. Given so mixed and unpredictable a sexuality, Moll's settlement in her declining years with one man—perhaps her only lover—bears considerable scrutiny. Like Elizabeth with Essex, perhaps, she blossomed late.

Leading a life by now established, Moll dwelt in her *milieu* with ease and trust. Her taverns, the adjacent Globe, the Bull, and the Devil (where she must surely have met Ben Jonson, and possibly John Donne among the "sons of Ben") lent her haven; her house in Fleet Street was packed with friends and refugees; and within her bailiwick she feared nothing. Outside was another matter: one anecdote relates a wager with showman Banks, daring her to ride horseback, straddling, from Charing Cross to Shoreditch. Trouble erupted at Bishopsgate when she was discovered for her infamous self, and she escaped narrowly from an ugly mob only by night, and with the divine distractions of a big wedding and a bailiffs' arrest. She admits being frightened.

203

Such notoriety could do Moll little practical good. Yet since 1610, in her twenties, Moll had been celebrated, or at least signalled, to an extent few statesmen, poets, or philanthropists of the age could hope to be. In August 1610 a pamphlet by John Day (now lost) was entered at Stationers' Hall: "A book called The Mad Pranks of Merry Moll of the Bankside, with her Walks in Man's Apparel, and to what Purpose." And within the year two formidable and prolific dramatists had framed a whole comedy capitalizing on Moll's sudden ascent into the popular eye. Presented at the Fortune by the Prince's Players, Dekker and Middleton's *The Roaring Girl* centered on Mary as a go-between, a raucous, irreverent, chaffing, but fundamentally well-intentioned and chaste "instrument," whose pranks and plots aid two lovers in their gulling of a vindictive parent. Moll herself is neither heroine nor sidekick, but the title of the play and most of its muddled action rely heavily on her presence. The earlier publication of Day is presumably under attack (was it slanderous, or derisive?) in Middleton's preface to the printed work (1611): "Worse things, I must needs confess, the world has taxed her for than has been written of her; but 'tis the excellency of a writer to leave things better than he finds 'em; though some obscene fellow, that cares not what he writes against others—yet keeps a mystical bawdy-house himself, and entertains drunkards, to make use of their pockets and vent his private bottle-ale at midnight—though such a one would have ripped up the most nasty vice that ever hell belched forth, and presented it to a modest assembly, yet we rather wish in such discoveries, where reputation lies bleeding, a slackness of truth than fulness of slander." Perhaps, in effect, *The Roaring Girl* was intended as a vindication of Moll's character, despite occasional innuendoes (see below), and its epilogue concludes with an extremely provocative pledge, apparently to produce

204

Moll herself on the stage for a personal appearance at an unspecified time:

> If what we both have done
> Cannot full pay your expectation,
> The Roaring Girl herself, some few days hence,
> Shall on this stage give larger recompence . . .

The Roaring Girl as published bore a woodcut portrait of Moll which we have described. No other extended characterizations of her before 1662 are extant, but there are a good number of casual allusions to her peculiarities by poets and dramatists over the next fifty years. Thomas Freeman treats her to an indifferent epigram in 1614; Nat. Field calumniates her in *Amends for Ladies* (1618); John Taylor praises her, perhaps ironically, in a passage on "fantastick gestures and attire" (1622), where Mary Frith "doth keep one fashion constantly/And therefore she deserves a matron's praise,/In these inconstant moon-like changing days." She is mentioned, in passing, in *The Witch of Edmonton* (Rowley, Dekker, and Ford, 1621), and as late as *Hudibras*, where she is compared to "Joan of France." By 1668, a decade after her death, her name still stirs memory in an adaptation of Thomas Corneille, *The Feigned Astrologer*, as the deceased "oracle of felony."

All this equivocal publicity was accompanied, or perhaps occasioned, by more than mere eccentricity of dress and behavior. The progress of Moll's criminal career was swift and sure, beginning with her fumbling initiation into purse-cutting, until she had achieved a kind of gangland preeminence rarely challenged either by law or disorder. She had early acquainted herself with all the variety of specialists in London's highly-organized underworld. Their need in common was for a trustworthy receiver, and Mary proceeded to become one: she was alike at home to petty thieves, pickpockets and "those grandees of this function of thievery, the blades and hacks of the highway, who, having heard from their inferior tribe this repute of my equitable dealing, did deposit in my hands some of their coin against a rainy day.'' Also welcome were ''heavers,'' who snatched account ledgers from the shops of drapers or mercers—ledgers were commonly kept on a desk near the doorway, and guarded carelessly during lunchtime by apprentices, who would in turn be glad personally to pay a small ransom for the precious records, rather than reap the wrath of the master. Simpler in *modus operandi* were the ''King's takers,'' who merely grabbed merchandise from the stalls or barrows, usually at the lonesome hours of noon or dusk, and ran away—faster than their pursuit.

For all these thieves Mary's services were available and necessary. It was she to whom the victims of robbery could come to redeem their property; she could advance cash against future takings, and ''bank'' stolen money for the more sophisticated highwaymen, avoiding always ''the luggage and lumber of goods purchased by burglary''—i.e., identifiable large objects—preferring of course money—''portable and partable.'' For all such purposes Moll soon established ''a kind of brokery or insurance office'' in her house in Fleet Street, ''within two doors of the Globe Tavern, over against the Conduit.'' Here felons could deposit and losers for a fee repossess their stolen jewels, rings, and watches; the whole process seems to have been relatively acceptable to all concerned, like the thriving slave market in fifteenth-century Christian Constantinople, where relatives or friends might ransom known captives, wherever in the Mediterranean they might be, through infidel but dependable middlemen. Mary herself complacently lauds her occupation, as ''a lawless vocation, yet bordering between illicit and convenient, more advantageous by far to the injured than the courts of justice and benefits of the law, and more equal to the wrong-doers, who by such an hazardous seizure have, as themselves think, an equal propriety in their spoil, by yielding and restoring it upon such indifferent terms as my markets and prices usually were." In *The Roaring Girl*, Moll in her accustomed garb accosts a pickpocket:

MOLL. Dost not ken me, man?

CUTPURSE. No, trust me sir.

MOLL. Heart, there's a knight to whom I'm bound for many favors, lost his purse at the last new play i'th' Swan. Seven angels is in't; make it good—your best, do you see? No more.

CUTPURSE. A synagogue shall be called, Mistress Mary. Disgrace me not: *pocas palabras* [few words]; I will conjure for you, farewell.

In Richard Brome's comedy, *The Court Begger* (1632, II. i.), Citwit has been robbed of his watch as he window-shopped "at the coranto shop [i.e., newsstand]," and declares "I'll go to honest Moll about it presently."

Now Moll's dwelling-place assumed the character of an "Algiers" or neutral base, safe for thieves and conventionally off-limits to thief-takers, but always subject to the lady's authority, and "arbitrement" as to price and equipartition, "so that I may be said to have made a perfect regulation of this thievish mystery [i.e., profession], and reduced it to certain rules and orders, which during my administration of the mistress-ship and government thereof, was far better managed than afterwards it was; nor were the robberies so frequent nor so grievous then, as when my discipline was cast off, and this sort of cattle left to themselves, when I became obnoxious to these *reforming times* . . ." Correspondingly loyal, the criminals in Moll's entourage turned to her first for settlement of private disputes, and she continued as "an umpire in their quarrels" as long as they shared her hospitality. Long since she had let out rooms in her home, admittedly by bribing the landlord, but in keeping with her policy of safety in crime "never harbored any felon under my roof."

For despite the apparent security of Moll's position, scrapes with the law were inevitable; her only concern was to keep them at a minimum. An early *contretemps* is typical: in 1612, accused by some "adversary," Moll was charged and tried at the Court of Arches for "wearing indecent and manly apparel." Her lawyer did little but spin out the case with technicalities, and in the end Moll was sentenced "to stand and do penance in a white sheet at Paul's Cross during morning sermon on a Sunday." Indeed she served this light punishment, but John Chamberlain says, or reports the report, that she arrived "maudlin drunk, being discovered to have tippled of three quarts of sack before she came." In the meantime, with a particularly insipid sermon behind her, certain of her "emissaries" amused themselves by slicing the pantaloons and capes of the gawkers who lingered to watch. It was all rather a lark; she did not alter her attire. A similar and again slight brush with the courts, at the instance of an officious cobbler, one William Wall, landed Moll overnight in the notorious "hole" of Woodstreet Counter, where Richard Vennard caught his death of a cold. The charge was no more than breaking curfew, the judgment a small fine only, but Moll's elaborate revenge against Wall occupies nine pages of her narrative.

More serious, however, was a later indictment for dealing with stolen merchandise. Here the fault was Moll's own carelessness in displaying in her "magazine" or brokerage window a stolen watch before it had had time to "cool." The victim noticed it, and rather than ransom it, raised the authorities. Matters might have gone very ill for Moll at the formal sessions, had not a familiar pickpocket snatched the very evidence in court and fled with it, leaving the judge to fulminate, reprimand, and threaten, but the jury with no choice but to acquit. Henceforth Moll kept closer within the charmed circle of her "Algiers," and attempts in the period of the Commonwealth to bring her to justice met with no more

208

success—although a kind of starvation program observably curtailed her operations.

For Moll was aging, and the old order of cavaliers and desperadoes, indifferent constabulary and tolerated corruption began, in the 1630's, to wobble, and finally, in the '40's, to collapse. We began for the first time to hear of a new career, initiated, she would have us believe, when her brokerage had dwindled to a mere trickle of business, something which Moll blames fervently on "legalized" robbery by the roundhead regime, but which we may more realistically put down to increased efficiency in the prevention of free lance thievery. "Now seeing how little hopes there were of my interlooping in stolen goods, I thought it the best course to keep me in my old age, which grew apace upon me, to deal altogether in prohibited wares . . ."

"Prohibited wares" were at a premium now, and although Moll claims never before to have involved herself in procuring or most certainly in personal prostitution, hints of such activity had been current since 1610: "Twixt lovers she's a fit instrument," observes Sebastian in *The Roaring Girl*, and Moll herself, in the same play, points out that "Moll" is the commonest harlot's name in all London. And the antagonistic Nat. Field makes no bones about voicing the accusation, among many others. But Moll insists that her entry into flesh-mongering was a late expedient, and one to which necessity drove her.

Characteristically, however, once committed to the course she made the best of it. She had "some familiarity with the mad girls and the venerable matrons of the 'kind motion'," among the rest most intimate with the "abbess" of Holland's Leaguer, an infamous brothel celebrated by Shakerley Marmion in his best-remembered play (*Holland's Leaguer*, 1631), and with a noteworthy courtesan named Damaris Page, "newly then from a whore rampant separated [heraldic image] to the office of a procurer or provider." Knowing these, and their thriving business, and observing that the Civil War did nothing whatever to disrupt such enterprise, that in fact "the voluptuous bed is never the less frequented for those hard and painful lodgings in the camp," Moll "saw also, that the former traffickers this way were very strait-laced and too narrow in their practice, as confining their industry in this negotiation to one sex, like women tailors, that if they were to be hanged cannot make a doublet for themselves. In this," she adds wryly, "I was a little prosperous, though to make good the simile, I never could fit myself."

What Moll finally explains is the organization of perhaps the earliest double-barrelled brothel in London, an elaborate and sophisticated palace of venery providing not only girls but "stallions," for the whim of masked ladies great and less, "the sprucest fellows the town afforded, for they did me reputation at home and service abroad . . . so that my house was become a double temple of Priapus and Venus, frequented by votaries of both sorts, to whose desires my answers (the oracles of a couch-chair where I sat as chief priestess) were always favorably accommodated." Nothing so ambitious of such nature had been attempted before, if we are to believe Moll, and no more inexorable mistress had ever broached the attempt. In no time she had outstripped, in all senses, the prominent establishments of Mistress Pike and Mistress Turner, providing herself with the most delicate fresh bait ("I had my purveyors continually abroad, who had always the prime of the market; whatever maidens came to town, there was none durst or might see them till my turn was served—my sisters of the tribe must wait for my leavings") and the most aristocratic clientele. One of the latter, an unnamed nobleman, later bailed her out of a ticklish situation provoked by her royalist sympathies, through his superseding a parliamentary warrant for her arrest. Such friends were a solace to Moll's later years, but for the continued business of brothel-keeping and procuring she exhibited in the end little enthusiasm. A last, rather pathetic anecdote of a gentlewoman's self-ruin is retailed, almost shamefacedly, and no more is spoken about the "house."

Indeed, by 1642 Moll was at least fifty-three, and her concerns verged more and more on the political and military; a staunch royalist always, even her gaming and criminal pursuits took on anti-parliamentarian overtones, one exploit in particular being addressed against the Earl of Strafford, Lord Deputy of Ireland, whom she "allegorized" in a sponsored bull-baiting, narrated by herself, at Bear Garden: the dogs were styled "Pym," and "St. Johns, and so forth." On another occasion she toyed with fire in fencing an enormously valuable watch stolen at church from Lady Fairfax. In 1638, at the return of Charles from his Scottish expedition, she had filled, so she says, the Fleet Conduit with free wine, an emblem of lavishness prefigured in fiction by Dekker, and in fact by the ecclesiastical authorities at Istanbul in 1606. And she involved herself both in civil protest against the early barring of the London gates to King Charles, and in mild sabotage thereafter; as much as a woman in her station could do, perhaps, Moll did for her cause, and for the time of its life devoted herself to the King with the same zeal which had informed all her earlier enterprises, whether by encouraging "royalist" highwaymen like Cheney and Captain Hind, whose dismal end— betrayed—she laments bitterly, by forgery of parliamentary writs of payment, or by philanthropy toward the victims of the administration in jails where her influence commanded perquisites. But here history itself stood in her path, and no downright blows or witty manipulations sufficed to derail it; she admits, at last, that her efforts have come to little, and traces the path to an ultimate retirement with retrospective regret:

... All things coming to confusion by the carrying on the Rebellion, I betook myself to a contemplative life, and retired myself at home, despairing to see good day again, lamenting the sad and miserable distractions into which we were reduced. Let no person think I had no sense thereof, for though I say it myself, I had as much English nature in me as anybody, and suffered as much in my way as anyone whatsoever. But that which more nearly grieved me was the absence and loss also of my great friends, who were of the other side. In this solitary condition, to alleviate and lighten the tediousness thereof, I played with those my several sorts of creatures of pleasure and imitation, such as my baboons, apes, squirrels, and parrots, with them and the recreation of their tricks to pass away the time and supply the defect of better converse.

Pets, lodgers, and even literature took up Moll's latter years, while her personal fortunes deteriorated to near nothing: "My trade I am sure was wholly at an end, and my money gone, get what I would, the cavaliers my friends were so needy; so as I was glad to stay at home and play at tick-tack for drink with one of my companions, and bemoan my decayed fortunes." Friends remained: Captain Hind had been loyal to her, the cavaliers still courted her, and one man indeed may have solaced her more intimately, although perhaps not so late in life: Ralph Briscoe, the Clerk of Newgate Prison, younger by far than Moll, who "had known him as a child," nevertheless "was right," she admits, as she admits of no other man in her narrative, "for my tooth and made to my mind, in every part of him." A rather tender relationship ensued, predicated in part on a mutual addiction to the Bull-Ring, where once Moll saved his life, "the bull having made a heave at his breeches, which broke and gave way." Ralph called her "Aunt," and "ever after we two were both one, he never failing of any duty, nor any service I required of him, which he was capable to do . . ."

As for literature, leading a new "sedentary life" shut up in her Fleet Street refuge, Moll turned her back on the popular black-letter trash of the day, "tale-books and romances, and the Histories of the Seven Champions, and the like fopperies," and took up "more serious writings and contemplations." Whether because she had altered the pattern of a lifetime or because self-indulgence had caught up with her, "grown crazy in my body and discontented in my mind, I yielded to the next distemper that approached me, which by my bustling and active spirit I had kept off a good while from seizing me. It was a dropsy, a disease whose cause you will easily guess from my past life, but it had such strange and terrible symptoms that I thought I was possessed, and that the Devil was got within my doublet." Poor Moll found herself so bloated as to be unable to wear her accustomed male garments, and forced to "do penance again," as at Paul's Cross, "in a blanket." Her skin withered, her blood thinned, her legs thickened, and with a swathed head she reminded herself ironically of the mythically ugly and ancient witch and soothsayer, Mother Shipton. The countless looking-glasses hung in the house seemed to mock her; there was none large enough to reflect her all in all. In such distraction and misery she passed her last months, dying on 26 July 1659, to be buried at St. Bride's, Fleet Street, on 10 August following. The *persona* of 1662 gives her age then as seventy-four, but if born in 1589, as suggested, she was just seventy. Her will, indexed in the records of the Prerogative Court of Canterbury under an alias ("Mary Markham," which she had used on various occasions), is dated 6 June of the same year. "Sick and weak in body," she bequeaths her soul to God, her body "to the cart, whenever it come," and the bulk of a modest estate to her married niece and executrix Frances Edmunds; twenty and twelve pounds respectively were left to two other kinsmen, Abraham and James Robinson, son and father. In spite of her supposed ability to read and write "perfectly" she signs with a mark—a confused, spidery "X" which extreme illness might account for.

Despite the firm evidence of the will, the equally specific *Life and Death* lists an entirely different set of legatees: ten pounds each to her three maids, and the rest, about seventy pounds, to "my kinsman Frith, a master of a ship, dwelling at Redriffe." She would have preferred, she says there, given the means, to have endowed almshouses, like the Elizabethan actor Edward Alleyn. Her autobiography concludes with an appropriate request, one which the scrivener might blush to include in a formal testament, but which sums up the lady and her lifetime far better than hand, seal, and witnesses three:

Let me be lain in my grave on my belly, with my breech upwards, as well for a lucky resurrection at Doomsday as because I am unworthy to look upwards; and that as I have in my life been preposterous, so I may be in death. I expect not, nor will I purchase a funeral commendation; but if Mr. H—be squeamish and will not preach, let the sexton mumble two or three dusty, clayey words and put me in, and there's an END.

"Is it not better to make a fool of the world, as I have done, than to be fooled of the world as you scholars are?"

"William Kempe,"
in *The Return from Parnassus*
(1600)

NOTES TO CHAPTERS

Chapter One

The first figure is the page-number; the figure following the decimal point indicates the line. The passage noted is identified within quotation marks.

4.26-7 "uncommonly well-documented" Manuscript and printed sources for chapters one and two are so numerous I think it best to list them chronologically at the conclusion of page-and-line notes.

6.16-17 "may confidently be ascribed to Francis Bacon" see Bacon, *Works*, eds. Spedding, Ellis and Heath, IX (1862), 108 ff. Tenison (X, 492) disputes the ascription, but was unaware of the contemporary corroboration to be found in More's *Historiae Prov. Angl.*, p. 220 (sidenote).

9.3-4 "can be to some extent confirmed" see *SPD*, CCLXXXIV, 34, 43; *SPD* Adds., XXIV, 41, 42; and MS. Stowe 167, f. 65.

11.21 "at Rome in 1594" see T. G. Law, *A Historical Sketch of Conflicts between Jesuits and Seculars in the Reign of Queen Elizabeth* (London, 1889), XXVIII ff.

18.9 "extravagant accusations" *SPD*, CCLXXIV, 53.

23.12-13 "the familiar ring of a campaign promise" Compare for example the similar and also unredeemed promise in *The Copie of a Leter* ("Leicester's Commonwealth")—which Fitzherbert himself may have translated into French—(London, 1584), p. 58.

36.31 "customary and legal" see David Jardine, *A Reading on the use of Torture in the Criminal Law of England, previously to the Commonwealth* (London, 1837), *passim*.

39.23 "there were justices" see Samuel Rezneck, "Trial of Treason in Tudor England," *Studies in Honor of C. H. McIlwain* (Cambridge, Mass., 1936), pp. 258-288.

45.8 "on 13 November" Martin Array's error ("23 November") has been perpetuated by a number of authorities.

45.31-2 "it is indeed possible that Walpole himself . . ." *SPD*, CCLXIX, 27 suggests that Walpole sincerely thought Bagshaw could be depended upon; see also the Petyt MSS partially calendared in HMC XI, Part VII, p. 266. Martin Hume, *Treason and Plot* (London, 1901), theorizes fancifully that the real point of Walpole's device was to ruin Bagshaw, and that Squire was no more than an unwitting agent on a fool's errand, bound to be caught, and likely to "betray" Bagshaw—a notion evoking the situation in John Le Carré's *The Spy Who Came in from the Cold*. Bagshaw in fact was almost certainly not involved in the episode: see William Watson's remarks in the CRS *Miscellanies*, I (1905), 73, and Law, *Historical Sketch*, LXXIX ff.

46.4-5 "henceforth the seculars" see above all William Watson, *Important Considerations*, 1601 [*STC* 25125]; also [Robert Parsons], *A Manifestation of the Great Folly of certain Secular Priests*, and W. C., *A Reply unto a certain Libel* [i.e., Parsons'] (1603); and *The Golden Balance of Trial* (1603), esp. the appended "counterblast."

46.7-8 "delight of all" e.g., George Abbott, *Answer to Doctor Hill* (1604), Thomas Bell, *Anatomy of Popish Tyranny* (1603), "O. E." (*alias* M. Sutcliffe), *A Brief Reply to a certain Slanderous Libel* (1600) and *A Challenge concerning the Romish Church*; also Thomas Diggs, *Humble Motives for Association* (1601). Pro-Catholic replies include Edmond Thomas Hill, *A Quatron of Reasons of Catholic Religion* (1600), and "E. O." (*alias* Philip Woodward, *A Detection of divers Notable Untruths* (1602).

46.31 "still visiting prisoners" *SPD*, CCLXXXIV, 32.

46.33 "working conversions at Seville" Foley, *Records*, II, 255 ff. See also Jessop, *One Generation*, pp. 297 ff., *Authentic Memoirs of . . . Father Richard Walpole* (London, 1773), and Lewis Owen, *Relation of the State of the English Colleges* (1626), the latter two *passim* for undependable calumnies.

MS Sources: Chapter One

Chamberlain to Carleton, 4 May 1598. *SPD*, CCLXVII, 5.

John Stanley to Robert Cecil, 22 Sept. 1598. Hatfield MS. *64*, 44.

John Stanley to the Earl of Essex, n.d., 1598. Hatfield MS. *67*, 83.

Relation of John Stanley, n.d., 1598. Hatfield MS. *233*, 5.

Examination of John Stanley, 23 Sept. 1598. *SPD*, CCLXVIII, 62.

Francis Bacon to Robert Cecil, 23 Sept. 1598. Hatfield MS. *64*, 48-49.

Chamberlain to Carleton, 3 Oct. 1598. *SPD*, CCLXVIII, 71.

Warrant to commit Richard Rolles to the Tower, 6 Oct. 1598. *APC*, XXIX, 219.

W. Waad to the Earl of Essex and Robert Cecil (containing "Discourse of Squiers of the Jesuits Dealings with the English beyond Seas"), 7 Oct. 1598. Hatfield MS. *64*, 92, 94.

Declaration of John Stanley, 18 Oct. 1598. *SPD*, CCLXVIII, 82.

Examination of Edward Squire, 19 Oct. 1598. *SPD*, CCLXVIII, 83 (copies, 84, 85).

Declaration by Edward Squire, 19 Oct. 1598. *SPD*, CCLXVIII, 86.

Chamberlain to Carleton, 20 Oct. 1598. *SPD*, CCLXVIII, 87.

Second Examination of Edward Squire, 23 Oct. 1598. *SPD*, CCLXVIII, 89 (copy 90).

Third Examination of Edward Squire, 24 Oct. 1598. *SPD* CCLXVIII, 91.

Examinations of William Monday and Richard Rolles, 3 November 1598. *SPD*, CCLXVIII, 103.

Edward Coke to Robert Cecil, 3 Nov. 1598. Hatfield MS. *65*, 40.

Robert Cecil to (Thomas) Edmondes, 6 Nov. 1598. Stowe MS. 167, f. 60.

Chamberlain to Carleton, 8 Nov. 1598. *SPD*, CCLXVIII, 108.

Trial and Conviction of Edward Squire, 9 Nov. 1598. P.R.O. MS. KB/8/55, cal. in D.K.R., IV (1843), App. II, pp. 291-292.

"The Manner how the English Jesuits do deal with our Englishmen which are brought prisoners into Spain" ("A Declaration of Edward Squire after his Arraignment") MS in the author's collection.

Richard Bayley to Sir William Stanley, 19 Nov. 1598 [Brussels]. *SPD*, CCLXVIII, 111.

Payment for conveying Rolles and Stanley to the Tower, 19 Nov. 1598. *APC*, XXIX, 294.

Chamberlain to Carleton, 22 Nov. 1598. *SPD*, CCLXVIII, 115.

The Council to the Earl of Bath, acknowledging receipt of "the examynacions that concerne Stanley the traytour that came out of Spain," 4 Dec. 1598. *APC*, xxix, 335.

Thomas Edmondes to Robert Cecil, 12 Dec. 1598. Hatfield MS. *66*, 58 (a copy: original in P.R.O. *S.P. Foreign*).

Francesco Contarini to the Doge and Senate, 22 Dec. 1598. *SPV*, ix, 758.

Relevant portions of the Account Book of Sir John Peyton, Lt. of the Tower, for 1598. MS. in possession of Sir I. Gollancz in 1925; extracts as printed in Tenison, x, 435 and 444.

Warrant paying the keeper of the Counter for Squire's room and board (seven weeks) before he was moved to the Tower, 28 January 1599. *APC*, xxix, 506.

Examination of Richard Gifforde of Chichester, 12 Feb. 1600. Hatfield MS. *68*, 35.

Printed Sources

[Francis Bacon]. *A Letter Written out of England . . . containing a True Report of a Strange Conspiracy.* London, 1599. This is reprinted roughly in George Carleton, *A Thankful Remembrance of God's Mercy,* rev. and enlarged ed., London, 1625 (not in the first ed. of 1624) and again in the anonymous compilation, *Authentic Memoirs of that Exquisitely Villainous Jesuit, Father Richard Walpole,* London, 1773; but possibly the text of the narrative in *Authentic Memoirs* stems from a manuscript (the postscript appended to the version there is probably spurious). Spedding's text follows Carleton, as he was unable to locate a copy of the original pamphlet.

M[artin] A[rray]. *The Discovery and Confutation of a Tragical Fiction.* Rome, 1599.

Parker Society. *Liturgies and Occasional Forms of Prayer set forth in the Reign of Queen Elizabeth,* ed. W. K. Clay. Cambridge, 1847, pp. 679 ff.

John Stow. *The Annales of England . . . until 1600.* London, 1600.

T[homas] F[itzherbert]. *A Defense of the Catholic Cause.* [St. Omer], 1602.

Robert Parsons. *An Answer to the Fifth Part of the Reports lately set forth by Sir Edward Coke.* [Douai], 1606.

John Speed. *The History of Great Britain.* London, 1611.

218

William Camden. *Annales: Tomus alter et idem* (book IV). Oxford, 1629.

Henricus Morus. *Historiae Provinciae Anglicanae.* Antwerp, 1660.

Secondary Accounts

Henry Foulis. *The History of Romish Treasons.* London, 1681.

White Kennett. MS. notes on Edward Squire. Landsdowne MS. 982, no. 139.

John Lingard. *The History of England ... to 1688.* Sixth ed., rev. and enlarged. 10 vols., London, 1855.

Henry Foley. *Records of the English Province of the Society of Jesus.* 7 vols., London, 1875-1883.

Augustus Jessopp. *One Generation of a Norfolk House.* London, 1879.

A. E. Pollard. "Edward Squire," *Dictionary of National Biography.*

Martin Hume. *Treason and Plot.* London, 1901.

Eva M. Tenison. *Elizabethan England.* 13 vols., Royal Leamington Spa, 1933 et seq.

Chapter Two

53.25-6 "citizens' petitions" Calendared in Irwin Smith, *Shakespeare's Blackfriars Playhouse* (New York, 1964), pp. 489-92.

56.17-18 "a seat of Catholic intrigue" see E. K. Chambers, *William Shakespeare* (Oxford, 1930), II, 165-9.

64.19 "at first suspected dead" see my "William Drury, Dramatist," *Recusant History*, VIII, 5 (1966), 293-7.

69.21 ff. "Goad" Some data on Goad may be found in John Crow, "Thomas Goad and *The Dolefull Euen-Song*," *Trans. Camb. Bibl. Soc.*, I (1951), 238-259, which deals primarily with the printing history of the pamphlet. For its relations with W. C., *The Fatal Vesper*, see my "*The Fatal Vesper* and *The Doleful Evensong*: Claim-Jumping in 1623," *The Library*, Fifth Ser., XXII (1967), 128-35. The conventional identification of W. C. with Richard Crashaw's father William is false.

73.9 my italics

83-4 *last and first line* my italics

84.29-30 "a last literary attempt" The attribution to Goad (by *DNB*) of *The Friars' Chronicle* (1625) is incorrect.

85.25-6 "willing . . . to his widow" Will PCC 159 Harvey, proved 18 October 1636.

MS Sources: Chapter Two

Calvert to Conway, 26 October 1623, *SPD*, CLIII, 103.

Henry Bannister to Lord Zouche, 27 October 1623, *SPD*, CLIII, 104.

Conway to Calvert, 28 October 1623. *SPD*, CLIII, 106.

John Maynard to Conway, 29 October 1623. *SPD*, CLIII, 108.

Valaresso to the Venetian Court, 31 October 1623. *SPV*, XVIII, 147.

Dudley Carleton, Esq., to Sir Dudley Carleton, 1 November 1623. *SPD*, CLIV, 2.

Mead to Stutevile, 1 November 1623. Harleian MS. 389, f. 375.

Mead to Stutevile, 8 November 1623. Harleian MS. 389, f. 377. With two relevant enclosures, *viz.*, f. 374, and ff. 378-80; the latter is printed in Birch, II, 428-431.

Chamberlain to Carleton, 8 November 1623. *SPD*, CLIV, 17.

Chamberlain to Carleton, 15 November 1623. *SPD*, CLIV, 28.

Mead to Stutevile, 15 November 1623. Harleian MS. 389, f. 381.

Chamberlain to Carleton, 21 November 1623. *SPD*, CLIV, 55.

Diary of William Laud, in *Works*, ed. James Bliss (Oxford, 1847-60), III, 143.

Diary of John Southcote, *PCRS*, I (1905), 99.

Diary of Mr. Foord, Vicar of Eltham, in Samuel Lysons, *The Environs of London* (London, 1792-96), IV, 410.

Diary of Walter Yonge, ed. George Roberts (London: Camden Society, 1848), p. 70.

Diary of William Whiteway, Egerton MS. 784, f. 35.

Autobiography of Simonds D'Ewes, ed. J. O. Halliwell (London, 1845), I, 238.

Printed Sources

W. C. *The Fatal Vesper*. London, 1623.

Thomas Goad. *The Doleful Evensong*. London, 1623.

Something Written by Occasion of that Fatal and Memorable Accident. N.p. [London], 1623.

I.R.P. [i.e., John Floyd]. *A Word of Comfort*. N.p., 1623.

[Matthew Rhodes]. *The Dismal Day at Blackfriars*. London, 1623.

John Gee. *The Foot out of the Snare*. London, 1624 (4 eds.).

——. *New Shreds of the Old Snare*. London, 1624.

——. *Hold Fast*. London, 1625.

Richard Hord. *Elegia de Admiranda Clade Centum Papistorum*. London, 1625.

John Wilson. *A Song, or Story, for the Lasting Remembrance of Divers Famous Works which God hath done in our Time*. London, 1626.

John Robotham. *Omen Romae*. London, 1627.

William Gouge. *God's Three Arrows*. London, 1631.

Alexander Gil. ΠAPEPΓA, *sive Poetici Conatus*. London, 1632.

Secondary Accounts

William Camden. "Annals of King James I," in *A Complete History of England* (London, 1706), II, 659.

John Stow. *Annales ... continued ... by Edmund Howes*. London, 1631.

Thomas Fuller. *The Church History of Britain*. London, 1655.

Anthony à Wood. *Athenae Oxoniensis*. London, 2 vols., 1691-92.

John Prince. *The Worthies of Devon*. London, 1701.

Henry Foley. *Records of the English Province of the Society of Jesus*. London, 7 vols., 1875-83.

Dictionary of National Biography, sv. esp. "Robert Drury," "John Gee," and "Thomas Goad."

Chapter Three

91.4 "Thomas Randolph" see *Hey for Honesty, Down with Knavery* (1651), IV, iii (*Works*, ed. W. C. Hazlitt, p. 470).

92.5 "By Macheath's time" see J. W. Hill, *Tudor and Stuart Lincoln* (Cambridge, 1956), p. 5.

93.28 ff. "Langford's troop . . ." see *APC*, XXXII, 292, 395; Carew MSS *Calendar*, 1601-03, p. 397; *State Papers Irish*, 1601-1611, *passim*. A summary of Ratsey's Irish career in the Shakespeare Association Facsimile of *The Life and Death of Gamaliel Ratsey* (London, 1935), v-vi, is quite inaccurate.

94.26 "a proclamation" *STC* 8333.

97.27 "A folk tale" see Frank Aydelotte, *Elizabethan Rogues and Vagabonds* (Oxford, 1913), pp. 101-2.

103.1 "William Harrison" see F. J. Furnivall, ed., *Harrison's Description of England in Shakespeare's Youth* (London: New Shakspere Society, 1878) pp. 108-9.

112.11 "Forty shillings" see Chambers, *William Shakespeare*, II, 323-7.

113.4 "to play" B. L. Joseph discusses playing for a wager in *Elizabethan Acting* (Oxford, 1951), pp. 152-3.

114.15 "two lost ballads" E. Arber, ed., *Registers of the Stationers' Company*, III, 287, 291.

Chapter Four

123.16-17 "As early as 1546" see Joseph Strutt, *The Sports and Pastimes of the People of England*, ed. William Hone (London, 1876), p. 304.

123.24 "'From the top of the spire . . .'" Wilberforce Jenkinson, *London Churches before the Great Fire* (London, 1917), p. 6, quoting *The Burnyng of Paules Church* (1563), G4ʳ.

124.1 "a Dutchman named Peter" Strutt, p. 306, quoting Holinshed.

124.8-9 "according to Thomas Deloney" Jenkinson, p. 7.

124.19 "'bend your course . . .'" Thomas Dekker, *The Guls Hornbook and The Belman of London*, ed. Oliphant Smeaton (London, 1941), p. 33.

125.10 "William Banks" Banks's first name has not previously been identified, although on occasion he is called John or Richard by nineteenth and twentieth century writers (e.g., Chambers). *DNB* and S. H. Atkins leave blank the first name, as do all of Banks's contemporaries and chroniclers. That he is in fact William is shown only by the petition for a victualing license (*SPD* CCLXXV, 10) of 2 October 1634 ("William Bankes") cited again below.

125.20 "Ralegh assures us" see Thomas Frost, *The Old Showmen and the Old London Fairs* (London, 1874), p. 23, quoting *The History of the World* (1614).

125.22-3 "Over sixty allusions" Most are collected by S. H. Atkins, "Mr. Banks and his Horse," *NQ*, CLXVII (1934), 39-44, following in part the lists provided by J. O. Halliwell-Phillipps, *Memoranda on Loves Labours Lost* (London, 1879), and C. E. Browne, "Banks and his horse Morocco," *NQ*, 5th ser., VI (1876), 387. See also E. F. Rimbault, ed., *Maroccus Extaticus* (London, Percy Society, 1843), adding an allusion by Dekker; Hyder Rollins, "An Analytical Index of the Ballad Entries (1557-1709) in the Registers of the Company of Stationers of London," *SP*, XXI (1924), 210, adding three more; R. B. McKerrow, ed., *The Works of Thomas Nashe* (corrected reissue, Oxford, 1958), IV, 266; also cf E.S., *The Discovery of the Knights of the Post* (1597) [*STC* 21489], B1ᵛ and the materials cited below.
Unless otherwise documented, statements or quotations from contemporary writers about Banks may be found in these compilations.

128.28-9 "'a well-educated ape'" Strutt, p. 331, quoting Jonson's *Bartholomew Fair* (Induction).

130.20-1 "a ballad (lost)" Rollins, no. 2430.

131.21-2 "apes . . . before 1572" Strutt, p. 330.

131.26 "dancing camel" see A. Davenport, ed., *The Collected Poems of Joseph Hall* (Liverpool, 1949), pp. 205-6.

132.2 "a fourteenth-century illustration" see Strutt, p. 339.

132.2-3 "in 1610 three showmen . . ." see *SPD* LVII, 43 (6 September 1610).

132.28 "260′ high . . ." Dugdale's figure, as quoted by Jenkinson, p. 6. Stow is slightly at variance.

132.32 "Dekker advises you ..." *The Guls Hornbook*, p. 37.

132-3, *last and first line* "a penny in 1609, and a penny still after the Great Fire" Dekker, p. 37; Jenkinson, p. 6, quoting Henry Peacham, *The Worth of a Penny* (1669).

133.28-9, ff. "a remarkably full account ... from a French observer." The entire French text is given by Atkinson; I have translated passages only.

136.9 "Isaac Casaubon" see Mark Pattison, *Isaac Casaubon* (London, 1875), p. 445.

136.13-14 "Bishop Morton" see Atkinson, p. 42 (no. xv).

137.32 "Already in 1604 ..." see E. K. Chambers, *The Elizabethan Stage* (Oxford, 1922), III, 279.

138.11 ff. "he ventured to open a tavern" see Atkinson, p. 43 (no. xxII); the career of the tavern is touched on by the documents calendared in *Remembrancia*, pp. 547-8; the royal petition is *SPD* CCLXXV, 10 (2 October 1634).

138.32-3 "a satirical squib of 1637" see Halliwell-Phillipps, p. 52, quoting MS. Ashmole 826.

140.16 "Mr. Daniel Lambert ..." see G. H. Wilson, *The Eccentric Mirror* (London, 1806), I, 19.

141.2-3 "almost certainly earlier printings have perished" The "1582" edition recorded by *STC* bears however a faked imprint and colophon, and dates actually from *circa* 1650 (see *BMC*); but a play (lost) about Long Meg was probably performed by the Admiral's Men for Henslowe on 14 February 1595: see Harbage and Schoenbaum, *Annals of English Drama* (London, 1964), p. 62.

142.24 "Harrietsham" so says Taylor, but the name does not appear in the Harrietsham or any neighboring parish register as transcribed by Streatfield (BM Add. MSS. 33914-15; indexes in Add. MSS. 33907-13). These are however incomplete, and Wood was perhaps of origins too low to figure in them.

143.12 "Sir Warham St. Leger" see *DNB*, L, 168: he was knighted in 1608, and sold Leeds Castle before his death in 1631.

143.22 "Baron Wotton's" either Edward, first Baron (d. 1626) or his Catholic son Thomas, second Baron (d. 1630).

146.1 "a flyer" unique example in the library of the Society of Antiquaries (Lemon 98; not in *STC*). See W. W. Greg, *Dramatic Documents from Elizabethan Playhouses* (London, 1931), VIII.

149.5 "John Vennard" referred to as a merchant and creditor, to a considerable sum, in 1578 (*APC*, X, 315).

150.25 "the deed of gift against the will" The course of government action concerning the Vennards and Lowe may be traced in *CSPD*, 1 December 1591 and 25 February 1596, and in *APC*, XIX, 452; XX, 97, 173, 196, 202, 207, 252; XXI, 42, 152, 168, 240-1, 332; XXII, 218, and 431 (1590-92). John senior's will is PCC 51 Rutland; John junior's is PCC 67 Leicester.

157.24 "certain 'Verses . . .'" now lost; the covering letter is at Hatfield House (*HMC*, IX, ix, 413).

159.30 "the request and its bearer" *HMC*, IX, xi, 24.

159.33 "Richard gratefully presented . . ." *HMC*, IX, xi, 538 ("1600").

161.26 ff. "A doggerelists' flyting match" Fennor's apology is *I am your First Man* (*STC* 10783); Taylor's counterattack is in *A Cast over Water . . . given gratis to William Fennor* (*STC* 23741). See also *Eliz. Stage*, II, 468-9. The verse quoted here is from *A Cast over Water*, B4ᵛ.

162, *last line* "an unidentified 'R. R.'" John Manningham, *Diary*, ed. John Bruce (London, Camden Society, 1868), p. 93.

164.28 "in 1603 a deposition . . ." *SPD* CLXXXVIII, 16 (n.d., but undoubtedly 1603).

166.2 "Vennard was still a rhymer" *A Cast over Water*, C3ʳ. It is conceivable that the hexaines in Fennor's *Fennor's Descriptions* (1616), B3ᵛ-C3ᵛ and D3ᵛ-[E1]ʳ are by Vennard; they are in his manner.

168.10 "sent him posting on horseback to nearly all parts . . ." Records of Ferris's service are calendared in *APC*, XI 178 (?); XII, 59, 78; XIII, 30, 31, 57, 69; XIV, 80, 119, 289, 295; XVI, 17, 138, 246, 419; XVII, 25; XVIII, 402; XXI, 361-2; XXII, 18, 52; XXVI, 290, 460, 469, 538; XXVII, 59, 61, 164, 338, 347; XXVIII, 554, 559; XXIX, 131, 664; XXX, 318, 767; X̣XXII, 241-2 (1579-1601), and one document of 1597 described in Hofmann and Freeman, *Catalogue Eighteen* (1967), item 10.

169.10-11 "*The most Dangerous . . .*" reprinted by J. P. Collier, *Illustrations of Old English Literature* (London, 1864), v. 2, and by Edward Arber, *An English Garner* (Bristol and London, 1877-90), VI, 155 ff. Only the Bodleian copy of the original survives.

173.7-10 [ballads] see Arber, *SR*, ii, 557, 558.

174.30 "a visit to Thomas Nashe" *APC*, xxvii, 338; see *Eliz. Stage*, iii, 154.

175.5 "one chance mention" *DNB*, sv. Ferris.

175.10-11 "a highly successful actor" see the standard accounts of Kempe's career in *Eliz. Stage*, ii, 325-7, in Edwin Nungezer, *A Dictionary of Actors* (New Haven, 1929), pp. 216-22, and in the introduction to William Kempe, *Nine Days' Wonder*, ed. A. Dyce (London, Camden Society, 1840).

176.17 "The morris" A full historical discussion is given by Francis Douce, *Illustrations of Shakespeare* (London, 1807), v. 2.

176.31 "in 1609 in Hertford" see *Old Meg of Hertfordshire for a Maid Marian and Herford Town for a Morris Dance* (London, 1609), reprinted in *Miscellanea Antiqua Anglicana* (London, 1816), v. 1.

181.32-3 "*Nine Days' Wonder*" The Bodleian copy of the original is unique.

Chapter Five

191.19 "The Duke of Würtemberg" see W. B. Rye, *England as seen by Foreigners in the Days of Elizabeth and James the First* (London, 1865), pp. 7, 14.

192.2 "Webster's 'character'" John Webster, *Works*, ed. F. L. Lucas (London, 1927), iv, 38-9.

193.7 "the first actress" see G. E. Bentley, *The Jacobean and Caroline Stage* (Oxford, 1941-66), i, 25.

193.16-17 "the most recent and authoritative account" Carrol Camden, *The Elizabethan Woman* (Houston, New York, and London, 1952), pp. 200-1, 224.

193. *last line, ff.* "*The Fleire*" Edward Sharpham, *The Fleire*, ed. H. Nibbe (Louvain, 1912), p. 6.

195.5 "about 1589" See *The Life and Death of Mrs. Mary Frith, commonly called Mal Cutpurse* (London, 1662), p. 3. This elusive

226

duodecimo (apparently the British Museum copy is unique) remains our primary source for Mary Frith's biography. Although it is cast largely as an autobiographical narrative, "Mall Cutpurse's Diary," pp. 27-173, how much is the "editor's" invention lies naturally open to question. The book itself, if even partly fictional, is a fascinating and readable forerunner of *Roxana*.

195.9 "the Barbican" see John Stow, *A Survey of London (1603)*, ed. C. L. Kingsford (Oxford, 1908), I, 70, 302.

195.20 "If Mary were baptized" There is no entry in the register of St. Giles (Guildhall MS 6419/1); the neighboring parish registers searched have been published by the Harleian Society.

195.22-3 "a jovial and eccentric pastor" Apparently not from London, as no Frith of this period appears in Newcourt or Hennessy's *Novum Repertorium*; nor is he mentioned by Fuller (Church History) Le Neve, or Neale, or among Cambridge or Oxford alumni. Possibly he is identifiable as Roger Frith, parson of Paul's Cray, Kent, who d. 1599 (will PCC 23, 24 Kidd; no niece is mentioned).

199.22 "By 1620" Camden, *Elizabethan Women*, pp. 263-7.

200.10 "One mid-seventeenth-century engraving" reproduced photographically in Thomas Middleton, *Works*, ed. A. H. Bullen, IV, facing p. 3. This may originally have been issued as an oversized frontispiece to the BM copy of *The Life and Death*, but has since been removed from the volume. Denis Meadows, *Elizabethan Quintet* (New York, 1957), p. 241, mentions "some painted panels recently discovered in an old house in Huntingdonshire," (i.e., at Hilton); and Meadows' vignette ("Mary Frith, the Roaring Girl," pp. 238-63), while the only substantial modern account of Mary, is quite peppered with errors and misconstructions; its author in fact appears never even to have consulted *The Life and Death* directly, but to have based his biography instead on extracts quoted by Dyce and Bullen. An historian now engaged in a study of Mary Frith has accumulated a few more data from MSS, and other opinion and detail are available in recent articles upon or editions of Middleton, Nathan Field, *et al.*, by, e.g., R. C. Bald, Robin Jeffs, and S. Schoenbaum. I have not wanted to reiterate these.

201.13 "her affinity for dogs . . . extravagent" see Middleton, *Works*, ed. Alexander Dyce (London, 1840), II, 431. Dyce's introduction (II, 427-31), following Boswell/Malone's notes to *Twelfth Night*, Reed's Dodsley, and Nares, and followed in turn by Bullen, is the best compendium of early allusions to Moll.

201.19-20 "imaginative commentators" Dyce, following the 1662 portrait, followed by Meadows, p. 255. But the "eagle" may be a parrot, and the very small whiskered "lion" instead Mary's "strange cat."

205.9-10 "a good number" all cited by Dyce.

207.2 "in *The Roaring Girl* . . ." Thomas Dekker, *Dramatic Works*, ed. Fredson Bowers (Cambridge, 1953-61), III, 89.

208.9 "John Chamberlain says" letter of 12 February 1612: see *Letters*, ed. McClure, I, 334.

213.23 "dying on 26 July 1659" *Smith's Obituary* (MS. Sloane 886), ed. Henry Ellis (London, Camden Society, 1849), p.51.

213.24 "buried . . ." Guildhall MS. 6540/1, register of St. Bridget *alias* Bride, London.

213.26 "Her will" PCC 119 Nabbs, proved 24 July 1660.

INDEX

Most written works have been indexed only by their authors; major nations (England, Ireland, France, Spain, etc.) are not indexed separately, nor are English counties, nor London, save for specific streets, parishes, buildings, etc.

230

Elizabeth II (Queen of England), 167
Ellis, R. L., 215, 228
Ely, Dr. Humphrey, 11
Erdestand (Herts.), 176
Ermine Street (Roman road), 177–79
Escorial, the, 37
Este, Thomas, 160
Eton College, 53

Fairfax, Lady, 211
Faulkland, 158
Fawkes, Guy, 51, 66, 68
Fayal, 27–28
Featley, Daniel, 69–70
Fenner, Captain Edward, 171
Fenner, Captain George, 171
Fenner, Vice-Admiral Thomas, 171
Fenner, Captain William, 171
Fennor, William, 161–62, 166, 167, 183,
    185, 225. See Bernard Quaritch
    Catalogue 953 (1975), item 17, for a
    note on Fennor and his origins at
    Leeds
Ferrer, Nicholas, 193
Ferris, Richard, 168–75, 187, 225–26
Field, Nathan, 202, 205, 209, 227
Fisher, Fr., 70, 78. See also Muskett, Fr.
    George
Fitzherbert, Fr. Thomas, 3, 6–7, 12, 16,
    23, 30–34, 36, 39, 42–43, 46, 215,
    218
Fleming, Thomas, 38
Florence, 194
Floyd, Fr. John (alias I. R. P.), 67, 74,
    221
Flushing, 14
Foley, Henry, 7, 45, 216, 219, 221
Foord, Mr. (Vicar of Eltham), 67, 220
Ford, John, 201, 205
Fosse Way (Roman road), 91
Foster, John, 86
Foulis, Henry, 219
Fowler, Mrs. (of Fetter Lane), 79
Frankfurt, 137
Freeman, Arthur, 217, 219
Freeman, Thomas, 205
Friars' Chronicle, The, 220
Frith, Captain (of Rotherhithe), 214

Frith, Mary (alias Mary Markham),
    194–214, 226–28
Frith, Roger, 195, 227
Frost, Thomas, 223
Fuller, Thomas, 58, 70, 221
Furnivall, F. J., 222

Garnett, Fr. Henry, 22–23, 46, 86
Gayton, Edward, 127, 133
Gee, John, 49–54, 57, 62–65, 68–86, 221
Gifford, Alexander, 201
Gifford, Richard (of Chichester), 24,
    30–31, 35, 220
Gil, Alexander, 85–86, 221
Gilbert, Thomas, 181
Gilbert and Sullivan, 171
Goad, Thomas, 59, 61, 69, 70–75, 78,
    84, 219–20, 221
Godfrey, Sir Edmund Bury, 86
Godrevy, 171
Golden Balance of Trial, The, 216
Gollancz, Sir Israel, 218
Goodwin, Meg, 176–77
Gouge, William, 53, 56, 61, 65, 68, 77,
    86, 87, 221
Gowrie Plot, 158–59
Gravesend, 117, 170, 185
Greene, Robert, 140
Greenway, Captain, 28
Greenwich, 3–5, 19, 26, 28–29, 31, 167,
    170, 183
Greg, Sir W. W., 225
Guadeloupe, 5
Guiana, 143
Guinness Book of World Records, 167
Gunpowder Plot, 164

H., Mr. (clergyman), 214
Hadley, 130
Hakluyt, Richard, 5
Hall, Joseph, 131, 223
Halliwell-Phillipps, J. O., 220, 223, 224
Harbage, Alfred, 224
Harrietsham, 142, 224
Harris, Fr., 78

232

233

234

235

238